"*Flight and Freedom* presents a vivid picture of Canada as seen by the refugees who have found a new home here. You'll see your country anew, when you read their tales, but you will also ask yourself: would they still get in today? This wonderful book is both a hymn of praise to a great tradition of Canadian generosity and a quietly scathing critique of how we have let this tradition decay. It's a celebration, but also a call to action."

    — Michael Ignatieff, Shorenstein Center, Harvard Kennedy School

"Ask almost any Canadian 'how did your family get here?' and you will hear an extraordinary tale – very often a tale of flight from a faraway conflict. We are, to a large extent, a nation of former refugees. Ratna Omidvar and Dana Wagner have looked beyond the statistics and the political crises to reveal the human texture of the refugee experience at the heart of Canada. At a moment when refugees are too often seen as an abstract threat, this book reveals them, in moving detail, as our neighbours, doctors, leaders, professors, business owners, and colleagues: the people who, when permitted to settle in Canada, become essential to the fabric and life of the country."

    — Doug Saunders, author of *Arrival City* and *The Myth of the Muslim Tide*

"This is a book that must be read to understand that, no matter how different the circumstances or reasons for the need to escape, refugees share remarkable resilience and strength, and have made enormous contributions to our country. Each story makes the reader both humble and proud to be Canadian. May our doors continue to be open to refugees for the benefit of us all."

    — Naomi Alboim, School of Policy Studies, Queen's University

"So many emotions tumble out after reading this rich collection of accounts of the suffering, determination, and resilience that is the refugee journey. These awe-inspiring journeys begin at different times and from places around the world, and they all end in Canada. This book is a very special reminder of the generosity and diversity of Canada. It is also a timely and urgent call to action to turn back the recent refugee laws and policies that have focused instead on restrictions and punishment."

— Alex Neve, Secretary General of Amnesty International Canada

"A timely and well-needed counterpart to much of the rhetoric around refugees, highlighting the remarkable personal stories of thirty refugees who have contributed and continue to contribute to Canada. These stories make a compelling case for a more generous approach, reminding us of the potential cost of more restrictive approaches."

— Andrew Griffith, former Director General of Citizenship and Multiculturalism, Government of Canada

"It is a privilege to learn, through these moving personal stories, both about people who helped build Canada into one of the world's most welcoming societies and the deliberate policies that made that possible. This book is also an important warning, however, that we not take these people and policies for granted and that vigilance is required to ensure Canada remains a country people in need can call home."

— Alison Loat, co-founder of Samara Canada

"These powerful stories show how Canadian society has benefitted from our country's generosity towards those fleeing 'climates of terror'. To me this is the essence of Toronto. For generations, that spirit of reaching out to refugees and the exceptional contributions they make have combined to shape our city making it the envy of the world. We must never stop."

— Barbara Hall, former Mayor of Toronto

"Giving migrants a voice, thus acknowledging their individuality, is the first step towards helping them fight for their rights and to facilitate their access to justice. We need to transform our own perceptions of migration, rejecting nationalist populist fantasies, myths, threats, and stereotypes. 'They' do not bring unemployment, illnesses, or criminality with them. The voices of Randy, Tarun, Humaira, Sabreen, and the other migrants in *Flight and Freedom* should help us to find the sensitivity necessary to appreciate the traumatic choices each of them had to make, to be 'in awe of their strength,' and to recognise their individual displacement as a dignity-seeking journey."

— François Crépeau, Faculty of Law, McGill University, and
United Nations Special Rapporteur on the Human Rights
of Migrants

"We can be indifferent until we see the individual faces of the families and the children. We have no choice but to engage when we hear their stories. This is a unique compilation of the stories of thirty individual refugees who escaped to Canada in recent years ... a must-read for anyone with a deep interest in refugees generally and for Canadians who are coming to understand the significant contribution of refugees to our diverse society. These stories are a key to understanding what makes modern Canada great."

— The Hon. Ron Atkey, former Minister of Immigration,
Government of Canada, responsible for the program for
60,000 Vietnamese refugees

FLIGHT AND FREEDOM

Stories of Escape to Canada

Ratna Omidvar and
Dana Wagner

Between the Lines
Toronto

For the families

Flight and Freedom: Stories of Escape to Canada

© 2015 Ratna Omidvar and Dana Wagner

First published in 2015 by
Between the Lines
401 Richmond Street West
Studio 277
Toronto, Ontario M5V 3A8
Canada
1-800-718-7201
www.btlbooks.com

Library and Archives Canada Cataloguing in Publication

Omidvar, Ratna, author
    Flight and freedom : stories of escape to Canada / Ratna Omidvar and Dana Wagner.

Includes index.
Issued in print and electronic formats.
ISBN 978-1-77113-229-9 (paperback).—ISBN 978-1-77113-230-5 (epub).—
ISBN 978-1-77113-231-2 (pdf)

    1. Refugees—Canada—Biography. 2. Refugees—Canada—History. 3. Canada—Emigration and immigration. I. Wagner, Dana, author II. Title.

JV7284.O45 2015   305.9'06914092271   C2015-903784-0   C2015-903785-9

Cover and text design by David Vereschagin/Quadrat Communications
Cover photograph © iStockphoto/ lilly3

Printed in Canada

As winner of the 2012 Wilson Prize for Publishing in Canadian History, Between the Lines thanks the Wilson Institute for Canadian History for its recognition of our contribution to Canadian history and its generous support of this book.

We acknowledge for their financial support of our publishing activities the Government of Canada through the Canada Book Fund, the Canada Council for the Arts, which last year invested $153 million to bring the arts to Canadians throughout the country, and the Government of Ontario through the Ontario Arts Council, the Ontario Book Publishers Tax Credit program, and the Ontario Media Development Corporation.

Canada Council
for the Arts
Conseil des Arts
du Canada

Canadä

ONTARIO ARTS COUNCIL
CONSEIL DES ARTS DE L'ONTARIO
an Ontario government agency
un organisme du gouvernement de l'Ontario

Contents

Preface

Ratna Omidvar

This book has been in the making in my mind for many years. Not simply because I share a narrative of flight with the others in the book (although mine pales in comparison to the danger and drama that unfold in their stories) but because I believe that as much as we are a country of immigrants, we are also a country of refugees. And sometimes we forget this.

Even though the official terminology of "refugees" as a distinct group of immigrants was only introduced into government legislation as late as 1976, Canada had been a safe haven for those fleeing persecution for many years before. Our first chapter tells the story of Adeline Oliver who fled the United States as a free slave in 1812 to start a new free life in Halifax, Nova Scotia. Our last story takes us to Israel's Negev Desert in 2006 and to Sabreen who escaped from her own family and death at their hands. Notwithstanding the time or the context, one commonality shines through—the will of the human being not just to survive but to be free.

As I read these stories I am left with some stark images. Zafar Iravan and his family hugging the sides of the mountains as they flee to safety from Iran to Pakistan. The shock of Sorpong Peou's family in finding a father they thought had died many years ago, only to "lose" him again to his new family. The sheer chutzpah and cockiness of Marko as he is confronted by soldiers from competing sides of the Bosnian War. The high stakes drama that plays out for Robi Botos and his family at the last minute, allowing them to stay in Canada. The image of Avtar Sandhu stepping onto a beach in Nova Scotia hungry and sick but eating a very Canadian peanut butter and jelly sandwich by noon. The unimaginable life of Humaira as she hides in one room with her children for five years.

I am also struck by the protagonists' first impressions of their relationship with Canada or Canadians. We come across as a people who are kind, fair, and compassionate, whether in the person of an English teacher in a camp, or an officer at the border, or a private sponsor in a city. In this we should take pride.

I am struck again by the lives of the protagonists in Canada. Many have been successful beyond imagination, in business, in academia, or as professionals. Others, in particular the more recent stories, tell of the struggle that takes place on arrival—the strangeness of a new country, the inevitable nostalgia for home and familiarity, the challenges of leaving the old behind.

And finally I reflect that no two stories of flight are the same. Escape is not a straight line. Some flights are made overnight, some develop over the course of a decade.

These stories are not meant to be read in one fell swoop. They are too full of history, complexity, human tragedy, and human resolve to be devoured in a short time. Rather I encourage the reader to take them one at a time, to read and re-read them to find answers to questions that will inevitably arise in your mind.

I also hope that these stories will serve to defrost the natural empathy and compassion of Canadians for those who find themselves in camps or at our doors. We have a proud history—starting from the War of 1812 to our response to the Hungarians, the Ugandans, the people from Vietnam, Cambodia, and Laos, to those fleeing war in the former Yugoslavia and many more. As the world finds itself confronting more human tragedies in new conflicts, this book should serve us as a reminder of the way forward.

I also believe that these stories need to be intertwined with other stories about our wonderful nation so that this strand becomes part and parcel of our national fabric and national identity. This book I hope will contribute in some small way to our understanding of what and who is Canada.

Acknowledgements

We first met and interviewed the people in this book between July 2013 and February 2014. In coffee shops, offices, a library, a school, many homes, and over two Skype calls when travel was not possible. They answered deeply personal questions about the experiences of persecution and escape that redirected their lives. Until this book went to press, they scheduled us in a second, third, fourth time, answered even more emails and phone calls, and walked us through their stories yet again.

We are in awe of their strength. They shared their stories with a capacity for openness that humbled us every time, baring the private rhythm of everyday, but also grief, pain, and past choices that people anywhere should live without having to make. We hope we convey even a small measure of their character.

Thank you to those who supported everyone in this book when, and in some cases before, they arrived in Canada: FCJ Refugee Centre, Covenant House, Action Réfugiés Montréal, Mennonite Central Committee, Supporting Our Youth, 519 Church Street Community Centre, Afghan Women's Organization, the Maytree Scholarship Program, and others. Their empathy and energy, especially in the years of arrival and adjustment, is not done justice here. A closer look at the otherworldly stage of arrival in Canada and the role of the settlement community is for another book.

The knowledge and incisive editing of Wayne Mutton, Ken Alexander, Mary Newberry, and others, brought the manuscript to life. For providing ideas, guidance, time, support, passion, and balance, we thank Peter Showler, a tireless refugee lawyer and good friend. Peter's contribution is nothing short of the backbone of this book. We also thank the lawyers Andrew Brouwer, Lorne Waldman, and Barbara Jackman for their analysis of the refugee cases within the stories, which space did not permit us to include, but can be found online.

The work of our colleagues at Maytree and Ryerson University are behind each stage of this book. Alan, Judy, Markus, Sarah, Marco,

Katarina, Bonnie, Vali, Stephanie, Evelyn, Kim, Alejandra—thank you. To our families, thank you for being early critics and supporters. To the team at Between the Lines, thank you for your excitement from day one and all your work after that.

Any error in historic or legal fact belongs to the authors. Where personal documents that are cited are still in possession, we have seen them. Direct quotes that are not referenced are verbatim and from firsthand interviews.

A book like this cannot exist without the willingness and courage of the people who own these stories to share them. Thank you.

> Ratna Omidvar and Dana Wagner
> Toronto, Canada
> 2015

Abbreviations

ASEAN	Association of Southeast Asian Nations
CIA	Central Intelligence Agency (US)
ESL	English as a second language
FMLN	Farabundo Martí National Liberation Front
HIV/AIDS	Human immunodeficiency virus and acquired immunodeficiency syndrome
IRB	Immigration and Refugee Board of Canada
IRPA	*Immigration and Refugee Protection Act*
KNLA	Karen National Liberation Army
LGBT	Lesbian, gay, bisexual, and transgender
MP	Member of Parliament
NGO	Non-governmental organization
POW	Prisoner of War
RCMP	Royal Canadian Mounted Police
RPF	Rwandan Patriotic Front
RUF	Revolutionary United Front
UN	United Nations
UNHCR	United Nations High Commissioner for Refugees (the UN Refugee Agency)

Introduction

Alan Broadbent

In the entrance of Istanbul's Rahmi M. Koç Museum is a large ceramic wall map of the region. As we passed the map, Ratna Omidvar paused and began to show me the route she and her husband Mehran followed as they fled Iran. She traced their path through the north of Iran into Eastern Turkey recounting the danger and difficulty. As she talked a small group of people stopped to listen, and began to ask her questions and engage with her in her journey. It was at that moment I realized the power of stories of migration, with their intense mix of personality, character, politics, and geography.

Ratna and I were visiting Istanbul in 2008 as part of a meeting of the European foundation community. At the time, I was chair and she president of Maytree, a private Canadian charitable foundation, and we were presenting our fledgling Cities of Migration program. We later spoke of this exchange, in front of the museum's map, and I think of that conversation as the genesis of this book.

My first experience, and later Maytree's first experience, with refugees began in the late 1970s and early 1980s when our attention was brought to the people fleeing the Pinochet regime in Chile. We looked at some data which showed that the arriving Chileans had much higher education attainments than the Canadian average, and that they had significant work experience in the professions, academia, and commerce. Anecdotal evidence also showed them to be highly motivated, energetic, and engaged in society.

We began to learn more about refugees generally and were struck with several things:

- Refugees are a threat to tyrants because they have economic, intellectual, or social power.
- Refugees are vigorous and ambitious, seeking a better life for themselves and their families.
- Refugees desire a better society, and are prepared to work for it.
- Refugees will find their way to a place with better prospects.

Those, we realized, were exactly the qualities we valued in our fellow Canadian citizens who were the leaders in our communities across the country. Canada has been built by people who developed economic, intellectual, and social power, who had the drive and ambition to build a better country as they helped their own families prosper, and who were practical enough to create success. The evidence is clear that refugees have been an enormous benefit to Canada over time. In fact it is as close to a sure bet as you can find, the kind of investment that the commercial world would call a "home run."

Canadian governments, though, have always been perplexed by refugees. In the 1920s Frederick Blair, assistant deputy minister in the federal Department of Immigration and Colonization, said about Armenian refugees, "A refugee coming to our shores ... naturally would have to be housed, fed and found employment or become permanently a public charge."[1] And he went on to note that refugees would likely become "a permanent problem to Canada." Later an unnamed immigration official, when asked how many Jewish refugees fleeing from the Nazis would be accepted by Canada, responded, "None is too many."

The Canadian federal government was slow to act on Hungarian refugees fleeing the repression of the 1956 Revolution before bowing to public pressure to remove health inspections and security checks to speed up intake. And the same reluctance to facilitate processing of refugees occurred following the 1973 military coup in Chile, which overthrew a democratically elected government. And even today government ministers seem suspicious of refugees, characterizing them as "bogus" and "phony" while withdrawing services in spite of a long history of provision that, in the case of legal aid, stems from Supreme Court rules. The Supreme Court may again be called upon to step in to decide the fate of federal cuts to health care for refugees.

But many Canadians have often been ahead of their government in their acceptance and embrace of refugees and other immigrants, and have eventually forced government to catch up. My own family in the 1950s took in Estonians fleeing from the Soviet Union's oppression of their country. Other Canadians have done the same over the years, often through church groups or neighbourhood associations. Showing us at our best, Canadians privately sponsored 34,000 refugees from Vietnam, Cambodia, and Laos in just two years between 1979 and 1980.[2]

This book confirms our discovery that each refugee has a story to tell that is inspiring and instructive. These stories are a validation that the great efforts required to move to a safer place indeed produce the ability to make a better life. And each story has the power to teach us a lesson of how we can help make these transitions better. They tell us that when we try to make things difficult for refugees, nobody wins. Canada needs to be, and is, alert to security and safety; our laws and security agencies are well equipped to manage these threats. We cannot let fear mongering and scapegoating put barriers in front of welcoming those who will contribute to the future success of our country.

Again this is where Canadians have been far ahead of their governments, with church groups or families taking in refugees, communities crafting welcoming environments, municipalities establishing effective settlement programs, small businesses finding jobs, or schools helping kids find new friends. Often this welcoming work has had to face down government process and regulation, and from time to time it has forced government to change. The present is a time for Canadians to help governments catch up, to match the humanitarianism, compassion, and pragmatism of Canadians. It is time to close the gap.

Maytree, and all those who have believed in this project and helped it grow beyond its Maytree origins, believe in the power of stories to shape our thinking and move our hearts. We know there is a limited audience for charts and data sets, important as they are to our understanding of complex issues. We also know there is a limited use for stories that are merely sentimental. I know the stories in this volume will inform and inspire. I hope they will lead you to believe as I do, that embracing refugees is a huge favour our country can do for itself. Moreover it will usher in a new group of citizens who can stand shoulder to shoulder with us to build an even greater country.

Who Is a Refugee?

In Canadian and international law, a refugee is someone who is outside their home country and is unable or unwilling to return to their country because they fear persecution. Persecution can include many forms of harm including death, torture, arbitrary imprisonment, or some form of severe physical or psychological harm. There must also be a motive for the persecution related to a person's race, religion, nationality, political opinion, or membership in a particular social group, which could include their gender, family identity, or sexual orientation. This limits the refugee definition. For example, people who fear flood, famine, or extreme poverty are not refugees. There are other legal elements to the definition, but the central idea that applies to almost every one of the refugees in this book is that they were outside their home country and asked for Canada's protection because they feared persecution in their home country.

How Does a Refugee Receive Canada's Protection?

There are two ways for a person to receive refugee protection: from outside Canada (the resettlement system) and from inside Canada (the inland system).

Under the resettlement system, we annually bring several thousand refugees to Canada from all over the world. They will be recognized as refugees before coming to Canada and most will already be living in United Nations refugee camps. Resettled refugees can be sponsored by the Canadian government or by groups of private citizens such as community or faith groups. In addition, for urgent refugee crises, Canada has historically established special resettlement programs to bring a specific number of refugees to Canada. Many of the refugees in this book were brought to Canada through specific resettlement programs.

In all instances, for resettlement, Canada gets to choose the number of refugees it brings from outside the country.

Under the inland system, asylum seekers fearing persecution ask for refugee protection once they arrive in Canada. At that point, they are considered to be refugee claimants. If they are eligible to make a refugee claim (more than 98 per cent of claimants are eligible), they are entitled to a hearing before a member of the Immigration and Refugee Board of Canada (IRB) who will decide their claim. Claimants cannot be removed from Canada before having their claim decided. With a positive decision, refugees may apply to be permanent residents and are on their way to Canadian citizenship. With a negative decision, after an appeal process, refused claimants may be removed from Canada. *Since, under its UN obligations Canada cannot expel someone who is legally a refugee, Canada does not get to choose the number of refugees it protects inside the country.*

1 Adeline Oliver

United States

As Told by Leslie Oliver

Leslie Oliver at Acadia University in Halifax.
Photograph by Chris Purcell.

Standing in Halifax's Black Cultural Centre, Leslie Oliver gazes at a picture of his father, an Order of Canada recipient for his work furthering social justice and equality in Nova Scotia. There's also a picture of his activist lawyer uncle, retired Senator Donald Oliver, the first black man appointed to Canada's legislative upper chamber.

How could this remarkable family of achievers ever have been on the run? It's bewildering. But two hundred years ago, they were.

1814, Maryland, United States

Adeline Oliver,[1] a seventeen-year-old black slave and her infant daughter, Laura, were hurrying through a dense forest in Maryland at a time when, throughout eastern North America, fighting raged between Britain and the fledgling United States. The war began in 1812.

Her husband, Moses Oliver, was already gone. The Olivers were runaway slaves, married, but the property of two different owners on separate estates. Now Adeline was fleeing with fourteen others to board a British ship anchored in the Potomac River. To avoid drawing attention to their escape, the Olivers split up. The plan was for Adeline and Laura to meet Moses later when their ship—like his—arrived in British North America, where the British government had promised they would be free settlers.

Though the United States had been a country for less than forty years when war broke out, the powerful British Navy struggled to blockade and control America's eastern waterways. The British knew that encouraging desertion by slaves could disrupt America's economy and battle strength. They were right. Some escapees chose to stay in America to fight against their former masters. Others, like the Olivers, slipped away to board ships bound for Halifax or Saint John.

More than two thousand free slaves landed in the Canadian Maritimes between September 1813 and August 1816.[2] Some are named on the Halifax List, a Nova Scotia record of black refugees, reminiscent of an earlier British Navy document The Book of Negroes. On the Halifax List, written in a slanting cursive hand, are the names of Adeline, Moses, and Laura.

After 1814, Halifax, British North America

United now, the Olivers set out to build a free life. Somehow they scraped together enough money to buy a chunk of land in Lucasville on what a taxi driver will tell you used to be called Windsor Road. Like Nova Scotia's better known enclave Africville, its settlers were mostly poor and black.

To survive in Nova Scotia, free slaves did grueling work. Women sold their household and childcare skills; men sold their muscle in the shipyards and construction sites of the busy port city. To thrive, however, people like the Olivers had to work one full-time job for others, then find whatever spare time they could to work their own land.

Not everyone had the fortune to own a bit of property. Those who did, like Adeline and Moses, could cut timber for heat, raise animals for the market, and move food straight from land to table. But it was exhausting, finishing a full day's work only to go back to work on a rocky and mostly barren plot. Halifax was segregated, and fertile land was unavailable to black people.

Adeline gave birth to a second daughter and then a son in the new colony. Having native-born children, however, was no guarantee you were finally home. Three years after Adeline and Moses arrived, Lord Dalhousie, governor of Nova Scotia, asked the British government to remove the black population to the United States, or to the recently created settlement on the West African coast, called Freetown and imagined by some to be an oasis.[3] The bid failed. A few years later, Dalhousie tried again (and again without success) to send them to Trinidad.

Endless work, poor land, botched expulsions ... and, of course, the experience of intolerance by the minority of 745 in a population of just over 11,000[4] in Halifax. But harder to bear, perhaps, was the tension within their community.

In Halifax in 1814, the black population included free slave refugees like Adeline and Moses, War of 1812 escapees. It included black Loyalists who had arrived several decades earlier during the American War of Independence. And, until slavery was abolished in British colonies in 1834, it included slaves. Every day in the dirt streets of Halifax, free men and women brushed up against them—and the dogged fact of slavery.

At this time, there was no single historical or cultural unifying force within Halifax's black population. Take the free slaves, with their eclectic lives stateside, in a city in Maryland, a farm in Virginia or a plantation in Georgia, who might have felt like strangers in this new northern colony. But cultures clash and regroup and grow. Across Nova Scotia, close-knit communities eventually sprang up, grafting together people whose torn roots were left behind over continents.

September 2013, Halifax, Canada

In the Halifax Black Cultural Centre on Main Street, Leslie Oliver, whose great-great-great-grandmother was Adeline Oliver, talks about how his mother had tracked down the history of Adeline and Moses on the British North American side. But their American past? It was sealed by war and time.

Until Leslie made a phone call in 2009.

Retired, Leslie now had time to reassemble the lives of his ancestors. He called the Maryland state archives, not expecting much. But a researcher returned his call.

"You won't believe what's on my desk," she said. Adeline Oliver was one of the biographies under development by the archives staff to mark the bicentennial of the War of 1812, and the file was bigger than most, thanks to Maryland court documents.

When the war ended in 1815, the British agreed to repay Americans for lost property. Owners could submit a claim for runaway slaves, and their estimated value had to be supported by witness affidavits. In the Maryland archives were affidavits on the Olivers. Adeline was described as healthy and aged between sixteen and nineteen years old. Laura was between nine and fifteen months. Witnesses thought Adeline was worth $300 or $450. Laura could sell for $50 or $100.

It was a jarring experience for Leslie, to see the dollar value on lives. "It really made you stop and think. It made it a lot more real," he says. "It certainly gave me a lot more admiration for what the preceding generations have done to try to get life stabilized."

Leslie Oliver was born in 1940 to William, son of Clifford, son of William, son of William, son of Adeline and Moses. That's six generations in Halifax, or seven including his two daughters. His two grandchildren would make eight, but they live in British Columbia.

Leslie has a copy of the will that shows Adeline's only son left no land to his son, also named William. Instead, William II perhaps opted to leave the plot to his four siblings while he settled on the grounds of Acadia University to work as a herdsman. Acadia once provided its students with homegrown food, but as the university modernized past animal husbandry, William rose to the position of head custodian of the buildings and grounds.

William's son, Clifford, succeeded him as head custodian. Though the work belonged on the fringe of academia, university life immersed Clifford and he passed a thirst for education to his children, including Leslie's father. This generation became the first of the line to attend university and Leslie's father was the first to graduate, a Bachelor of Arts and Divinity from Acadia. William, who took the first university job as a herdsman, died on the day of this first university graduation, but he died knowing the profound family achievement.

Leslie's parents raised their five sons to assume university was in their future so the relationship with Acadia continued. After an undergraduate degree in math from Acadia, Leslie worked in the infant field of computer programming. He returned to school and finished with a PhD in computer science from McGill. Acadia invited him back as a professor in 1985 and he taught there until his retirement.

"For me," Leslie says, "Moving to Acadia to teach, it was closing a big loop that had started with my great-grandfather going there as a herdsman." Leslie was not the only Oliver set on a university path by that decision. His uncle, Senator Donald Oliver, a lawyer and activist, became the first black man appointed to the Senate.

Today, Leslie is over seventy years old and he just switched to a MacBook. His research was once the stuff that led to a patented algorithm to detect heart tissue. Now he's interested in history and picked up where his mother's notes stopped. When she died, Leslie inherited the boxes of family history and began to digitize.

Leslie works in retirement at the Black Cultural Centre that was founded by his parents. Inside, you can stand at the centre of a circle of overhead banners, photos of the celebrated. Among them is Viola Desmond, the Canadian Rosa Parks who ignored the rules and took a white-only theatre seat; Richard Preston, a founder of the province's

Baptist community; and William Hall, the first black man and Nova Scotian to receive a Victoria Cross. Leslie sketches their lives like a tour guide, still with wonder.

In another room is a photo of Leslie's mother surrounded by young girls. Poverty disproportionately affected the black community in the province for a long time. It still does today[5] and building girls' belief in a big future was her passion. Leslie recalls the many professionals, the women, who filled the pews at her funeral. On another wall is a photo of his father William with his high school hockey team. He only played the home games because travelling included hotel stays, and most hotel managers turned away black clients.

In 1984, Leslie's father became a member of the Order of Canada for his work on social justice and equality in Nova Scotia. The achievement had Leslie looking backwards, all the way to Adeline and Moses. "This is built on people who, for generations, did something that contributed to allowing you to develop and evolve," he says.

That's why history matters. "It's healthy for people to have some idea of their heritage, so they understand they're not alone, they didn't come from nothing."

2 Mampre Shirinian

Ottoman Empire (Turkey)

As Told by His Son, George Shirinian

George Shirinian at the Zoryan Institute in Toronto.
Photograph by Ryan Walker.

1915, Geyve, Ottoman Empire (Turkey)

Posters appeared in the spring of 1915 across the Ottoman Empire[1] with an order for Armenians to leave immediately. At gun point, they gathered whatever belongings they could carry at a moment's notice for a trip with no clear route or destination.

To the Young Turks still in charge of the crumbling empire, the Christian Armenians posed a threat to the state. Some Armenian nationalists had taken up arms against the empire and so the Young Turks, setting a precedent for skittish leaders of the coming century, declared that Armenians were not ethnic Turks. To "Turkify" the empire, Armenians had to leave, even though there was nowhere for them to go.[2] Of course, there was a plan, and keeping to it, they died along the way.

All over the empire, across what is now Turkey, convoys of men, women, and children moved on foot, sometimes with donkeys and wagons, as Turkish escorts brutalized them at will. Beatings and theft were common. Some Armenians were raped or watched family dragged off to be raped, and many, ultimately, were killed. There are accounts of people being shot at close range, bayoneted, drowned, burned alive, and bludgeoned to death.

Mampre Shirinian was around five years old when his family left their village of Geyve on official orders. His uncle and brother would not survive the march. The night his uncle died, Mampre lay awake listening to his final breaths, by then a rasping wheeze. It was probably pneumonia, one of the diseases like typhus and dysentery that also threatened to wipe out the Armenians.

If they managed to guess the purpose of the march before setting out, some parents chose to quietly leave their children behind in Greek households. That is, until the Turkish authorities caught on and cut this line of support by broadcasting that hiding their fellow Christians would cost the good Greek neighbours their lives. Another option was an orphanage.

That's where Mampre arrived sometime between 1918 and 1923, at an orphanage in the capital Constantinople, present-day Istanbul. He survived part of his family's march, and remembered that bit, but he could never recall how he wound up in the capital. His home village, Geyve, is around 150 kilometres east of Constantinople, and sits on the old Silk Road linking China to the Mediterranean. It's possible Mampre moved along this historic route in the care of Christian missionaries, after his mother, desperate and with one of her sons already dead, gave him over. Mampre was one of many Armenian orphans with living parents, at least for a time. He had just one visit from his mother at the orphanage and for years after, heard nothing about her.

———————

The events after Armenians left their homes on Turkish orders were later called genocide. In fact, it was the Armenian massacres that in part prompted a man named Raphael Lemkin to coin the word decades later. The expulsion, designed to destroy a whole people,[3] eventually killed between one to 1.5 million Armenians by force or starvation and illness.[4] Not even orphanages were safe. In a January 1916 memo, the Turkish interior minister wrote:

We hear that certain orphanages which have been opened receive also the children of Armenians. Whether this is done through ignorance of our real purpose, or through contempt of it, the Government will regard the feeding of such children or any attempt to prolong their lives as an act entirely opposed to its purpose, since it considers the survival of these children as detrimental.[5]

Before long, the minister's policy trickled down into effect. Mampre remembered one incident in Constantinople, when he ran into Turkish soldiers while outside his orphanage foraging for extra food. When the soldiers saw the wiry kid, they taunted him—an Armenian, a Christian, and uncircumcised. They threatened to do the job in the street, before Mampre managed to sprint away, trailed by guffaws of laughter.

Whenever possible, the missionaries moved children outside the country and Mampre next landed at an orphanage on the Greek island of Corfu. He left without saying goodbye to his family or knowing if anyone was still alive.

All this took place as Turkey, along with Germany and the Austro-Hungarian Empire, fought the Allied countries in the First World War. The Armenian massacres could have gone largely unnoticed, lost in the shadow of the bigger, global battle. But some Allied governments did react and two responses involved Mampre.

The mayor of London, England, created the Lord Mayor's Fund to rescue and resettle orphaned Armenian children, and aided by that money, the Canadian government, with a handful of others, agreed to import a small number of the children from orphanages in Greece.

The distant killing of Christians found a way into Canadian headlines, even during war. At first, Canada was reluctant to receive any refugees, especially non-Anglo Saxons (a senior bureaucrat in Ottawa predicted refugees would pose a "permanent problem"),[6] but church and relief groups lobbied for a response to the crisis. They argued that money alone wouldn't help. People needed out.

The lobby won over the government, and the first group of 50 Armenian boys arrived in Canada by ship, the *Minedosa*, on July 1, 1923. A second group of 40 boys docked in Halifax on September 30, 1924, after sailing on the *Brage* from the Greek port Piraeus. In Halifax, they boarded a train to Georgetown, Ontario. They were orphans, mostly children, some had survived a desert march or an overcrowded, filthy freighter from Turkey to Greece, and some had witnessed the slaughter of their families. There were 109 boys by the end of 1924.

In the second group of arrivals was fourteen-year-old Mampre.

October 1924, Georgetown, Canada

Their new home, at a time when many Canadians still lived in the country, was a two-hundred-acre farm in Georgetown. The newly formed Armenian Relief Association of Canada purchased the farm on behalf of the boys under a program designed to house, educate, work, and launch them as Canadians.[7] But a very specific type of Canadian. They would all be trained as farmers. There was no precedent for this refugee project, so it was termed "Canada's noble experiment" and the children became "the Georgetown boys."

When Mampre arrived at the farm in the second cohort, the fifty boys already there were old hands in Canadian ways of eating porridge and using flush toilets. He adopted their habits. The days were filled with classes on regular school subjects, plus farm chores or work in the kitchen or dormitories. The boys played, ate, and slept at the farm— always supervised by the live-in superintendents and teachers, some seconded from Ontario public schools. They even had free visits from local doctors and dentists.

A lifestyle emerged at this special boarding school. There was a swimming hole, garden plots, and a farm paper. The boys took field trips outside Georgetown to the Canadian National Exhibition in Toronto, attended summer camps, and visited concert halls (the boys onstage) during Christmas. By this rounded routine, the plan went, the boys would become model Canadian farmers.

Despite good intentions, a radical pilot is bound to have flaws. In hindsight, it was a mistake for the farm directors, who had Ottawa's blessing, to decide on renaming the boys something crisp and pronounceable. New English names would replace their Armenian ones. Mampre excitedly breathed his new name,[8] and when Onnig Varteressian became John Oliver, and Haroutoun Jizmejian became Robert Grant, they too laughed and bowed to each other, practising formal introductions. But later, after lights out, the boys began feeling something else that was not excitement. They discovered they didn't want to lose their Armenian names—almost the single constant in the life of an adolescent orphan and survivor of genocide. Somehow, their names tied them to a family and culture already gone. They stayed up late that night deciding what to do. Within days, the mood on the farm was tense, and soon the boys refused to respond to the English names.

The adults were defenceless when the boys explained themselves. On behalf of the younger Mesrob Hagopian,[9] who was fighting back tears, one of the older boys told the farm directors in nascent English: "When he young baby, Armenian priest put water on his head and named him Hagopian after his father and mother. Then he lost his father, his mother and also his country, and all he left is Hagopian." In the end, the boys kept their Armenian names, and they kept their numbers, too, taken from lists that accompanied them from Greece to Canada (like Number 73: Mampre Shirinian). At first the numbers had the thrill of code names, but they stuck and became a bond and shared identity. Years later, Mampre could still name the number of every Georgetown boy.

Mampre moved from the farm to Toronto in the late 1920s to attend Jarvis Collegiate. He wasn't alone in this. It turned out many of the orphans, now teenagers, had ambitions that didn't include shovelling manure. Mampre worked for his food and board during school, once as a doorman at the central King Edward Hotel. He fell in love with Mariam Mazmanian, another orphan of the genocide who'd come from Corinth, Greece, after a brother came to Canada as one of the first Georgetown cohort in 1923. The International Red Cross had matched the pair in an epic effort to reunite scattered parts of families. A smaller group of orphaned girls was resettled to Canada, and fairly quickly parcelled out to domestic jobs from the farm, but less is known about them today. Their files remain buried in classified Ottawa archives.

In Mariam, Mampre found a fellow survivor who shared his history and language. They married and by the time they had two young sons, George and Lorne, they had opened a grocery market in Toronto. Mampre decided to sell the business in the 1950s, anticipating the end of market-plus-butchery shops, and ventured into real estate, his slogan, "The Gateway to East End Homes."

Mampre and Mariam raised their two boys to be "good Canadians." They spoke Armenian to each other but mostly English with the children. Mampre was an active member of the East York Kiwanis Club. And once, the family even considered another name change. In the 1950s, Toronto had diversity, but didn't yet embrace it. Anti-Semitism was still chronic and Mampre thought his surname, Shirinian, sounded too Jewish. He had already experienced racism and losing clients who thought he was Jewish, but finally decided against dropping it.

At his peak, Mampre owned nine real estate offices in southern Ontario. He never looked back at farming. He was honest and warm, a charmer, and deeply trusted by his clients, mostly Armenian and Greek immigrants. But others, too, trusted "Monty" Shirinian, who in the end changed half his name for the sake of Canadian business.

January 2014, Toronto, Canada

Mampre is survived by his sons, both of whom chronicled the Armenian genocide in their professional lives. George told this story. His older brother, Lorne, began studying the genocide first, but it took George years longer to touch the subject. George studied classics at the University of Toronto and was drawn to ancient Armenia, but he shunned modern history because it inevitably covered the horror around 1915. "I couldn't wrap my head around the genocide. I didn't want to," George explains. "It was very upsetting and very distasteful. I did not identify myself with this victim group, the Armenians."

He could avoid the genocide at home because his parents, Mampre and Mariam, talked very little about their childhood. George began to understand why in his late twenties. In the 1970s, when affordable tape recorders appeared, George became interested in oral history. He had also begun, cautiously, to step closer to 1915. He once asked his mother and an Armenian friend of hers, another orphaned survivor, for permission to record their stories. They agreed to sit down, but within minutes, both women were crying uncontrollably, their bodies shaking and unable to speak. George switched off the recorder. It was a glimpse of the pain his parents almost never spoke about.

George knew even less about Mampre's mother, his grandmother, who Mampre discovered much later, lived in Varna, Bulgaria. She had remarried and had children—daughters. They corresponded from time to time, and she passed away in the 1950s.

During university, George was a volunteer manager of his church congregation's small library and that led to a job at York Public Library. One of the employees he hired became his wife, a woman who stunned him with her knowledge of literature, her beauty, her Polish accent. She had a son who George found himself easily chatting with, who he would call his own son one day. George's career steadily advanced in the library and when he left in 1998, he was acting chief librarian. On his own time, he volunteered with the Zoryan Institute in Toronto, a think tank with a focus on Armenia. He was first impressed by its focus on Armenian identity, and later, by its mandate to educate about genocide prevention, not only by research on Armenian history but on all genocides.

At Zoryan, George was finally immersed in the details of the Armenian genocide, including survivor accounts and the declassified papers of the Turkish and other involved governments.

"Just reading modern histories about it is painful enough," George says. "Then when you actually delve into the evidence, the documentation, the horrible, horrible graphic detail, it does something to you." He is more emotional, he says, and more sensitive to the pain of others. George could finally grasp what happened to his parents, though Mampre and Mariam had long since passed away.

They did live to see their sons growing into good men, whom they would have called "good Canadians." Today, Lorne is a retired English professor of the Royal Military College in Kingston, historian, playwright, and poet.

George is now the executive director of the Zoryan Institute. He is editor of several books on the genocide, including one, which arrived from the printer during our interview, that exclusively looked at declassified records detailing the involvement of Germany, an ally of Turkey during the First World War. George holds the inches-thick hardcover for a few moments in silence, then softly says, "Fourteen years in the making."

This book is partly why George does what he does, because of its impact: a Turkish journalist, in an early review of the book for the paper *Hurriyet*, wryly challenged Turkish officials to refute this latest cache of evidence. He wrote, "I know you will remain silent."[10]

Piecing together events that began in 1915 is delicate work, primarily because the official position of the Turkish government is denial. As a result, Western governments that consider Turkey an important ally have been reluctant to wade into Armenian history. For George, the best riposte is balance. In 1999, when a Canadian parliamentary subcommittee asked the Zoryan Institute for a balanced report to help decide if Canada should recognize the genocide, the drafting fell to George. He returned a neat executive summary appended by dozens of pages of evidence. Seven years later, in 2006—nearly a century after killing began—the Canadian government formally recognized the Armenian genocide.

Of the genocide, George could list manifold lessons. Of the noble experiment in Canada, he pinpoints one: "At the critical time when they had the choice to erase the identity of these Armenian orphans or let them be Armenians and Canadians, the government made the right choice." Their family names survived.

3 Loly Rico

El Salvador

Loly Rico in Toronto.
Photograph by Ryan Walker.

1979, San Salvador, El Salvador

Loly Rico was so lucky. Born into a wealthy San Salvador family, enrolled in a private school, she had never wanted for a thing. She thought aloud once about taking piano lessons. Her father promptly went out and bought her a piano. Loly was privileged—and that's why it was so confusing. She had become a member of a popular movement opposed to El Salvador's government, a repressive regime that was supported by families like hers.

Her country was a powder keg. A huge number of Salvadorans lived in poverty after being shoved off their land so a rich minority within the country could get even richer, monopolizing the landscape to grow crops for the booming markets in coffee and sugar cane.[1] And it wasn't safe to protest. With some regularity since the 1930s, El Salvador's landless and poor rose up only to be crushed by the military. But in 1972, something different happened. An opposition leader almost won the presidency. Many still believe an unofficial record shows he did win. Then adjustments were made. That's when the government began regarding the popular movement with deadly seriousness. In the 1970s, there were more protests and violence. By 1980, there was civil war. In the following more than a decade, before there was peace, an estimated seventy thousand would die.[2]

Opposing the government, but using very different tactics, were peaceful activists like students and some left-wing parties, and not-so-peaceful guerilla groups. But the right-wing government lumped them all together. So civilians, pacifists, armed fighters, even street corner complainers all faced disappearance, torture, and execution—sometimes in that order.[3] That strategy only served to drive opposition groups, including many pacifist cells, onto one team: the Farabundo Martí National Liberation Front, the FMLN, the main threat to the government.

War money came from familiar reserves. The United States funded and supported the military government; the Soviet Union, through Nicaragua and Cuba, funnelled funds to the Marxist-Leninist FMLN.[4]

At home, Loly's parents agonized over her left-leaning politics. They were equally concerned about Francisco, her university law student, activist boyfriend, articulate, passionate, charismatic, and outspoken. They believed their daughter was in dangerous company. So, after graduating high school and pressured by her parents, Loly, eighteen, stopped seeing Francisco and left for Mexico City in the fall of 1979 to study occupational therapy.

What her parents may not have appreciated was the role they had played in Loly's political development. To instill good conservative values, they had sent their thoughtful, compassionate daughter to an elite Roman Catholic boarding school. And that's where one priest in particular widened her eyes to her own privileges. In so many words, he taught her that to whom much is given, much will be required. Even while girls of her upper-class background sat separately from the poor girls there on scholarships, the priest spoke to Loly about social justice, the needs of the poor, and the responsibility of the advantaged few to use their status and education for good. Before she finished school, something happened that seared his words in memory forever. He was assassinated for his views.

From the priest, she learned about social justice. From Francisco, Loly learned how much raw determination you need to change anything. She fell in love first for his passion, then she saw how hard he worked, this law student who was forever agitating, forever organizing his peers to join protests against El Salvador's deep inequalities.

Whatever the pleas of her parents, Loly was a long-gone revolutionary.

While older, worldlier (it seemed to Loly), and poorer, Francisco was in fact quite like her. The son of teachers, Francisco was studying to become a law maker, and he was gaining notice for his writing and political abilities. Except he was attacking *el systema*. Small wonder Loly's parents found him threatening. So did others. Loly's uncles were among a small group of deans running the University of El Salvador on behalf of the government. Francisco, a student there, was protesting this political hand in university affairs—a direct challenge to Loly's family.

In Mexico City, Loly was detached, from Francisco, but increasingly from politics at home. School work was consuming her life.

Then, on March 24, 1980, a man with a rifle strode into mass in the Church of the Divine Providence and with a single shot, killed Óscar Romero, the archbishop of San Salvador, at the altar. Romero had been the voice of the poor (a powerful one in a country named, in Spanish, for "The Saviour" Jesus Christ). Romero told Salvadorans they could live better *now*, in this life. He appeared on television to appeal for an end to government massacres of civilians. He lost friends in the Roman Catholic Church by attempting to turn it away from complacency, even complicity, into an agent of progressive change. Now, for his politics, he had been killed. News of the archbishop's death travelled the world: *Another bold hit by the right-wing death squads? A CIA plot? A turning point for the Salvadoran opposition? A game changer in Latin America?*

During Romero's funeral, demonstrators filled the main square in San Salvador, setting off bloody clashes with police. For Loly, it was the second death of a spiritual leader, a personal leader, "Monsignor Romero." A holy man. If the regime could do this, it was capable of anything.

She joined the Salvadoran solidarity movement that had spread to campuses across Latin America. She became a courier, carrying letters from exiled Salvadorans to friends and family back home. It was perfect. With her low political profile, her privileged family background and credentials, she could cross the Mexican border south through Guatemala and be waved into El Salvador without interrogation.

Meanwhile Francisco, who had fled to Mexico shortly after Loly left, decided to find her. It was like nothing had changed. They had not stopped loving each other, only family and events had gotten in the way. In 1982, she gave birth to Giovanni, their first child. She quit travelling and two years later the Ricos returned to El Salvador. It was a risk. The civil war was four years old.

"We said, well, if the revolution is going to be longer, what are we doing outside?" Loly says.

Francisco got to work with the archbishop's legal office as an independent observer, documenting extrajudicial killings and other human rights abuses. His reports went to the media, probably the reason that in August 1985, Francisco went missing. Loly, nine months pregnant, was terrified. She knew what happened to the "disappeared." A military jeep would skid to a stop and uniformed members of a death squad would leap out to pull a bag over the target's head. Then they'd be gone and the street would be quiet. Families, reeling from whispers of others killed, burned, and gone without a witness who would talk, were left with a life of endless questions. Salvadoran NGOs estimate eight thousand people were disappeared during the civil war.[5]

But Francisco was alive. The Red Cross, during an unannounced visit to National Police Headquarters, had recognized him because they knew his work. Along with pressure from the church, Red Cross staff convinced the guards to release him after just two weeks behind bars. The police kept watching him, however, and in 1987, after a death threat, Francisco fled to Costa Rica, leaving Loly and their two children behind.

––––––––––

Back in San Salvador, Loly raised her family and became director of a centre for children with Down syndrome. Typical Loly, she also began quietly organizing for a group of women whose husbands, sons, or fathers had been disappeared. In 1989, Francisco returned to El Salvador. There was a lull. The military and guerillas were discussing a possible end to the strife. Loly and Francisco moved into a working-class neighbourhood, and Francisco continued his independent reporting.

Loly wondered, could this be the beginning of a normal life? She pictured raising Gio and Ana in this neighbourhood, in a job she loved, in their home country. But then the negotiations broke down, followed by Francisco's name appearing in the newspaper on a list of public enemies. He was now a probable target, one of those whose tortured bodies would be found dead, doused in gasoline and set ablaze to incinerate identity. Years later, Gio and Ana would remember seeing these burning remains lighting up the dark roadside.

The other ominous signs? A stranger appeared in the neighbourhood, asking people about the Rico children. Then a group of five men showed up. They asked the nanny—through the front door she wisely kept locked—about the children. Sensing the worst, Loly and Francisco moved everyone out of their home. Two days later, thugs ripped through the home, leaving its contents ruined.

"We were not thinking to leave the country until they came to our house," Loly says. "I believe they understood they were threatening us with our children."

It seemed Loly could not have an uneventful pregnancy. Five months pregnant with her third child in December 1989, Loly, with Gio and Ana, were jumping from one safe house to another, hiding with relatives. Francisco was on his way to Guatemala. He had contacted the Canadian embassy in San Salvador about requesting asylum, but they told him they should flee to Guatemala where, outside their country, the family could become refugees and apply for help at the Canadian embassy there. There were only two hiccups: a safe way out and, before the family could follow, passports for the children. They couldn't apply through the normal channels, not while in hiding. Francisco's sister came to their rescue. A civil servant, she arranged passports—and, sweetly, even a government vehicle—to move Loly and the children across the border.

Canada accepted the Rico family and skipped the usual refugee processing time by issuing ministerial permits. But even Guatemala, home to Salvadoran government supporters, was dangerous. Canadian embassy staff agreed with Francisco that the Ricos had to leave. On January 18, 1990, just three weeks after leaving El Salvador, the family was on a plane to Toronto.

January 1990 and October 2013, Toronto, Canada

Walking on Dundas Street in the early days in Canada, Loly saw an SUV swing into a parking spot ahead of her family. She had her arms around her children in a second, her face white. Francisco said softly, "Calm down Loly, we're in Toronto."

Loly had only known pregnancy as high-risk. She had high blood pressure while pregnant with both Gio and Ana, meaning a risk of complications. But all signs were normal when she delivered Manuel four months after arriving in Toronto. She didn't realize the effects of stress until she lived without them in a peaceful country.

A support cast of doctors, nurses, ESL teachers, housing staff, and employment counsellors cushioned the family's arrival in Canada. The congregation Sisters, Faithful Companions of Jesus (FCJ), provided their first home on Hamilton Street. Loly and Francisco became volunteers at the shared house, helping translate for new Spanish-speaking arrivals or sort out legal aid.

Loly slowly realized, again, how lucky her family was. As government-assisted refugees, resettled from abroad, they received support unavailable to those who claim asylum within Canada or at its borders (inland claimants). That gave her an idea. She asked the FCJ sisters if she could convert the rented house into a full shelter, and the sisters agreed. Hamilton House became a dedicated shelter for women who were inland claimants.

The Rico children were raised and shaped at Hamilton House. Early on in its operations, there was a miscommunication and a new resident arrived at the shelter while Loly and Francisco were out, driving to pick her up. When Loly realized the mistake, she called home and Ana, now about seven years old, answered the phone: *Mom, don't worry.* She and her brothers had prepared a bedroom and were about to sit down to dinner with their new guest. "That was the first time that I felt, well, our children are getting our own beliefs," Loly says. "We need to keep open the house for anyone who needs it."

The shelter moved to a bigger house on Oakwood Avenue and is today called the Faithful Companions of Jesus Refugee Centre.

The house was still waking up the morning of our interview. The young man at the front desk, once a resident and now a volunteer, offered a seat for a few minutes because the staff, including Loly and Francisco, were finishing breakfast with the residents. More than a thousand families have passed through FCJ and Loly is still in touch with several hundred of them, many of whom volunteer in the refugee settlement community on top of their own careers.

Loly and Francisco remain the shelters' live-in codirectors. Their children have moved out, all pursuing related fields. Ana is a family lawyer representing abused women, and Gio, who does pro bono work for FCJ as a community legal worker, is heading for law school next. Manuel is at college for social services.

Beginning in 1992, after a peace deal ended the twelve-year civil war, the Ricos have been returning regularly to El Salvador. Loly said she lives a dichotomy. She is pursuing goals in Canada, where her family became citizens in 1998, and in El Salvador, where she wants to open a community centre for women. She no longer has just one country.

In Canada, she says, "I can be open, I can speak up, I can do what I believe is for social justice, and that makes me who I am." She continues, "I want to go back to keep giving what I learn and what I have back to my country, to other women, but at the same time, I have my life here. This is still my haven."

A frontline shelter worker in Canada, Loly spots ways to make her new country even more compassionate. She recalls taking a Congolese woman to get fingerprints before her Immigration and Refugee Board (IRB) hearing which, because of changes, was scheduled within sixty days of her leaving a violent past and asking for asylum. Still coping with trauma, she panicked when she saw the equipment. Loly had to explain the fingerprinting didn't mean she was about to be jailed. It was flat out unfair, Loly says, making her talk before a board that would determine her future so soon. "How will she be ready to talk? She has to prove everything. That's not justice."

Loly's values are still the ones that motivated her in the 1980s. Her father saw this on a visit to Toronto after the Ricos had settled in. He had disapproved of Loly's activism as youthful experimentation, a passing enthusiasm. Beware of youthful impulses, he had once warned his daughter and her young boyfriend. But seeing their lives in Toronto, he told Loly and Francisco: I was wrong. Their passion had never changed.

4 Ken (Khanh) Do

Vietnam

Ken Do at home in Toronto.

Photograph by Ryan Walker.

June 1979, Off the Coast of Can Tho, Vietnam

A girl had collapsed but no one could help. They could barely move from sea sickness. They were packed in, the dark heat inside the hull suffocating. This first night was miserable, because of the stench of vomit and of not knowing who else had made it.

Hours earlier, Khanh had squatted in the brush at the shore of Can Tho, ready to obey his father. His eyes fixed on a boat carrying authorized exiles soon to weigh anchor. *Run to the boat, don't look back. Let go of your brother and sisters if they get shot and keep going. Get on the boat. Go to the bottom and don't move.*

But onboard and feeling the nightlong weight of heat, the smells of sickness, and the pressure of sweating bodies, thirteen-year-old Khanh had to break his father's rules. He pushed himself up from the sticky, pitching floor toward the hatch. Ocean air filled his lungs. After a few deep breathes he dipped back under to search for his family.

The Do family began planning to escape in 1977, two years after North Vietnamese tanks rolled into Saigon in April 1975. The following year around Tet, the Vietnamese New Year, Khanh awoke to soldiers inside his house collecting an inventory of everything, toothpaste, soap, salt, sugar, gasoline, rice. Whatever his family owned that was over the lawful limit was taken.

Both Khanh's parents were professors in the southern capital before the communist victory over South Vietnam ended three decades of war. They gave their five children the world, which at the time was a nurturing, comfortable home and French private schooling. Khanh was ten years old in 1975, the third child but eldest son. Under the communist system, he was quickly forced to become an adult. He helped earn the family food on the black market, selling cigarettes and other odds and ends while his parents split their days between work and communist re-education class. When the family decided to escape Vietnam, not a single chair was left in the house. They had sold everything for food and there was still never enough to eat.

Escape by boat was not the Do family's first choice. Khanh's family— his brother, three sisters, parents, and dozens of relatives—had already plotted an overland flight through Laos and Cambodia into Thailand. It had worked for others. They planned for over a year and then travelled north to where the country narrowed, pinching the distance to the

Laotian border. But after two weeks waiting there, they sensed local police had guessed their plan. Khanh's parents backtracked with their children to Saigon, but the others took a chance. They crossed into Cambodia, where the Khmer Rouge was exterminating that country's elite and where Vietnamese were especially unwelcome. The entire group was killed except for Khanh's young cousin, Lan.

Following Lan's solitary return home, "We grieved and continued planning to escape," Khanh says.

There was no money left to finance an escape but there was a family friend who needed to learn English if he was to later impress an immigration official outside Vietnam, most likely an English speaker. Khanh's father agreed to coach him in English in exchange for his providing his connections that would get them as far as the beach in Can Tho. English was their ticket out, their chance to make a short sprint to a moving boat.

Sea

Sixteen of Khanh's family made it aboard in June 1979, the five Do children and both their parents among them. Twenty-five others didn't run fast enough, or grab hold tightly enough, or have the strength to drag a hungry body over the boat's edge. Khanh learned later everyone was jailed, including his grandparents and Lan.

Aboard there were two types of passengers: illegal runaways and those authorized to leave. Ethnic Chinese living in Vietnam were able, or rather pushed, to pay for the right to exit. Ethnic Vietnamese, like the Dos, were inmates of their country, subject to be shot or imprisoned for attempting to escape. But once at sea, group differences faded; they were, together, surviving or dying from starvation, dysentery, and pirates.

Khanh's boat carried one hundred and thirty people during eleven days at sea. Eleven days of spherical blue, of not knowing how many more waterborne days were coming. Then a dot would appear on the horizon. Thai pirates attacked Khanh's boat eight times. On the fifth raid, the pirates smashed the boat's engine, enraged after finding no gold in any hemline or cavity. It is anyone's guess who onboard suffered most. Maybe it was parents watching a sick or starving child's body shrink and discolour, or the family who saw a mother, wife, sister, daughter raped by a pirate, or children seeing for the first time frail and powerless parents.

Khanh remembers standing against the engine exhaust pipe for warmth, thinking the blue world was endless. When the Do family left in 1979, tens of thousands of Vietnamese had already fled by boat. They knew the stories of suffering and yet, they decided to try.

"Should we take that risk for a better future, or stay here and get killed, disappear out of this earth for no reason?" Khanh says. "We chose to go."

Land

On the eleventh day, during the night and in the rain, the ocean ended. It was Kuku Island, one of thousands that form Indonesia. The adults lay sodden and sick on the beach, while Khanh, his siblings, and cousins collected shellfish at low tide and tasted leaves at the shoreline, searching for anything edible. Their boat was one of the first to arrive, but the occupants of Kuku grew and with them so did the squalor of an overcrowded and improvised refugee camp.

Kuku was one of dozens of spontaneous camps clustered mainly in Malaysia, Indonesia, and Thailand. By late 1978, before the Do family left Can Tho, 62,000 Vietnamese boat people were living in refugee camps across Southeast Asia.[1] By mid-1979, there were 550,000 asylum seekers from Vietnam, Laos and Cambodia.[2] The crisis provoked an international conference in July 1979, where safe countries including Canada agreed to basic principles of asylum and later, through government commitments, to offer permanent resettlement. Canada would accept around 60,000 of the refugees in just two years from 1979 to 1980, with more to follow.[3]

On Kuku Island, a Canadian immigration officer interviewed Khanh's father. Since many countries were accepting refugees from Southeast Asia in 1979, the Do family had some choice of where to go. Theirs was a democratic family, so the choice was up to the children. They chose French-speaking Canada. Though their father spoke English, Khanh and his siblings spoke only French and Vietnamese. They reasoned that if they left for a foreign-speaking country like Germany or the United States, they would need to start from scratch. They imagined a debilitating retreat to the first grade. In the refugee camp and wearing the same clothes as on the day they escaped Vietnam, the children reasoned that their first priority was school. Their escape had been possible because their father knew English, thanks to years of schooling abroad. To these children, education was survival.

February 1980, Scarborough, and June 2013, Toronto, Canada

They picked Canada for the French language but the Do family wound up in Scarborough, soon-to-be Anglophones, and the darlings of a support group twelve families strong. These strangers—Canadian families, church, and community groups—responded in the tens of thousands to sponsor refugees in the years after Saigon fell. The Canadian government matched the private response and brought in even more. It was called Operation Lifeline and it was unprecedented. It still is.

Three days after arriving in Canada, Khanh was breathlessly pronouncing his only English sentence, "I am a new student," in front of ninth grade (not first grade) teachers. Three months later, his mother found work in a factory, and three months after that, his father did too.

In his application essay for teacher's college at the University of Toronto, Khanh—he now goes by Ken—re-imagined his history as a path to a career in education. "When I'm at the bottom, I realize that no matter what, education is the key to keep you going, to give you hope." He has lived his personal theory, and continues to live it by laying education's potential before the minds of Northern Secondary School students in his office, where the nameplate reads Vice-Principal Ken Do.

"Whenever I talk to students, it's not about discipline," Ken says. "I'd rather tell them my personal story, I want to share to them that you struggle and I understand that. I struggled too. And we can overcome that. The key is to get education and the doors will open for you."

Kathleen is the eldest of Ken's three daughters. She's named after an English teacher Ken had in Scarborough—"My Canadian mom and mentor." Kathleen began grade nine in the fall of 2013 and Ken took the year off to volunteer at her high school. Her experience was not like his ninth grade transition, but he wanted to be there for her all the same.

Kathleen, Katrina, and Kamilla, three girls with lacquer-black hair in the image of their Vietnam-born mother, love to hear the adventure stories of their parents. It's important to Ken that they know their family history. Their own history, once removed. Like Vietnamese—a mother tongue, once removed—learned during evening language games in a mix of tones and giggles.

5 Hodan Ali

Somalia

Hodan Ali in Hamilton.
Photograph by Sheryl Nadler.

February 1989, Mogadishu, Somalia

You never know how a trip will turn out.

"See you in a month!" Hodan Ali called out to her parents, younger sister, and two brothers from the departures gate at Mogadishu's international airport. It was 1989, a warm February day, and twelve-year-old Hodan was travelling with her pregnant aunt, uncle, and their two young children to the United States. Her aunt had a history of difficult pregnancies. She wanted American doctors to handle this one and Hodan was along to babysit her cousins.

It was the last time they were all together. When the government of Somalia collapsed two years later, Hodan's family would join thousands of others who cleared out of the capital. And not everyone would survive.

Not even a shadow of these coming events crossed Hodan's mind. She was going on a vacation.

She had been abroad on a family trip to Italy once, but wasn't ready for the airport in Washington. Dazzling lights, stores, stairs that moved like conveyor belts then folded neatly into the floor. And rushing in all directions were people, every race, every colour, looking like they had walked here from every country in the world.

Hodan gaped. "What are they all doing here?" Her aunt chuckled and said, "They're Americans."

In Mogadishu, there were only people who looked like her. Hodan's mother was an accountant, her father, a businessman. The world of a girl in a middle-class family in Somalia was splendidly simple. There was private school and Islamic classes during the week, and on weekends, shopping trips downtown with her parents and siblings. There were movies and family gatherings with the men chatting about politics during lazy afternoons, while the children turned white stone floors into a make-believe stage. And always at her fingertips near their home was the "Côte d'Azur of East Africa," the white sand beaches, and adventure.

She remembers eating a burger in Washington, like nothing she had tasted. Then for Hodan it all became very confusing. The family group were not heading to an airport to return to Somalia in March 1989, but north, to Buffalo, New York, to the Canadian border. Hodan and her cousins waited in a separate room, while in another room her aunt and uncle were asking border officials to allow everyone into the country as refugees, though Hodan didn't know it at the time.

The adults had decided not to risk returning to Somalia with an almost-due newborn. Militias had formed across the country bent on forcing out longtime dictator Mohamed Siad Barre. The gun battles that would signature the next two decades had begun.

A different series of events made the spring of 1989 memorable for Hodan. A Canadian couple who belonged to a church in Fort Erie, across the Niagara River from Buffalo, brought Hodan's family to a motel where they spent ten days. Hodan ate cereal for the first time. The Fort Erie congregation helped find a house and register the children in school, and before long her aunt gave birth to a healthy baby girl. Hodan and her aunt's family were accepted as refugees in 1989. Hodan scarcely noticed. That was just background noise to a new house, a new grade six classroom, a new favourite teacher, and, within half a year, a new language: English. She was back in a place where people looked, well, the same. Except for her. She was the first African her classmates had ever met.

In Mogadishu in January 1991, with rival militias inside the city, the state dissolved. People living in the capital fled, many on foot, mostly south to rural Somalia or west into Kenya. But the world wasn't watching an entire capital nearly empty. It was watching live coverage of events some 3,400 kilometres north—Baghdad lit up by rockets, dust rising from columns of tanks, airstrikes, burning oil fields. Reporters broadcast Operation Desert Storm in real time and a Somali coup passed by unnoticed.

Hardly any news was being sent from Somalia. Rumours had replaced outbound communication and Hodan had no idea where her parents and siblings were. She and the family had to rely on word-of-mouth scraps that made it to Canada. She heard that her father was injured. That he was not injured. That he had been killed. That he was alive.

On a spring day in 1992, the phone in her aunt and uncle's home in Fort Erie began ringing. Hodan's mother had reached eastern Kenya and finally found a phone line. Hodan's father was dead, killed in Mogadishu. That was enough to hear but her mother had more: Hodan's younger sister was also dead. Sadia fell ill during the march from the capital. Hodan's mother, after losing her husband and burying her daughter, pushed on, escaping with her two sons.

There had been no warning, not even rumours about Sadia. "I had kind of prepared for the death of my father, but my little sister ..." At first, Hodan refused to speak about the news. "But then, you know, a year passes by, a year passes by, and she's in heaven, and same with my father, and you just come up with a peaceful way of accepting it, eventually. But there's no easy way, even when I talk about it, my throat fills up."

Sadia was seven years old when she died in the rural south of Somalia with a high fever and a stiff neck, what Hodan could later call malaria. It was a treatable illness, but there were no pills once war began.

September 2013, Hamilton, Canada

If a child with an infective bite by an Anopheles mosquito is not treated within twenty-four hours, malaria can progress to severe illness and then death. Ninety per cent of malaria deaths are in Africa.[1]

Hodan could diagnose and treat malaria today. She is a nurse practitioner at St. Joseph's Hospital in Hamilton where she moved with her aunt's family in 1992. Her mother and two brothers joined them in Hamilton in 1995 as privately sponsored refugees. Hodan is also a mother of two young girls, aged ten and twelve. When she's not with her girls, she's working. Nursing is her full-time passion.

In 2011, the year before Hodan began a master's degree in nursing at McMaster University, thousands of Somalis were again dying from famine, the lethal companion to war. Hodan volunteered with a relief agency, Islamic Relief Canada, to raise money, but Somalia needed her skills too. When the agency asked, she agreed to two weeks of work in Mogadishu. It was her first time back and she entered a war zone.

From Nairobi in neighbouring Kenya, a small aircraft brought Hodan and two Canadian doctors to Mogadishu. Armoured vehicles painted black awaited them with a driver and gunmen at the front, rear, and centre, and they raced through the remains of city blocks at highway speed to avoid sniper fire or an outright ambush.

Hodan had left her country whole, but it was unrecognizable now. Everything was rubble or bullet-sprayed ruins, left unkempt for twenty years. The city was bloated with fighters but felt hollow. The clinics where Hodan spent her days were full-empty too: full of hundreds of people each day; empty of the bare essentials of medicine. Hodan heard anguished stories of migration north to the capital, the opposite direction her family took in 1991. The patients, mostly women, came on foot from rural lands cleared by famine, cracked and dry, guarded by war lords.

Hodan remembers the mothers, some who had buried their children along the way, others who sat in the clinic queue cradling small, still bodies.

Standing beside the armoured car at the end of a long clinic day, Hodan asked the driver for bearings. Where was she? What building had they converted into this clinic? He told her it used to be a school, told her a name. That's when she recognized the mangled doors of what had been her primary school. Hodan had never experienced Somalia's war. All she had were romantic memories of the city, the way someone remembers a cottage where sunny months of childhood were spent. The revelation of having worked all day in her blown-out school snuffed out that version of Somalia like nothing else yet had. She climbed into the car, shaking and in tears.

Just months after returning to Canada, Hodan began her master's studies. During the next two years, "I was just itching to finish because you see what you want to do," she says. Hodan's ambitions had been growing for decades, maybe starting with her sister's death and gaining focus with Somalia's slump into chaos. Returning to Mogadishu sealed it. She would concentrate on helping people, anyone on the fringes who might not otherwise get care.

Hodan and two doctor friends opened a clinic for refugees in downtown Hamilton in 2011. Refuge Hamilton Centre for Newcomer Health is a non-profit, volunteer-based operation where Hodan works two days a week, and the rest at St. Joseph's. The clinic offers primary care but doubles as a life counselling centre. The patients are mostly newly arrived families and need help with everything from learning a new language to finding a pharmacy, maybe finding a school for their children. Visits with the doctor are typically in-and-out, but Hodan and the staff spend around thirty minutes with first-time patients.

On top of her two jobs, Hodan helped pilot a volunteer health network that sends nurses to high schools in Hamilton's poorer neighbourhoods, where teenagers might not have a family doctor or information about basics like nutrition and mental health. This is exactly what Hodan was itching to finish her degree to do, expand the reach of health-care providers, like herself, into the community.

But a predictable thing happens with frontline work. The drive to help gets stronger because new problems unroll at the feet of service providers. Since the Refuge clinic opened, there are more patients without insurance and more people who Hodan's staff have to turn away, part of the fallout from recent federal health-care cuts for refugees and refugee claimants. Hodan now sees people having to choose between paying rent and buying groceries or visiting a doctor. "It's not good health policy, but it's not a humane policy either," Hodan says. "It bothers me so much when people can't access because we choose for them not to have access."

The issue of choice angers her even more because she's been to a place where choices are few. In Somalia, after twenty years of no training or updates, Hodan saw surgeons working with their bare hands, without operating rooms or proper surgical techniques, and with no infection control—the near-total absence of health-care services. She knows that Somali children are among the most likely, worldwide, to die before they turn five. Many deaths are caused by treatable illnesses, like malaria. "To me, that's such an injustice. Their lives are just as valued." But they were born in a place like Mogadishu, not at St. Joseph's.

Hodan calls herself lucky to have a Canadian passport, and might use it again to return to Somalia. After her first trip, "I vowed that I'll continue to do what I can here, and eventually, maybe go back and see what I can do to be part of the rebuilding."

6 Claudio Durán

Chile

Claudio Durán at home in Toronto.
Photograph by Christopher Manson.

I want to write a long poem
like a nomad of this world's lands
where life consumes itself and is consumed
where trees planted their millennial lineage
where animals wanted to live dying
and among them those like me
who can seat themselves and write about their lives
sowed two different apple trees
that of discord and another not yet reached
in this environment of fleeting or eternal spring
–Claudio Durán, *Autobiography*
(Translation, Francisca Durán)

September 1973, Santiago, Chile

On the evening of September 10, 1973, as he often did, Claudio Durán met with three colleagues to discuss *El Mercurio*, at the State Technical University, the only left-leaning one of Chile's then seven universities, where Claudio was vice-dean of the Faculty of Education. For several hours each meeting, the foursome combed the newspaper for clues. *El Mercurio* was a right-wing mouthpiece for those opposed to the government of President Salvador Allende, and like a political forecast, it occasionally held hints of party manoeuvres.

The researchers had predicted accurately before, and now one of them guessed that something big was coming tomorrow, September 11, possibly a bombing of the presidential palace. It was the same day the president was scheduled to visit Claudio's university. A few members thought the evidence was ambiguous, however, and the researchers went home.

Early the next morning before Claudio left for work, Marcela, his wife, stopped him. She said there was news of a bombing at his school, the State Technical University. Claudio grabbed the phone and rang the radio station reporting the news, and he found an even bigger story: there had been a coup. His study group had been right to predict an event, but they wildly underestimated its scale.

By 9:00 a.m. on September 11, Augusto Pinochet, the general in charge of defending Chile against a military coup, had deposed the democratically elected government and seized control. The presidential palace was bombed later that day and Allende, the president, shot himself.

Although Santiago had been on edge for months, Claudio says "the coup came as a huge, big, terrible surprise." Months earlier, Claudio and his family had moved from an upper-class area because the homes of left-wing supporters like them were targets for vandalism and assaults by anti-Allende vigilantes.

Still, Claudio had disbelieved anything as extreme as a coup could disrupt democratic, pluralist Chile. In the early days of September, Claudio heard a colleague say a coup was inevitable. "I produced a twenty-minute-long speech demonstrating to him that it was impossible." (Years later, Claudio received a letter from the man, in exile in Mexico, with the words: "Remember when ...")

At news of the coup, Marcela took their six-year-old daughter, Francisca, and infant son, Andrés, to stay with her parents while she stayed with an aunt. Marcela's family had conservative ties and unlike her and Claudio, they were against the deposed president. "But still, relatives are more important than ideology," Claudio says. As for himself, the only fixed plan was to keep moving, so Claudio left home on the morning of the coup still resolved to get to the university, but he saw that the military had already filled Santiago's downtown streets. He made for a friend's home instead, deciding his own was unsafe.

Claudio knew he was a target. Left-wing intellectuals were a natural threat to right-wing strongmen like Pinochet, especially one scrambling to consolidate his newly gotten power. Claudio belonged to the Communist Party, but his politics were nuanced. He had supported Allende, the now dead leader of the Socialist Party, for building a coalition across polarized Chile. It was the *Unidad Popular* (Popular Unity), a mix of centre-left and Marxist parties, including the Socialist and Communist parties, that brought Allende to power in the 1970 election. Like the president, Claudio wanted a socialist *and* a democratic country, even while hardliners in the Chilean left urged an autocratic style of government.

Nuance didn't count for much under Pinochet. Four days into martial law, with a major crackdown underway, police raided the empty Durán home and asked neighbours if they knew Claudio Durán, a dangerous communist from the State Technical University. Before leaving, they piled his books on the front lawn and lit them on fire.[1]

Claudio switched beds every few days, sometimes arriving unannounced at the home of a friend or colleague, always before the military's 6:30 p.m. curfew. While he knocked at each new door, the junta broadcast radio messages calling on citizens to alert police should they see a stranger in the neighbourhood. A stranger, they said, could be a terrorist.

One early evening, as he entered another friend's home, Claudio noticed a young girl watching him before she turned and ran away. Would she report a terrorist? It was nearly curfew, but Claudio and his friend decided to risk the streets instead of a police raid. Claudio climbed into his friend's car at 6:20 p.m. In ten minutes, they were in a main artery in the city. "Totally empty. Nothing, nothing, nothing, nothing," Claudio says. Standing alone at the apartment of yet another acquaintance, Claudio rang several times, but there was no answer and the concierge threatened to call the police.

It was after 7 p.m. when Claudio walked back into the street, aiming for the home of Marcela's parents, some twenty blocks away.

September is spring in Santiago and pink light still bathed the city. Long shadows fell from houses on the north side, built without space between walls and sidewalk. Claudio brushed against the bricks, keeping himself in the shadow. The direct route took him past the National Stadium, noisy and surrounded by military trucks and jeeps. He knew it had become a detention centre, but like most residents, only later learned of the extent of atrocities within. It was a house of interrogation, torture, and execution. As those convulsive days of September wore on, the *desaparecidos*, or disappeared, kept increasing but people still hoped their loved ones—academics, members of left-wing parties, and other intellectuals—had not been killed, just detained. The National Stadium alone held some seven thousand political enemies of the junta that September.[2]

Claudio walked the twenty blocks unmolested as darkness fell. He spent the night at his in-laws and was off again the next day.

———

Two weeks after the coup, Claudio discovered his name on a list created by the right-wing extremist group Fatherland and Freedom, one that was involved in assassinations even before 1973.[3] Still, Claudio and Marcela agreed to stay put in Chile, telling themselves the junta would surely hold elections within two months. "We thought if we can hold out, we'll be okay," he says.

Then on September 21, Claudio heard about sympathetic diplomats at the Canadian Embassy and something clicked. It was time to go. He and Marcela, with their daughter Francisca, headed outside again. Their son Andrés was safe with his grandparents, who could deliver him later. The Canadians let the family sleep at the embassy that night, and the following day, on Saturday, September 22, embassy staff moved the group of now fourteen hideaways to the Canadian ambassador's residence.

Seven years before Canadian diplomats in Iran aided the extraordinary escape of eight Americans during the 1979–81 hostage crisis, the Canadians in Santiago scrambled to organize an exit for twelve Chileans and two Brazilians sheltered at the ambassador's residence. The first idea was to help them get to Peru or Mexico, but those countries declined, busy with their own share of refugees. So, on October 5, the embassy announced plan B. The group was going to Canada. Tomorrow. Claudio, Marcela, and Francisca had spent just over two weeks sleeping on mattresses in a large room upstairs (Andrés joined them before takeoff).

Canada had a patchwork refugee policy in 1973. To process the group, the diplomats arranged for the nearest immigration official, stationed in Buenos Aires in neighbouring Argentina, to fly to Santiago and process the group as immigrants, and they would arrive in Canada on ministerial permits. The official arrived at 8 p.m. on October 5 and held interviews nonstop that evening. He interviewed Claudio and Marcela at 1 a.m. Undaunted by circumstance, his first question was: "Why do you want to go to Canada?"

October 1973, Montreal, and October 2013, Toronto, Canada

The front page photo in the *Montréal-Matin* on October 8, 1973, shows a Chilean mother and son arriving at the Montreal-Dorval International Airport. It's Marcela and Andrés with a caption that says "les yeux de l'exil"—the eyes of exile. Montreal had welcomed Ugandan Asians just one year earlier, and this second emergency airlift not long after drew reporters and a crowd of several hundred people to the airport.

There were members of church, labour, and Latin American groups, cheering at the arrivals gate. Their activism had tipped the reluctant Canadian government to protect at least some political enemies of General Pinochet, a new statesman who Canada (and its ally, the United States) did not want to insult.[4] The Chilean refugee crisis fit what historian Gerald E. Dirks observed, "ideological considerations" had replaced race as the discriminatory feature of Canada's refugee policy.[5] Because Chilean refugees were a sensitive bunch for Canada, the success of public pressure was worth celebrating. And from an initially tepid reaction, Canada would go on to accept nearly seven thousand Chileans.[6]

Claudio felt upended. The dictatorship unfolding in Chile had not gained the solid lines of history. The fate of his missing friends and relatives was still unknown. Everything was confused. Who was disappeared or killed? And why? Being in Canada raised other questions. How close was this country to the United States and the CIA, suspected to be complicit in the Pinochet coup? Was he correct, that Canada too was a far-right country? And if not, why had tanks rolled through Montreal streets only three years ago during a so-called October Crisis?[7]

The Canadian government revealed its own blurred judgment of Claudio and Marcela when an RCMP officer interviewed the couple in Montreal. He asked why they chose Canada instead of the Soviet Union if they belonged to the Communist Party. The Cold War was still more than a decade from ending and communism was mistrusted in Canada. "I said I couldn't go to the Soviet Union because I don't want to live under a dictatorship," Claudio recalls. "I teach psychoanalytic theory and this is anathema in the Soviet system. I believe in democracy. I believe that socialism and democracy are perfectly compatible." The officer stood to shake their hands at the end of the interview. He welcomed them to Canada, not as an officer, he said, as a citizen.

After a week in Montreal, the Durán family moved in with a friend in Toronto. A number of Chileans were at the University of Toronto, and the family's first rented apartment was a graduate residence on Charles Street. They became citizens in 1978.

Andrés, then a one-year old, has no memories of September 1973, and Francisca has very few. She doesn't remember when she hugged

Claudio tightly, burying a sombre, six-year-old face the night he hurried past the National Stadium to arrive at his in-laws'. Francisca is now an artist and filmmaker, and Andrés is a lawyer. They both have children of their own.

In Canada, Marcela returned to school for a master's degree in education. She was soon hired by the North York Board of Education for what was then an innovative program, to help the increasing number of immigrant and refugee children in North York adjust to Canadian classrooms. Today, she teaches at York University's Faculty of Education, and coordinates a community practicum she helped design for future teachers to orient themselves to the cultural communities of their students.

Just one year after he arrived in Canada, Claudio became a professor of philosophy at York University. Half-joking, he credited a shortage of doctorates to fill the demand in teaching positions leftover from the 1960s boom of new universities in Ontario. He discovered that Canada was not a country on the far right, but one with deep social roots—where he saw with amazement that a hospital in downtown Toronto could treat his middle-class mother and a homeless man from his neighbourhood, with whom Claudio once stopped to share a coffee in the hospital lobby.

Claudio is now retired but still a presence at York University. When he's not in Toronto, he's teaching graduate courses in philosophy at the University of Chile in Santiago. The brutal rule of Augusto Pinochet ended in 1990 after seventeen years. Claudio continues to monitor *El Mercurio* with old colleagues and, always, to answer how a dictatorship ever emerged in Chile. "I made a point then in 1973, that I would spend my life as an academic trying to understand what happened."

The democratic collapse symbolized in the death of Salvador Allende on September 11 shocked Claudio in a lasting way. "He was a leader with a tremendous following and very dear to the working class. Especially to the working class." As a boy, Claudio went with his father to welcome Allende at the airport in Antofagasta, the northern city where Claudio grew up and where his father, a civil engineer, was posted to oversee the province's roads. "It took many, many years to really understand what had happened. It was difficult." Claudio recorded the shocks in his life with poetry. He began after he met Marcela. "I married an angel," he wrote in *Antofagasta*.[8] He published a translated book of poems in 2008 called *Childhood and Exile*. Simple, vivid lines reveal the personal disruption caused by the coup. Of the city where he and Marcela returned a decade after they escaped, he wrote:

> *Santiago, your buses carry me today.*
> *I go through the world with your symbols.*
> *I carry your structure in my bones.*[9]

7 Rabbi Erwin Schild

Germany

Rabbi Erwin Schild at the Adath Israel synagogue in Toronto.
Photograph by Ryan Walker.

November 1938, Würzburg, Germany

As dawn light crept into the sky, Erwin Schild watched a fire burning outside his Würzburg seminary. A Nazi mob had stormed his dormitory, smashing everything, but leaving the students mostly alone. Erwin had made his way to the main building, hoping to find some calm and order. Instead, he saw a great bonfire in the courtyard leaping higher as uniformed storm troopers dumped on armfuls of books.

Erwin didn't know it yet, but attacks against Jews had swept through Germany that night. It was November 10, 1938, the morning after Kristallnacht, the night of broken glass, when shards of glass littered the streets from Jewish-owned shops, buildings, and synagogues. More than one thousand synagogues were burned and seven thousand businesses destroyed.[1] Dozens of Jews were killed.

Erwin returned to his wrecked dormitory to wait, and, soon after, he and his trembling schoolmates were marched at gunpoint down the narrow Würzburg streets to jail. Days later, Gestapo officers herded them onto buses. The destination: Dachau concentration camp. Erwin felt numb.

He was eighteen years old and even before this, life had been wrenched out of his control by Adolf Hitler, who rose to power in 1933 and, law by law, stripped away the rights of Jews. Erwin had left his hometown of Cologne to study at the Jewish seminary in Würzburg because Jews were barred from attending university.

This loss of freedom was different. On the bus ride to Dachau, Erwin silently begged for a collision, anything to offer some chance of escape. Concentration camps had been in the news, described almost as holiday camps, but other rumours had spread among Germans. Erwin knew the camps were for political enemies of the Nazis and the name Dachau stirred "naked terror," yet he was incapable of imagining his days there.

He entered the camp gates as if under fever. Nothing made sense. They shaved his head and took his clothing away. Orderlies hosed his body with cold water. Someone pushed striped fatigues with a small patch, a yellow Star of David, at him. All of it happened with freakish order. Somewhere between bureaucratic disinterest and disgust, the SS officers handled Erwin like paperwork.

Simply surviving became an indignity. Guards tossed the inmates' meals on the ground, so Erwin ate potato peels covered in dirt. During roll call, he didn't move a muscle to help when another inmate collapsed on the parade square. Prisoners had been shot for doing less.

Another prisoner, an acquaintance, brought word about his family—his brother, sister, and parents back in Cologne—and told him his father Hermann was here too, in this camp, in a different section. Erwin worked his way to the area. He saw his father and stood watching him for several seconds. Then his father saw him. "He looked pitiful in his miserable uniform," Erwin wrote later. "I tried to hide the sinking feeling in the pit of my stomach, my fury, my despair, my mental anguish. And my poor dad—the look on his face when he saw me! Of course, he had not known what had happened to me, but neither of us were prepared for a reunion—and a very fleeting one at that—in Dachau. It was very hard. My father broke down and cried."[2]

Erwin learned that his mother, Hetti, and siblings Kurt and Margot were still safe in Cologne. For now, only he and his father were in danger.

Seven weeks after entering Dachau, during roll call, Erwin heard his name shouted out, one of a list of prisoners to be released. Working diplomatic channels, Hetti had managed to get her son one of the little-known documents that could still save Jews from the camps. A diplomatic affidavit from the consul of the Dominican Republic in Cologne named Erwin eligible for an immigration visa. It was a paper promise by a foreign government to take Erwin off Germany's hands.

In 1938, Hitler had not yet decided on the Final Solution. Jews were allowed out of the country as long as they had permission to enter another. Immigration, however, was a disappearing option. Countries tightened entry rules as more people became desperate to leave.

With the affidavit obtained by his mother, Erwin walked out of Dachau. But there was a caveat: he would be returned to custody if he didn't leave Germany immediately. Though no date was attached to this order, Erwin knew it meant he could be rearrested whenever the Nazis chose.

The Dominican Republic was only admitting a small number of German Jews so Erwin applied to Britain and Netherlands, and the Dutch paperwork arrived first. He spent his last dregs of time in Germany at home with his family, including his father, also saved from Dachau by the wit of his wife. Hetti had twisted a Nazi order into opportunity. A new decree forced Jewish firms to be sold to non-Jews, so

Hetti told Dachau authorities that she needed Hermann, the head of the family shoe store business, to sign away their property. It worked. Erwin's father was temporarily free.

Erwin crossed into Netherlands by train on January 26, 1939, eight weeks after his release, to attend agricultural college in the small Dutch town Enschede. He was there for only five weeks when his application for a student visa to Britain came through. He left for London in March. He felt liberated in this home of Shakespeare and Parliament and Oxford, and because he now had the English Channel between him and Germany. Netherlands had been too close. Erwin enrolled at the Torath Emeth yeshiva in North London, and quickly picked up Yiddish. He was already fluent in German, French, English, Hebrew, and Latin.

His sense of calm was brief. Britain declared war against Germany in September 1939, and Erwin felt the Nazi threat creeping closer to London. But it wouldn't be Nazis who targeted him next.

On May 16, 1940, two British policemen arrived and took Erwin to a makeshift internment camp at the Kempton Park Race Track outside London, a stopover before he was shipped to a second, more secluded camp on the Isle of Man. Paranoia had gripped Britain and politicians spoke openly about a "fifth column" of Nazi spies loosed on the country. A refugee but German national nonetheless, Erwin was declared a threat to British security.

Canada and other Commonwealth countries agreed to share Britain's ever-growing burden of military prisoners, but somehow the diplomatic lines of communication got seriously crossed. What Canadian officials heard was they were getting inmates, prisoners. Whatever the term used for those incarcerated, the Canadians took it to mean the arrival of German and Italian enemies. British officials, meanwhile, told Erwin and the other refugees that they were being shipped to freedom.

Erwin and the other Jews lined up in rows on the quay in Liverpool were not told their destination—a security measure at a time of continuous U-boat attacks—but the interned would sail to either Canada or Australia. A British officer counted them into two groups. The cutoff came just two rows behind Erwin. His group went up a gangway into one ship, the other group into a second. On the ocean, Erwin learned his ship, the *Sobiesky*, was bound for Canada.

Joy crept through him in a way he hadn't known since 1933. "Up to that point, there were no choices, there were no alternatives," Erwin says. "It was total absence of self-determination." *Nearly free,* Erwin thought, as he and his yeshiva mates on board spoke rapturously about the future in Canada, about how it would feel to again determine one's life.

July 1940, Quebec City, Canada

They docked in Quebec City on July 15, 1940, and Erwin discovered this was not a free land, not for him. Canadian soldiers and barbed wire received the *Sobiesky* passengers like enemies. Many of the internees spoke English and French, and as they were herded from the dock to the railway platform, they tried explaining the mistake, repeating the promises of freedom made by British officials.

A Canadian sergeant listened in surprise. He was a young man from Montreal and he was a Jew. Speaking in Yiddish, he told the refugees he would alert the Jewish community in Montreal. (He even told them quickly in Yiddish, "Keep everything in your pockets! What you have in your pockets nobody will take away."[3] Then he gave the order in English: "Empty your pockets!")

From Quebec City, they travelled by train to Trois-Rivières. Tantalizing forest and farmland streaked past the windows. Erwin detrained at a place called Camp T and he and the other refugees filed through the gates of yet another internment camp, to be met by the jeers of the resident internees. Anti-Semitic jeers. The camp was filled with true Nazis, who recognized the Jewish newcomers—who also instantly recognized them. The Nazis broke into familiar songs of the Third Reich. *When Jew blood spurts from the knife, all goes twice as well.* Erwin and the others panicked and surrounded their guards to plead for separation. It was granted by way of a barbed wire fence, quickly erected, to bisect the camp. The Canadian soldiers recognized, as their government apparently did not, that these were two very different groups under their command.

Camp T was one of several created by the Canadian government to accommodate prisoners of war. Over three thousand German and Austrian Jewish refugees, all unmarried men, were shipped from Britain to Canadian internment camps as Prisoners of War Second Class. The wrongful internment is an uncomfortable page of Canadian history, lesser known than the notorious policy to refuse Jewish refugees, summed up in the remark of a senior bureaucrat in Ottawa that "none is too many." There could be little basis, legal or moral, to imprison Jewish refugees in Canada, but POWs were fair game, so despite an outcry about their real identity from the Jewish internees, the Canadian Jewish community, and even (eventually) British officials, many were confined for nearly two years until Ottawa reclassified them as Interned Refugees.[4]

After five weeks at Camp T, Erwin was transferred to Camp B, near Fredericton, where life was better. Because the camp was half-built, Erwin's group was put to work cutting timber in the thick bush. Among the Jewish internees were scholars, professors, musicians, engineers, and even chefs. A school sprang up and a working self-government. There was initial chafing when soldiers' orders conflicted with religious observance, like working on the Sabbath, but these problems were usually resolved in the refugees' favour. Still, no pleasures of study or fellowship, or the slow trickle of civilian rights, could erase the outrage of internment. "The deprivation of freedom is difficult to bear, to be imprisoned as the enemy whom you hate ... and at that time, I hated Germany with every fibre of my being," Erwin says.

He was moved a final time to Camp I on the Richelieu River in Quebec. Ten days later, word came from Ottawa that the Canadian government had designated him a refugee. After that, internees were slowly released, with the help of sponsors. Two windows opened for Erwin: one sponsor in Ottawa, and this came with a spot at Carleton University (then a college); the other in Toronto, where he could attend a yeshiva. For the first time since 1933, Erwin had a true choice. He picked the yeshiva and walked free in February l942, nearly two years after arrest in London.

February 1942 and February 2014, Toronto, Canada

Erwin's free life was before him. As for his family, Erwin knew that his brother Kurt was in the United States, and after the war, they learned their sister Margot and their parents had been sent to Latvia, sometime after 1941, and there became separated. Margot survived and got to a Swedish refugee camp at the end of the war, but their father died in 1943. The fate of his mother was lost, except that she was sent to a labour camp where, Erwin could only believe, she died.

In his early years studying in Toronto, it did not take long for Erwin to excel, and at the prodding of his rabbi, he enrolled at the University of Toronto in the fall of 1944. Within four years, Erwin earned a bachelor degree, began teaching courses at the yeshiva, and married Laura Saxe, a born Montrealer, on a snowy day in December.

At the time of their marriage, Erwin was stateless. He was a permanent resident in Canada and his German passport had expired. In the custom of the day, a woman took her husband's nationality, so Laura became stateless like him.[5] Erwin spent two years interned as a Nazi sympathizer and yet, he says, "that was one of the most shameful things I encountered as an immigrant, that my wife lost her Canadian citizenship." Laura regained her status within months, and Erwin was naturalized in December 1946.

In his late twenties, life unfolded in beautiful complexity of choices and decisions. After graduate studies, the University of Toronto invited him to join its faculty. Or he could choose to enter the rabbinate, which Erwin chose, becoming the rabbi of Adath Israel synagogue in Toronto. He was only twenty-seven.

Erwin and Laura would have three children, and when those children were old enough to stay home alone, they visited Germany together in 1972 for the first time. Erwin returned over the years, often on invitation to lecture before Christian and Jewish audiences. He decided to devote himself to keeping different faith groups in dialogue, to develop a community. It was an obligation he believed came from surviving the Holocaust and having the chance to make another life in Canada.

This sense of duty is common among refugees, Erwin says. "These are the people who take a more elevated view of life, the preciousness of life, and the obligations that come from being rescued."

For his work building interfaith relations abroad and in Canada, in 2000, Erwin was awarded the Officer's Cross of the Order of Merit of Germany, and in 2001, made a Member of the Order of Canada.

Erwin turns ninety-four in 2014 and still occupies an office at Adath Israel synagogue in retirement. He sits behind a large desk piled with books and loose sheets of his writing, the Order of Canada insignia, the maple leaf on a hexagonal snowflake, pinned to his lapel. He hands a book across his desk, an autobiography published in 2001 for his children, grandchildren, and great-grandchildren. It's a record of deep loss and extraordinary events, and how someone gets by after that.

He wanted to show them how precious life is, and urge them to act on every opportunity to help other people. Erwin's blue eyes are clear behind his glasses, like the blue veins of his folded hands. "If God expects anything of us, that's what he expects—that we do something for others."

Randy Singh

Guyana

Randy Singh in Toronto.
Photograph by Christopher Manson.

2003, Georgetown, Guyana

The oceanfront of Guyana's capital, Georgetown, namesake of the British king and colonizer George III, is lined against the fits and cycles of the grey-blue Atlantic by a long concrete wall built for that purpose. The seawall's unintended use has been as a runway for children, a bench for lovers, and, when he was fifteen years old, a bed for Randy Singh.

When Randy told his family at age fourteen that he liked boys, not girls, his mother reacted the only way she knew how. She beat him. She was outraged and ashamed, and his five brothers, especially the four older ones, joined in the abuse.

Guyana was partly to blame for what she did. Like Randy, half the population of Guyana is Indo-Guyanese, the descendants of indentured workers from India. The next largest demographic is Afro-Guyanese, descendants of African slaves. Guyana is a Caribbean country, although not an island, and English is the official language. Politics and society have developed along colour lines, and Guyana still struggles with racism. People are conscious of their identities, their differences, and especially their deviations.

Randy's mother swore she wouldn't have an "anti-man" for a son and turned to the Pentecostal Church to cure what she called his "disease." This brought the pastor to visit their home, to pray and to cleanse Randy by feeding him mixed concoctions—they tasted like plain olive oil. But the shaming didn't end at home. Randy was dragged by the pastor to the front of the congregation, to the altar, and used as a visual aid to sermons on Sodom and Gomorrah.[1] The teenager submitted to all this; he wasn't certain, maybe he really was sick.

"I just went along with it ... I just wanted to find out who I was," he says.

Under Guyanese law, sex between same-sex partners is punishable by life imprisonment.[2] Added to this were the very real threats of stigma and that a gay man brought shame on the whole family and would certainly contract and die from HIV/AIDS.

For most Guyanese, it would be hard to confront their non-traditional sexuality. For a teenaged boy whose only experience with sex was forced by other boys and men, it felt hopeless.

When Randy was five years old, his older brother used to "play games that hurt." That's how Randy described it, being too young for the concept of rape. His first memory of his mother beating him was after he told her about the games. Whether she lashed out because she thought her youngest son was in some way to blame, or simply because she didn't know what else to do, it taught Randy silence. When he was raped again in the following years, by his brother and eventually by four of his cousins, he told no one.

When he could hide it no longer, he did finally tell his family about his sexuality. They were already suspicious. What followed were six months of abuse and humiliation, until Randy left home for a street life and sleeping on seawalls. He'd had enough of submission, not that this had been replaced with confidence or a comfort with himself. He tried suicide with drugstore pills.

Street life brought Randy a surprising comfort though—he received no abuse. But it was cold and he was often hungry. He walked back to the family home early every morning from the seawall for leftover food, which his mother allowed to disappear from the fridge. Randy would eat quickly, alone, then leave.

Among his entire extended family, Randy had only his stepfather and younger brother as allies, and after nearly twelve months living on the street, it was his stepfather who convinced Randy, by now a high school dropout, to move back home.

When he was seventeen, Randy began his first intimate and consensual relationship with a man named Travis, who was a first-time boyfriend, too. They had a good relationship, and Travis persuaded Randy to go back to school. After writing an entrance exam to the School of Nursing at St. Joseph Mercy Hospital in Georgetown, Randy was accepted to the three-year program without a high school transcript.

In a second new beginning, he was allowed to convert the basement of his mother's home into his own apartment, where he and Travis could spend their nights together. His mother had softened when it became obvious to her that Randy was not her feared stereotype of a gay man: a drag queen and prostitute. Randy still ate dinner separately from his family but his mother and two of his brothers were at least civil. He enjoyed his nursing courses and for a time, Randy was happy.

Then, in his second year of nursing, he dropped out. "I just went blank," Randy says. "I had no one there. Whatever happened to me when I was small just kept replaying, so at one point I was thinking about it all the time and just couldn't focus." His relationship with Travis ended just before Christmas in 2009.

On a walk one evening to escape his thoughts, Randy saw a poster for a free movie screening of *Kinky Boots*. He didn't recognize the organizer or the rainbow-coloured flag in the corner but he attended the film. He liked the people there, from the Society against Sexual Orientation Discrimination (SASOD). He learned that movies with gay characters existed, and that the flag stood for LGBT pride—and what LGBT meant. Randy attended a few more films and then SASOD meetings, always taking a taxi in case the wrong people knew where he was going. They talked about the discrimination and violence that lesbian, gay, bisexual, and transgender people were up against, and how to make it better in Guyana. He had found a community. Randy knew, "This is something I wanted to be a part of." Again, life improved and he went back to nursing school in July 2011.

Two years later, Randy was the face of SASOD, a growing group with international backing. He became a literal poster boy when a designer used his image for an event poster. Randy was now taking on bigger roles for the group. He organized a candlelight ceremony in May 2012 at the towering wooden St. George's Cathedral in Georgetown in memory of lives lost to HIV/AIDS, and he appeared in a media blitz beforehand. After the ceremony, for the first time, people began to recognize Randy on the street. Strangers called him "faggot" and worse.

Randy didn't change course; he became even more visible. He agreed to give video testimony on treatment of LGBT Guyanese to a visiting Canadian activist from Toronto and the next month, in April 2013, Randy flew to Toronto to speak at a conference on child sexual abuse.

Back in Guyana on a warm evening in May 2013, a car pulled to a stop beside Randy and three men stepped out. He struggled when the strangers grabbed him, but they forced him into the backseat and someone pressed a metal blade against his skin. They threatened to kill him if he made a sound or another move, and Randy believed them. He closed his eyes while all three men raped him, one after the other. He opened his eyes only when he felt himself thrown face down towards the pavement, catching his fall on his elbows and knees.

In another country, perhaps, or maybe without his history, Randy would have gone to the hospital or police station. But because he was a student at the hospital, because he had the family he did, and because of the stigma that would infect his relationships at work and at home, Randy walked to his basement apartment and showered. He cleaned the wounds where the pavement tore his skin and examined his body as best he could. Randy told his stepfather a few days after, but not his mother; the fallout from his first story at five years old was still enough to silence him.

Randy didn't tell his best friend, either. Stanton (her nickname) lived nearby and discovered she liked girls around the same time Randy was grappling with feelings for boys. She was outspoken, a partier, and she became like his sister. They liked to dress the same to go out, in matching jerseys and tight jeans. In June 2013, the month after Randy was raped, two men approached Stanton and threw acid in her face.

She ran, blind and screaming for help. Stanton came to George-town Public Hospital, a few minutes from the private hospital where Randy worked. "It hurt me daily to look at her and see the pain," Randy says, but he was beside her bed every day, monitoring her care in the morning before school, over his lunch hour, and long into the evening after course work.

Stanton lost an eye, and the damaged skin covered more than half her face. Scarring reached down across her chest, stomach, and arms. International friends working in Guyana helped her apply as a refugee to Canada. She was accepted on humanitarian grounds and flew with her young son to Toronto in September 2013.

It should have been impossible, but things got worse for Randy. Just before Stanton left, he received a dismissal letter from school. The official reason was poor attendance—he had missed a lot of class time caring for Stanton—but Randy suspected he was thrown out for another reason. Stanton's case was a big news story in Guyana and their friendship tied Randy to the LGBT label he had tried to keep quiet at the hospital.

The first threatening call to his cell phone came in early October 2013. The caller talked about deforming him. They were serious threats, but Randy didn't know how seriously to take them until he answered and the unknown caller described Randy's outfit, his jeep, and the exact intersection he was passing. Randy drove straight to the police station. An officer listened to his story and estimated it would take about a year to trace the call. Randy walked out and arrived home more panicked than angry. He told his mother and she reacted the same, both thinking what happened to Stanton could happen again. She helped Randy buy a plane ticket to Canada.

October 2013 and February 2014, Toronto, Canada

Randy arrived in Toronto on October 19, 2013, with a plan to stay for six months, on the same visa he had used for the conference in April, and then go to the United States where he figured he could get another visa, and then return to Guyana. Something had triggered a series of horrific events in 2013 and if he removed himself, Randy thought, whatever it was might cool down.

Friends in Toronto had another idea. They encouraged him to apply for asylum.

"I didn't know of a refugee process," Randy says. "I thought that when you filed for refugee protection, you had to be damaged." Like Stanton had been. His friends also helped him find a lawyer, El-Farouk Khaki, one of Toronto's top lawyers on LGBT refugee claims.

Randy entered the Canadian system the year a new set of refugee laws were first tested. Among the more controversial changes was a mandatory processing period, meaning an initial hearing is held thirty to sixty days after an asylum claim is filed (replacing an open-ended system with an average wait time of nineteen months).[3] Randy had his Immigration and Refugee Board (IRB) hearing scheduled sixty days later, in January 2014. His was the more generous timeframe, and yet, one of the best refugee lawyers in Toronto managed to submit the final evidence for Randy's claim just three business days before his hearing, causing the judge on his file to refuse several of the last-minute documents, including his psychological report, a critical piece used to gauge credibility.

The hearing began at 8:30 a.m. and ended seven hours later, when the judge finished her questions.

"She kept pressing on about when I was raped and when I was abused," Randy says. "The stuff I didn't want to recollect or recall and even though she would be talking to me and I would be crying, she wouldn't even say, 'I'm sorry and we're going to take a break,' she just kept pressing on."

At the end of the hearing, Randy was amazed to hear a positive decision.[4]

For weeks afterward, Randy felt low. He couldn't eat or sleep properly. He felt agitated. He wouldn't let Ken, his boyfriend, get close to him. Partly, it was the realization of the finality of what had happened: "That you can't go back home, you're here now." He Skyped daily, as much as possible, with his younger brother or his parents. He missed them, and the hardest times were Christmas and New Year's.

He is a status refugee, but a month after his successful hearing, in February 2014, Randy was still waiting for his permits, unable to work or study. It's a brief but frustrating state that shows in his strained voice and clasped hands. Once he can, he'll apply for a personal support worker program and save, through part-time work on the side, until he can afford nursing school. For now, he volunteers with the non-profits Supporting Our Youth, 519 Church Street Community Centre, and the Black Coalition for AIDS Prevention. Although he feels stalled professionally, these groups are a lifeline to Randy. At least in the meantime he can help others.[5]

The pace of Toronto is growing on him, while the tolerance already has. "I can hold his hand walking down the road," Randy says, motioning to Ken across their bachelor apartment. "If I feel like kissing him on the road, I can do that."

9 Marguerite Nyandwi

Burundi

Anonymous portrait of Marguerite Nyandwi at the Donald
Berman Maimonides Geriatric Centre in Montreal.
Photograph by David Kawai.

October 1993, Rutana Province, Burundi

Marguerite Nyandwi lay in a hospital bed in October 1993, an IV needle in her arm, her head throbbing with a malarial fever ache. Suddenly, her high school friends were all around her bedside. Were they visiting? No, they lifted her upright, detached the IV. Someone tipped a glass of milk to her lips. "You have to come," they said in thick voices. The malaria drugs had dulled Marguerite's hearing.

She half-walked, was half-pulled back to school as her friends explained what happened. The president of Burundi, Melchior Ndadaye, an ethnic Hutu, had been assassinated.

Marguerite's school was in Rutana Province of southern Burundi, a fragment of the African continent wedged east of Lake Tanganyika and cut through by hills of the East African Rift. Burundi sits beneath Rwanda and shares a great deal of that country's history, even called Ruanda-Urundi under the German and then Belgian colonial governments. Burundi and Rwanda were home to distinct nations long before Europeans carved up Africa in 1885. What the countries share are the two dominant ethnic identities, Hutu and Tutsi, and as do neighbours everywhere, they also share the results of events across the border.

Under the post-colonial Hutu governments in Rwanda, Tutsis were targets of systematic violence spanning decades. In 1994, it would become full-scale genocide.

Burundi appeared, as writer Philip Gourevitch described, like Rwanda through a "bloody looking glass."[1] It was Hutus, not Tutsis, who were targeted by what were Tutsi governments. The tiny country of nine million had already witnessed large-scale killing for much of the century. Attacks in 1965, what Burundians call genocide in 1972, attacks in 1988, and a few violent coups in between.[2] Over the years, both Hutus and Tutsis were massacred in Burundi, often sparked by violence across the border in Rwanda (a reverse process too).

It was a great victory when Ndadaye won the majority of votes in 1993, given the dominance of Tutsis in other government offices, including the military and police. Like his election, the fact he was a Hutu loomed large over his assassination on October 21. Violence was immediate.

At times like these, Marguerite, seventeen and a Hutu, understood it was only safe to be with her kind. That's why friends pulled her from her sick bed. It was the beginning of civil war, and not even hospitals were safe.

Marguerite's high school had divided into survival groups. Tutsis chose to stay and Hutus chose to run, fearing the arrival of the Tutsi-dominated military. Marguerite ran from school with her friends, still dizzy with fever. No one in their group carried a thing. No bags, no food, no weapons. There was no destination in mind, it only felt safer to be moving.

The landscape was a chilling spectacle. Like the *mille collines*, or thousand hills, of Rwanda, Burundi is a rolling country with closely grouped humps of red earth and green stretching endlessly at every angle. Marguerite could see the fire dropped by the military or Hutu rebels travelling fast over the dry ground, and at times her bare feet carried her on burning grass. Worse than fire, she could see people moving together on nearby hills. There was no way to tell if they were friend or foe.

Several days into running, Marguerite and her friends ended up captives, having stumbled upon the wrong group. There were six of them placed under arrest including Marguerite. Although her group was larger early on, people had fallen to the ground along the way, unable to walk farther. "You abandon people. You love them but there's no other thing you can do," she explains softly.

Sitting on a rock and surrounded, Marguerite was told to pray. Someone sharpened a machete called a *panga*. She thought she would die this way. Then a group appeared on the crest of an adjoining hill and they charged toward Marguerite's Tutsi captors, who turned and fled. Without thinking, Marguerite took off with them, her flight instinct in charge. It didn't matter that the incoming group were Hutu like her; they were new attackers waving pangas.

When they caught up with Marguerite, she realized they were Hutus, but they roughly restrained her, not believing her cries that she was Hutu too. Marguerite is tall and slender and has a narrow nose, supposedly traits of a Tutsi woman, but like so many, Marguerite is an exception to this identity rule.

They eventually let her go. Marguerite continued on, now with just a handful of friends. Between a crouch and run, they passed bodies, and sometimes just body parts, and all the dogs and birds that would fatten in the feeding frenzy of the coming weeks.

After three months of running and hiding, Marguerite arrived in Shanga, her home village in Rutana. She was almost unrecognizable, unbathed, her hair in clumps.

Both of Marguerite's parents passed away when she was a child, but her older siblings had taken over, giving her a bed and paying her school fees. It was school she had in mind now. "When you don't go to school, you're nothing," Marguerite explains. But it had to wait. Security came first.

When Marguerite next left her village to finish school, it was a year after the civil war began between the Tutsi-dominated government and various Hutu rebel groups. She found a tenuous peace in class. Marguerite fixed her eyes on the teacher, pretending to ignore the student beside her who had softly placed a grenade on the desk. She sat stiffly facing forward even when another student held a machete in his lap and gazed sideways at her. These were not light threats. People at her school had already been killed. Things were so bad that on some nights, Marguerite went to bed fully dressed so she could slip out and be far from the building when an attack began, and cautiously return at dawn.

The pace of war tossed people from one period of violence into another. Marguerite didn't finish high school until 1999, continually removing herself during the outbreaks.

After graduation, Marguerite had her mind set on attending university, but Burundi had in place a military service requirement for students. Another service wanted her too. Hutu rebel groups were recruiting fighters throughout the country to power an insurgency against the Tutsi government. At first, the recruiters cajoled, and then they bullied—calling her a traitor—and finally, they terrorized. She wasn't alone, men and women were being forced into service, sometimes kidnapped by rebels and used as soldiers, slaves, or human shields.[3] When death threats came, Marguerite left her brother's home to stay with her aunt and uncle. For housing a dodger, her aunt was killed at home during the night. Marguerite and her uncle found her.

Still, she refused to enlist with either the government military or the rebels. It was against her nature. "I said no ... for me, it's something which cannot go in my blood."

Then, in 2002, Burundi lifted conscription for university students. Marguerite jumped at the chance to enrol at the University of Burundi in Bujumbura and to live in the capital, where she hoped to find anonymity. One day, however, someone did recognize her in a street market. He was a friend, he knew Marguerite from Shanga and told her about his work with an organization that helped refugees. If she ever needed anything, he said, she could call. She took the offer and with his help, Marguerite got a Burundian passport with a visa to Kenya.

August 2002, Nairobi, Kenya

Marguerite had tracked down the address of a girlfriend's family in Nairobi and they met her at Jomo Kenyatta airport. She would stay at their home in Kawangware, a sprawling slum in Nairobi's west end, just beside the gated homes of Lavington. Still, Marguerite describes them as, "Not poor, only a little bit," because a corrugated roof was better than none.

In her first few days, the family showed Marguerite around Nairobi. The city's newness and contrasts to Burundi's capital overwhelmed her. Compared to Bujumbura, everything was fast. The small transit buses, *matatus*, tore through downtown boulevards at high speed, their touts hanging from open doors, catcalling clients. Pedestrians too seemed to move faster, even in queues they jostled forward. It was unthinkable that her bag could have been snatched from her arm in Bujumbura, so unlike tourists who are taught what to do, Marguerite didn't cling to it and suddenly, it was gone, along with her passport.

The United Nations High Commissioner for Refugees (UNHCR) was a large presence in Kenya because of surrounding conflicts in Somalia, Burundi, Rwanda, Democratic Republic of Congo, and beyond. Marguerite had planned to register with the agency as a refugee, and the bureaucratic steps multiplied without her passport. Her identity mattered now for a different reason than it had in Burundi, but she had nothing to prove herself. She was one more face in Nairobi's paperless crowd, the great undocumented. For sixteen months, Marguerite went to the office on Rhapta Road in nearby Westlands, at first daily to queue outside with dozens of others, and then for countless appointments, until she could get her case accepted.

Marguerite wasn't living in a designated refugee camp, the rule in Kenya.[4] The full consequence of this wasn't yet clear. In effect, she was rescinding her refugee status. Marguerite had been to a camp before, in Burundi in 2001, when she was hiding from rebel recruiters. She thought the camp might be safer, and then she was raped there, twice.

The first time, the Burundian soldiers stationed there dragged her to the showers, telling her she had no right to refuse her protectors. The second time, when women were collecting firewood outside the camp in the early morning, armed men appeared around them. They accused the women of sleeping with the government military, and said that now it was their turn. One woman tried to run and they shot her dead, so Marguerite didn't struggle.

She knew about Kenya's rules, but refused to ever go back, "Me—I don't go to refugee camps."

While staying in Kawangware, someone from the UN Refugee Agency found Marguerite to deliver a message from a brother who she hadn't seen in more than ten years. He now lived in Canada and was searching the UN database for his family. After finding Marguerite, and along with the Action Réfugiés Montréal, a Canadian non-profit, he launched a private sponsorship application in 2004 to bring her to Canada.

Life in Nairobi became more comfortable. Marguerite now had money wired from her brother, and her refugee status gave her a clearer idea about her future. At least she would not be deported to Burundi. The war that dumped her out of a hospital bed in 1993 would somewhat end with a ceasefire in 2006, although mass disarmament would not begin for another two years. While she waited for Canada, Marguerite enrolled in a medical lab certificate course at the Technical Institute in Nairobi, already feeling like time for school was escaping her.

Word arrived in the fall of 2007 that Canada had accepted her, five years after arriving in Kenya. She could leave as soon as October the same year. But the rest of 2007 passed and Marguerite was still in Nairobi, stuck, unable to leave because of the problem in her paper-work—she was not a resident of a refugee camp. The United Nations was bound by Kenya's rules, and so Marguerite couldn't get the signatures she needed to leave. "At that time I was almost crazy," she says. The door, so unexpectedly opened to Canada, seemed now to be closing.

So began a seven-month long stream of letters and phone calls among Canadians, Kenyans, and UN staff, led by Glynis Williams, a Canadian reverend based in Montreal and working with Action Réfugiés Montréal, until the stalling parties in one or more bureaucracies agreed to release Marguerite. In April 2008, with mere weeks to go before her Canadian visa expired, she was back at Jomo Kenyatta airport, boarding a plane.

April 2008 and December 2013, Montreal, Canada

Topping Marguerite's agenda after landing in Montreal was a visit to Rev. Glynis and at first, she could only manage to cry. She sank onto the woman's lap, this stranger and rescuer. As soon as she could, she enrolled in school. She decided on nursing, and in May 2008 Marguerite was in a classroom at the Centre de formation et de placement en santé, training to become a nursing aide, one month after arriving in Canada.

Marguerite began a nursing program at Montreal's Saint-Laurent College in 2009 and graduated four years later, taking just a year longer than her peers to adjust to the Québécois French language and new system. She is now a registered nurse working night shifts at the Donald Berman Maimonides Geriatric Centre and she glows, speaking about her work. "It's something which is in me."

Marguerite's living room faces a snow-covered suburban street in Montreal. Ducking in and out during our interview, George, her husband leaves to dig their car from the snow outside, then disappears into the kitchen to fix dinner. They met at Rev. Glynis's church in Montreal, but the two share a history in Kenya. George was born in Kenya and their first conversation covered Marguerite's unflattering impressions of Nairobi, which he heard with empathy. As Marguerite says, "He has a story of his own."

When she met George, he was an asylum claimant very close to being deported. As Marguerite fell in love, she carried the fear and stress of his uncertain future the way she had carried hers. Soon, his future was hers too. They married in August 2010, and three years later, in August 2013, George heard he could stay in Canada.

Marguerite became a Canadian citizen in March 2013. To her that means, "I'm free." She can study without interruption, she can feel indistinguishable among Montrealers, and she can be critical—especially of conditions in Burundi, a capacity she didn't know she was missing until she arrived in Montreal. "I can go back home and speak out, things which I see which are not right, but before I could not do it ... I can only do it when I'm a Canadian."

Another change Marguerite discovered in Montreal was her ability to trust men. She thought that was over, broken somewhere between the woods and a muddy shower stall in Burundi. She surprised herself when she found George.

"He's amazing. I can go to sleep, he cooks—you see? He's busy, he's always busy," she points to the kitchen, smiling. "He's an amazing man."

10 Andrew Hidi

Hungary

Andrew Hidi at his office in Toronto.
Photograph by JC Pinheiro.

November 1956, Budapest, Hungary

Andrew Hidi and his fiancé Suzanne had decided to leave Hungary, but not before getting married and honeymooning for one night at the Grand Hotel on Budapest's Margaret Island. They paid a bribe to schedule a same-day civil ceremony on November 3, 1956, and before a few relatives and close friends, they became husband and wife.

The Danube River's famously blue waters wind around Margaret Island and here the newlyweds could withdraw into a world of 1870s-era elegance, gardens, leafy walkways, and medieval ruins. A moment to remember all their lives while, around them, Budapest was holding its breath.

Weeks earlier, impromptu student marches escalated amazingly into a revolt against the brutal Soviet-backed communist government. Andrew was twenty-one, a fourth-year engineering student at the University of Budapest, when the revolution stunned even its orchestrators in October 1956. He marched with thousands of students from the university to Bem Square and, later that week, to the Western Rail Station. He watched Soviet tanks roll over the cobblestones, saw Molotov cocktails smashing in flames, and saw students dropping in the streets. He heard bullets whistle over his head. The world was watching. Photojournalists wired home images of the daredevil protestors, guns strapped over their shoulders, surrounded by rubble and Soviet machinery. In late October, the Hungarian government collapsed.

Shocked by the resistance, the Soviet tanks and troops withdrew to the countryside. In that early November lull, Andrew and Suzanne married. There was time to honeymoon because they were leaving the next morning. Except the tanks rolled back into Budapest that night.

By Sunday morning, November 4, the bridges to the mainland were closed and Andrew and Suzanne were marooned. One day too late.

Andrew was not completely surprised. He knew the military and secret police would regroup. As a protestor, punishment would be swift. There was no choice. He had to leave. And he was also in love, giving another reason to leave. Both their family connections left them unloved by the communists—Andrew's father was an accountant, an occupation authorities rated below the factory worker or peasant farmer. But accountants were useful and considered acceptable. So their children, like Andrew, had better access to education. Suzanne's family operated a bourgeois independent business, and from all they had heard, her chances of getting into university were low. Bright and ambitious, she felt she had no future in a communist Hungary.

On the island, when the bridges reopened, Andrew and Suzanne immediately tried to get out. Befriending two foreign journalists, they crammed into a Volkswagen Beetle and sped toward the Austrian border, only to be quickly stopped and turned back to Budapest by Russian soldiers. Their second attempt came days later, aboard a truck headed for Austria's capital, Vienna, but that was aborted when Andrew fell sick.

Their third try was by train heading west to the border town of Szombathely, where they left the station and began hiking through woods again toward Austria. Overland escape would work for over two hundred thousand Hungarian refugees,[1] but not this time, for Andrew, Suzanne, and three friends accompanying them. Close to the border, Russian patrols were everywhere. The group was stopped and loaded into an army truck, in the care of a squad of soldiers so drunk they were slashing the air with machine guns like clumsy swordsmen. The detainees were taken to jail but released after one night, because of overcrowding more than leniency.

The reckless energy of the protestors matched against Soviet steel brought some three thousand deaths in under three weeks in 1956. Then began the roundup of survivors[2] and attempts to tidy the revolution into oblivion by arrests and by physically sweeping the streets. But the evidence still littered Budapest like abandoned party favours: beheaded statues, lopsided window frames without glass, stray tires, concrete blocks, and finer rubble—a coating of gritty dust. Curious onlookers made tracks around burned-out tanks.

On November 24, after three failed attempts, Andrew and Suzanne tried it again. This time travelling by truck to a spot past the city of Gyor, about an hour's drive northwest of Budapest. The truck driver—who was to be caught later and executed—stopped and pointed ahead into the darkness. Austria was that way. They began walking. Less than an hour later they stumbled up to the edge of a huge swamp, impossible to cross at night. It was a dead end. They headed back to Gyor.

Within hours the newlyweds would be making a last desperate attempt. With the help of a local man said to be able to help escapees reach the border, Andrew and Suzanne set out at 5:00 a.m., when the fewest number of border patrols would be out in the predawn cold.

Following their guide, they hurried over fields cleared of landmines less than one year before. The Russians had dug up the mines as a goodwill gesture to Austria. The ground forward was clear. But with protestors on the run, the Russians were sending up flares into the gloom to illuminate the would-be escapees. Moving beneath this eerie light show, each time a flare burst in the sky, they fell to the ground. Anyone left standing was a stark silhouette. A hundred metres from where they lay like stones, Andrew saw soldiers surround another group of escapees exposed under the light.

As they haltingly advanced toward what they hoped was Austria, their guide, a total stranger, kept asking for more money, more valuables to keep going. Could he be trusted? When the fields had been mined, they knew that some groups were guided into the arms of a waiting patrol. Those guides were double agents. Hoping for the best, and with more bills or another watch, Andrew and Suzanne and their guide kept moving.

After two hours of walking and dropping to the ground, the darkness was fading and the sky becoming paler and paler. Andrew and Suzanne, still with their guide, believed they were nearing the border until they heard Hungarian voices nearby. They froze, thinking their guide had trapped them. But it was not a trap, not a patrol, only a translator working with the Austrians who were searching for refugees. They had reached Austrian soil. Aid workers spirited them to Vienna in dry clothing, and from there, they joined over 37,000 Hungarian refugees accepted to Canada as a special class of subsidized immigrants.[3]

The newlyweds sailed from the Italian coast on the *Castel Bianco*, although not exactly a luxury cruise. This was December 1956. They, at least, fared better than most passengers, who spent the two-week Atlantic crossing below deck with thirty to a room. Suzanne spoke English and worked as a translator for the ship's Italian doctor. As payment, the couple shared a private cabin. Suzanne spent her days working. Andrew, seasick, lay prone on the deck. He smiles at the memory of Suzanne finding him at the end of the day, his face paper-white with dried ocean salt.

———

January 1957, Saint John, and August 2013, Toronto, Canada

Andrew and Suzanne arrived in Saint John, New Brunswick, on January 4, 1957. They took a train to Montreal where friends of friends were waiting to drive them to Toronto.

Canada, what a difference: slushy streets, flashy cars with huge tail fins, the election of someone called John Diefenbaker, Hollywood movies like *Bridge on the River Kwai* and *Twelve Angry Men*. News covered Canadian troops peacekeeping in Egypt, the Sputnik 1 satellite launched by the Russians, and coming in April, Elvis Presley playing two concerts at Maple Leaf Gardens.

Andrew and Suzanne were young, twenty-one and nineteen, about to test themselves in a new country. They wanted to go to school, but first, they needed to find work. Andrew took a job cleaning the Yorkminster Park Baptist Church, a Gothic giant on Yonge Street, and Suzanne became a receptionist with Bell Canada. When Andrew was accepted into third year engineering at the University of Toronto with two years of his Hungarian education recognized, Suzanne funded his tuition. Years later, after he graduated, he did the same for her. Ten years after arriving in Canada, Suzanne earned her PhD.

They now have a family, two boys (who speak Hungarian) and six grandchildren (who do not). Their children grew up with grandparents because Andrew and Suzanne sponsored her parents, and her grandmother, to follow them to Canada.

At the age of forty, Andrew started a company. His engineering consultancy firm grew from one employee to one hundred and thirty, and the buildings the firm has worked on dot downtown Toronto. One is the Ritz-Carlton on Wellington Street. Farther afield is Gresham Palace, a Four Seasons Hotel in Budapest. His son Jamie is his business partner and now the company's president. His second son, Andre, runs the global mergers and acquisitions division at the Bank of Montreal—but only after a stint in pro-hockey. Andre played for Canada at the 1980 World Junior Championships. In the NHL, he skated seven games for the Washington Capitals. After leaving hockey, Andre earned an MA from Stanford University's Business School.

Hockey and skating turn up more than once in Hidi family history. Andrew's grandson is studying on a four-year university hockey scholarship. And skipping back two generations, Andrew and Suzanne first met on an ice rink when he was sixteen and she fourteen. In 1950s Budapest, the rinks were strictly for counter-clockwise skating so Andrew can't cross to his right side. Can't shoot a decent puck either. "I leave hockey to the kids," he grins.

Andrew and Suzanne first travelled to Hungary in 1964 and returned many times since, but never for good. Andrew explains, "In simple terms, I'm a Canadian. I feel like a Canadian."

11 Sorpong Peou

Cambodia

Sorpong Peou at home in Newmarket.
Photograph by Ryan Walker.

April 1975, Battambang, Cambodia

Sorpong Peou desperately wanted an end to war in Cambodia. He wanted it to stop and change course smoothly like the water of the Tonlé Sap, flowing one way on an evening in June and another way in the morning.

Sorpong was the oldest of seven children. Their father, Nam, was an apolitical civil servant in the Ministry of Interior, in the governments of King Sihanouk and his successor Lon Nol. The job brought the family to Battambang from Phnom Penh, the capital city where Sorpong was born, where the Tonlé Sap and the Mekong meet.

Fighting between Khmer Rouge insurgents and government forces had raged for years outside Cambodia's cities like Battambang, but by early 1975, even these urban strongholds felt increasingly at risk. As a precaution, and if the family had to flee, Nam had rented a house in Bangkok, Thailand. In Battambang, the family even had a trench dug beside their home in case artillery arced in their direction. Two years earlier in the capital, Sorpong's maternal grandfather lost part of a leg and his grandmother and an aunt had been killed when a shell hit.

The war ended on April 17, 1975, when the Khmer Rouge marched into Phnom Penh. Sorpong's family came close to leaving for Thailand, but didn't. Rumours said the government would soon fall, and there would be no drawn-out, bloody end as expected. In the beginning, Sorpong and his parents, like many, believed the Khmer Rouge slogans about installing peace and a new type of democracy. Their relief the war was over outweighed any misgivings. The Khmer Rouge was a radical group that everyone seemed to know in the abstract, but whose goals and leadership were obscure.

And then the marches began. There was logic at first to the Khmer Rouge order, at gunpoint, that city residents leave their homes and file out on roads that turned to rice paddies and jungle. The soldiers said it was a temporary inconvenience, necessary because of the threat of bombing by Lon Nol's American allies, and that there was no need to carry many belongings. "We bought that," Sorpong said. "I even believed we would come back in five days or a week."

Sorpong was seventeen, still in high school, and excited. With a four-wheeled cart packed with blankets and food, his family moved easily from village to village, away from the city. He was surrounded by thousands of people, flickering through trees when they crossed a jungle or bulging in winding lines through the fields. They slept in pagodas if there was space, or else outdoors in the warm night. For Sorpong, there was an air of adventure. But days became a week and still the soldiers pushed them onward. April turned to May, the month of dry heat before monsoon rains, and as he walked, Sorpong's eyes stung from blowing dirt that stuck beneath his eyelids.

They stopped after—was it fourteen days? They had reached a village, not much more than some thatched homes and a pagoda, where Sorpong lay on the cool wooden floor and felt his eyes pulse.

His eyelids had swollen closed from dirt so Sorpong only heard his father crouch at his side to tell him that he and the other civil servants were being ordered back to work—he guessed returning to help the Khmer Rouge build a new government. Nam kissed Sorpong on the forehead and said, "Papa will come back in a few days."

A few days passed and unease settled over the groups of families. They were all waiting. Some were recovering from the march, some like Sorpong's mother, Chhea Vath, were watching every group of new arrivals stumbling into the camp, scanning the tired faces. But Nam did not appear.

Slowly, the villagers and the new residents from the city were organized into work groups. Sorpong and two or three other young men pulled a plow, in place of buffalo they didn't have, while a single man behind them steered the blade through the earth. They worked from sunrise to just before sunset, but sometimes went straight until midnight. Workload didn't vary much by age or strength. His mother was assigned to the common kitchens. Two younger siblings were assigned to youth groups used as travelling labour for a dam project or an understaffed field. The youngest, Sorpong's six-year-old brother, was sent to dig small canals.

Sorpong slept on the floor of a pagoda hall with dozens of other men. There were no walls, just pillars supporting a vast, carved roof. His youngest brother arrived from the fields even later than he did, exhausted, his slim torso caked with dirt. If Sorpong had any excitement left for the rhetoric of building Cambodia on human strength and labour, it disappeared at the sight of his hungry brothers and sisters.

Sorpong lasted for three months and then collapsed, falling unconscious in the harness of the plow. He was ill and already, his skin stretched taut over his bones from hunger. At that point, he should have been killed. That was the Khmer Rouge practice with people no longer able to work, echoed in their mantra: "To keep you is no benefit, to destroy you is no loss." His life was spared, however, because the village leader had a curious soft spot for Sorpong and his siblings, for the mundane, almost silly reason that they were cute. It was help they didn't look for, but didn't object to, either. Without the village leader, the whole family would have been compromised by Nam's former job. Khmer Rouge believed intellectuals poisoned the country's "old people," meaning the rural, illiterate peasants. "New people" who exhibited signs of education or basic literacy were to be eliminated. There were few exceptions; among them, Sorpong and his family.

Once he regained some strength, Sorpong was trained as a blacksmith.

Despite the central plan for three harvests per year, Cambodia dropped quickly into famine. Sorpong's constant hunger and sickness (from malaria and abdominal pain), the long days of work, exhaustion, and unrelenting fear for his family changed his version of time, so that weeks and months were not separate things to mark as they passed; there was just each day, with another day tomorrow.

He saw people fall sick to the ground, passing from work to death in moments, and he saw others marched away by soldiers to private executions. The Khmer Rouge took a man who slept near Sorpong from his bed during the night. He knew it was likely that his father died the way these people did, shot and buried in the pit that caught their fall. Sorpong lost his paternal grandparents too. His grandfather from starvation, his grandmother, he believes, from a broken heart.

———————

Vietnamese soldiers entered the village in late December 1978. Sorpong and other villagers could only watch as the battle seemed to begin and end in the space of a field, the Cambodian soldiers running and the Vietnamese advancing and shooting them down. The village leader who spared Sorpong's family was executed. Phnom Penh fell to Vietnam a month later, in January 1979. Almost four years had passed.

After the Khmer Rouge, Sorpong devoted himself to feeding his family. There was no use for money, whatever bills survived abolishment in 1975 were devalued to junk. But goods were traded for food, and Sorpong used his blacksmith training to craft metal covers for wooden wheels and other items in demand. They stayed in the village because they had nowhere else to go.

This new routine of survival ended when Sorpong received a tip that the Vietnamese, the new masters in Phnom Penh, suspected he was a spy for the anti-Vietnamese liberation movement. He was given no explanation why.

Sorpong didn't want to leave Cambodia or his family, but landing in jail would be worse for them all. Thailand was the safest bet, even though he had heard stories of Cambodians being caught at the border and forced as a lesson to retreat through minefields. He found his way to a refugee camp on the Cambodian side of the Thai border, after carefully picking his way along foot trails that crossed those minefields. There, the Vietnamese suspicion turned into a self-fulfilling prophecy. Sorpong joined a newly formed resistance group, the Khmer People's National Liberation Front, battling alongside remnants of the Khmer Rouge, against the Vietnam-backed regime. "I went to the border by myself, I was twenty," Sorpong explained. "I had to join something, a movement, to get food at least."

He didn't stay long. He returned to the village for his family, walking during the night, and with his six siblings and mother in tow, he retraced his steps back to the border, to a refugee camp.

Sorpong and his brothers crossed back and forth from Cambodia to Thailand, smuggling out goods and selling them in the camp. It was during this time, in early 1980, that Sorpong suffered beyond all the Khmer Rouge had inflicted. His family was going hungry in the camp, so Sorpong returned to his old village to dig for food in the furrows of the latest harvest, this time alone. That's when he got news that the camp where he had just left his family was destroyed by Vietnamese artillery. All the refugees had dispersed or been killed. Sorpong heard nothing from his family for months. "That was the lowest point in my life. Forced labour is bearable, losing all your family is not." He considered suicide.

And then he heard from a relative returning from the border, "Sorpong, what are you doing here? Your family is looking for you in Thailand." Sorpong found them, all of them still together, six siblings and his mother. After that, they stayed in Thailand in camps run by the United Nations High Commissioner for Refugees (UNHR), and Sorpong took odd jobs with the agency, once as the chief radio operator for the network of refugee camps along the roughly eight-hundred-kilometre Thai-Cambodia border. He learned English on the job.

In early 1982, he volunteered with an American embassy unit doing refugee resettlement. He befriended a few Americans and when they failed to persuade their own country to take the Peou family, the Americans called their counterparts at the Canadian embassy in Bangkok and asked for their help. Within months of that phone call, Sorpong and his family were on a plane to Montreal-Mirabel International Airport.

September 1982, Ottawa, and January 2014, Toronto, Canada

The family landed in Ottawa in September 1982. As government-assisted refugees, they spent their first few nights in a budget hotel. From April 1975 until he stepped on the plane to Canada, Sorpong had been consumed by basic survival. Now, it was once again an invisible occupation. He used his newfound spare time to thumb through the universities section of the hotel phone book. He dialed a few to ask how to apply. He felt giddy with optimism. "I can dream again," he explained. "Because in Cambodia, you cannot dream."

Sorpong was now twenty-four and life in Ottawa began to fall in place. His family moved into a house near Chinatown on Somerset Street, his younger siblings enrolled in school, and Sorpong got a job as a dishwasher and started volunteering at a Cambodian church—an arm of the old Metropolitan Bible Church on Bank Street. The congregation did not sponsor the Peous, but some members acted like they had by helping them find a home and driving them to the umpteen appointments that new immigrants file through.

All this came first. Sorpong still hadn't applied for university. Would anyone accept him, given his age? Plus he hadn't a shred of paper to prove he'd almost finished high school. University felt steadily more unrealistic until a church member (his godmother, he came to call her) encouraged Sorpong to look up a program for mature students at the University of Waterloo. He did and applied. He had only a few hundred dollars in his bank account when he opened an offer to become a political science undergraduate.

Sorpong worked part-time to cover rent and living. Student loans paid for his tuition. His days began with a morning shift before class cleaning restaurant washrooms. He went to bed late, after homework. In his first year, he scored a few Fs and Cs and wondered if he'd made a foolish choice. But his second year improved, and by fourth year, he had straight As. When he applied to nine graduate schools, he received nine acceptance letters. He shifted from loans to scholarships and earned a master's degree at York University in Toronto, and then a doctorate. After that, he accepted a job as Canada-ASEAN Fellow teaching politics with a focus on international security at the Institute of Southeast Asian Studies in Singapore.

In 1994, he married Chola, a Cambodian Canadian, and she moved with him to Singapore. They stayed for just over four years, until Sorpong had an offer at Sophia University in Tokyo, where he became a full-time professor. Japan is a special place to Sorpong and Chola. It is the birthplace of their two daughters. And it was in Japan where Sorpong recognized with new intensity what he felt when he became a Canadian citizen in 1986—that Canada was home. Unlike under Canadian law, Japanese citizenship is not granted to children born inside the country by non-national parents, so his girls were stateless until the Canadian embassy issued their passports.

After eleven years in Tokyo, the University of Winnipeg called. Sorpong had an offer to head the politics department, and he gladly brought his family home.

Today, Sorpong chairs the Department of Politics and Public Administration at Toronto's Ryerson University. His is an extraordinary career: the head of a university department, with a significant body of work on security and peacebuilding in the Asia-Pacific, after surviving a regime that tried to butcher the entire Cambodian intelligentsia.

In 2011, Sorpong felt his life unexpectedly rerouted again. That year, his younger brother made a discovery on a visit to Cambodia. Sorpong's father, Nam, was alive. He had been shot, as his family had guessed, and heaped onto a pile of other executed civil servants, but he was still breathing and managed somehow to escape. He was later caught and tortured, and he survived that too. Sorpong, his other siblings, and his mother boarded a plane for Phnom Penh when they heard. They had not seen Nam, the gentle father who used to scoop his children off the ground into hugs, for thirty-six years. And Nam had lived that time believing that his wife and seven children had been killed.

Sorpong found an old and very poor man, but a man who still moved with the same gentleness. Everything had changed, of course. Nam was missing a familiar, damaged fingernail because Khmer Rouge torturers pulled out his nails and new ones grew in their place. And there was a new family: Nam's new wife and six children.

Phnom Penh was different too, not in the spatial way cities transform. The buildings were not much higher or more magnificent. It was its youthfulness. The Khmer Rouge had wiped out the parents and grandparents of a generation.

The short visit came to an end. Nam would stay in Cambodia with the mother of his younger children, and Chhea Vath would return to Ottawa, having lost her husband for the second time. She had held onto a single photograph of Nam during the Khmer Rouge years and throughout all the refugee camps, and it now sits in a frame in her bedroom. Some days, she stares at it for hours.

"When I talk about my mother, I just want to cry," Sorpong said, for her sacrifices and the risks she took to keep her children alive, like stealing food for them during her shifts in the village kitchen, something punishable by death. Because her children survived, she will only express gratitude for the way things turned out. Sorpong called her before speaking at an event in Toronto about his family's experience as refugees. He wanted to know how difficult it was for her arriving in Canada. She insisted, "No problem at all! Tell everyone I'm thankful!"

Sorpong's daughters are still young but they know parts of his story. They know all about the church members, friends, and colleagues who helped him make a life in Canada, and as they learn about that, they learn that helping others is noble. Peace, kindness, mercy—these are dinner table topics, simplified lessons from the Khmer Rouge terror. "Don't look down on other people," Sorpong will remind his girls. "Because Daddy came from that background."

12 Tarun

Sri Lanka

Anonymous portrait of Tarun at Ryerson University
in Toronto.
Photograph by Christopher Manson.

1983, Jaffna, Sri Lanka

Tarun[1] was born in 1983, the year civil war began in Sri Lanka. Across the northern part of the island country once known as Ceylon, the Liberation Tigers of Tamil Eelam (Tamil Tigers) were in a brutal fight to establish a free state. Tamils, a Sri Lankan Hindu minority, opposed the (Buddhist) Sinhalese-dominated Sri Lankan government, and thousands would die in coming years. The conflict was built on decades of grievances, and each death pushed the groups further apart.

Tarun had no experience of a country at peace. He grew up with the sound of warplanes groaning overhead and the sight of bodies along the green roadside in Jaffna, capital of the northernmost province. But because his father was a teacher, Tarun and his younger sister rarely missed a day of school. That is, until 1994, when classes stopped and a long, untidy line of people began filing into the school grounds, refugees escaping the government bombs dropped over parts of the city controlled by Tamil insurgents. The school was now one of several makeshift refugee centres.

His family recoiled from the chaos. Tamils themselves, they lived in a government-controlled stretch of Jaffna, trying desperately to be non-partisans and to avoid taking sides. Almost an impossibility.

One day, standing outside his home by the main road, Tarun watched a cortege of bloody, misshapen people, some draped across motorbikes, on their way to an overcrowded hospital. It was something he'd seen before but this time was different. These were hundreds of Tamils who had sheltered in a cavernous church just as the Sri Lankan military bombed it to rubble.

"Those were events that pushed everyone to the edge," Tarun said. "To say, 'You know what, it's enough. We should fight against all these attacks.'"

But to fight, really? And on whose side? With his cousins and neighbours, Tarun struggled to decide. They could gather intelligence for the army or, more likely, they could join the insurgency.

Certainly the Tamil Tigers complicated civilian life, endangering everyone, suddenly appearing in the night at Tamil homes, pressuring people to join, and fighting in the city's streets. But the military was careless and vindictive, bombing Tamil civilians and insurgents alike. What's more, government troops singled out young Tamils, obsessively suspicious, especially of kids like Tarun as they grew up and into the corner called "fighting-age male." To authorities, Tamil teenagers were a threat.

To avoid trouble, Tarun hardly left the house, except to attend school. But it didn't matter. The Indian troops posted in Tarun's neighbourhood under a defence pact with Sri Lanka seemed convinced he'd joined the Tamil Tigers. He was pulled aside, questioned: *We heard they came to your house last night. The Tamils recruited you. You're one of them. What information do you have?*

The soldiers took him again and again to the army barracks for interrogation, which meant torture. *What information do you have?* As though it were something that enough hits from a baton could force up, as though it could seep out like blood. As though, by plunging his face in ice water, Tarun, gasping for air, would exhale it—the information. Unless he had none, as Tarun kept repeating. The soldiers always let him go after a few hours, a night at most.

Two of Tarun's neighbours joined the Tamil Tigers (and later died) and recruiters pressured him to do the same. Just as his government interrogators accused, the recruiters arrived at night under cover of darkness to make their pitch, but Tarun resisted. He was angry like anyone else, but he wanted no part of it. Instead, his thoughts turned to leaving Sri Lanka altogether. "I wanted to do good in the future. I have my dreams and my career goals. I just wanted to do something with my life."

By the late 1990s, the fighting worsened. The Tamil Tigers surged south, surprising everyone by defeating the Sri Lankan Army in successive battles. It made all sides more edgy, more likely to interrogate or recruit, or both.

As Tarun neared the end of high school, his sister was just entering her teens. She was five years younger than Tarun, and her fate seemed dangerously tied to his. Both he and his parents feared that the men who kept calling for Tarun—from the army and the Tamil Tigers—would one day leave with his sister. So after Tarun graduated in 2004, the family decided, for everyone's safety, he had to leave home.

He went south to the capital. But Colombo, on the southwest coast, was not immune to war. Before there was a Ground Zero in New York City, suicide bombers were innovating across Sri Lanka. In Colombo, the Tamil Tigers blew up politicians, transit lines, the Central Bank, aircraft sitting at Bandaranaike International Airport, and part of the Sri Lankan World Trade Centre.

In that climate of terror, newcomers to Colombo got noticed. It was not long before the police, like the soldiers at home, asked Tarun to come in for questioning. Their tactics were not much different, except they didn't let him go. Tarun was hung upside-down by a rope tied around his legs and beaten. He begged them to listen. *No, I'm not against the government, no I'm not a terrorist.*

For nearly three weeks in prison, Tarun only spoke to his torturers. He didn't breathe a word to other inmates when they called out from their cells. "That was my first time in Colombo. I was too scared to talk to anybody." Tarun had nothing to confess and no information. He was released only because of his father's money, 200,000 rupees (around $1,800) wired to police. Outside prison, Tarun didn't feel much safer. What good was freedom, he thought, when there would certainly be a next time?

"I said, 'Okay, I can't go home, I can't stay here, so I have to leave the country.'"

To do that, Tarun asked his parents for help. They made careful arrangements, even picked his destination. Tarun didn't learn about the plan until a man, "the agent," came to his apartment and told him he was going to Canada. The flight was the next day.

His father had paid over $25,000 to the agent, a package deal that included a fake passport and a plane ticket out of Colombo, where Tarun had only been for a full three months. Tarun, a fighting-age male with a police history he hadn't deserved, needed the new identity to get a visa. He listened to his agent's plan a bit dazed. There was no time to get to Jaffna first, to say goodbye to his parents and sister, and even if there were, he might not find the will to leave them again, this time permanently.

The flight was to New York City, and Tarun's agent would accompany him that far, but his parents had arranged Toronto as a final destination. It was the home of an uncle, and the family had heard good things about the way Canada treated refugees. It was Tarun's first time on a plane. He was awed and scared, the agent always at his elbow: *Stand here, say this, don't look down.*

Tarun landed in New York in August 2004, and with final instructions to tear up the fake passport and flush it down the toilet after passing customs. He was then to catch a bus for Buffalo's east side, not far from the Canadian border, and find Vive La Casa, a former Catholic elementary school remodelled as a shelter for refugees passing through American airports on their way to Canada.[2]

Tarun stayed at the shelter for two weeks and then took a taxi to the Peace Bridge border crossing into Fort Erie, Ontario.

At the border, with the help of a translator, he told his story. The Canadian officials asked why he didn't stay in the United States. He told them he had an uncle in Toronto, and that Canada was safer. They asked if he joined the fighting back home, and when he said no, they wanted to know why.

"If I stayed longer, I would have done it," he told them. "I'd have no choice, right? But to join." Unlike so many others, Tarun chose not to fight. He was lucky. He never reached his breaking point during the war.

October 2013, Toronto, Canada

Tarun, a son in a close-knit Hindu Tamil family, is now engaged to a woman his family have never met. When he became a Canadian citizen in 2009, four years after a judge decided he was a refugee, Tarun applied to sponsor his parents and sister to immigrate to Canada. It has been five years and his parents are still moving through the immigration system, but nearing the end, he hopes.

He has seen his family twice since he left Sri Lanka. The first time, in 2008, they met at a halfway point, in Singapore, where Tarun felt safe. Then, in 2013, four years after the twenty-six-year war ended in 2009, Tarun returned to Sri Lanka for his sister's wedding where, for the first time, he also met his new brother-in-law. His hometown, Jaffna, still showed scars from the end of the war. It had been a long bloody finish, what many thought was punishment from the victor, the Sri Lankan military. Buildings were rubble, and the once lush green neighbourhoods now had an earthy, tired hue.

Harder to absorb were the stories. Tarun listened to an old woman explain how she walked in chin-deep water for three days to survive the rebels' last stand, and he learned about friends who were missing or dead. He heard more accounts of the vicious events at the war's end, how the advancing army shelled to death an estimated forty thousand civilians deliberately, futilely used by the Tamil Tigers as a human shield.[3] Neither side finished the war with honour.

"One thing is that you get angry, and the other side is, it's so sad to see all that," said Tarun, who didn't see those things, but watched people remember them. He's unsure if he'll ever go back to Sri Lanka.

If he does decide to visit, Tarun would find the time and money. He arrived in Canada with $50 US. Today, he drives a Lexus.

Tarun was twenty-one when he stepped off a bus in Toronto, eager to continue school. He took ESL classes and six high school credits to earn his Canadian high school diploma, rooming with his uncle. He next applied and, with scholarships, entered Ryerson University's engineering faculty. In his first semester, Tarun worked nights sorting mail at Canada Post before heading to full days of class. He felt robotic from lack of sleep, but in second year, a professor, impressed by Tarun's skill at math, offered him a job as a teaching assistant. Tarun quit his night job and worked as a TA for the rest of his five-year degree. By graduation in 2011, he had an engineering job to walk into.

Tarun has a warm smile, more noticeable because he speaks softly. Sitting across from him, you lean in. He said he's good at talking to people, and makes a point of getting to know his managers. He recently switched companies for a better position, an analyst in energy systems and design. Tarun eventually wants a leadership position and thinks an MBA could be his next step.

He left Sri Lanka wanting this: the freedom to set goals and reach them. Holding a coffee cup in Scarborough, he quietly explained how close he came to missing the opportunity. He almost didn't risk escape because in 2004 leaving his family was nearly unthinkable. Tamil parents like his have deep emotional ties to their children and keep them close, usually living in the same house until marriage.

"That's one of the things I remember," he said. "When I was leaving, I couldn't see how I could leave because of that." Now, his parents are nearing passage to Canada and they plan to do things in reverse. Living together will begin, not end, with his wedding.

13 Yodit Negusse

Ethiopia

Yodit Negusse at Scissors in Ottawa.
Photograph by David Kawai.

June 1984, Addis Ababa, Ethiopia

Yodit Negusse, a teenager in Addis Ababa, opened her front door to a young boy, a messenger sent by a family friend. He said militia from the neighbourhood *kebele*, a powerful local arm of the government, would be searching for her tonight, part of a regular after-dark roundup of opponents. Yodit, home alone, thanked him, shut the door, and grabbing the only valuable in the house, her sister's gold ring, she fled.

Yodit had joined demonstrations against the government, handing out pamphlets on the street. When militia came pounding on doors before, she simply climbed up onto the wooden boards beneath the rafters in her mother's home and lay, tangled in electrical wiring. Her mother was still alive then and her older sister, who refused to be involved in politics, scolded Yodit. *Think of the stress on our mother.* But Yodit could counter, *think what the president and his men are doing.*

Thugs with guns were central to the military dictatorship in Ethiopia, better known as the Derg (the Committee), since coming to power in 1974. Their tactics worsened under Mengistu Haile Mariam, who brought the Red Terror, the official name of an anti-opposition campaign he unleashed on Addis Ababa in 1977 after taking the presidency. His agents began going after students like Yodit and other real or imagined dissidents.

Even before high school, Yodit was part of a four-member opposition cell. Only the designated leader of the cell had a contact, someone in the echelon above. That person too stood blind in the hierarchy of the underground opposition. It had to be that way. The police could torture a name from anyone. Secrecy was survival, Yodit knew. She had already spent eight months in prison after being arrested by Mengistu's men when she was a tenth grader.

She was on the run now, wondering if that night would find her behind bars again. Or in the morning, would people be walking around her splayed body on the street, as she had hurried by her own friends discarded this way before? No, this time, she decided, she would disappear.

Carrying her sister's gold ring to exchange for fare, Yodit met three friends, one woman and two men, at the train station, other teenagers leaving behind family and a once-loved city. No longer. In the first year under Mengistu, from 1977 to 1978, over ten thousand people were killed in the capital alone.[1] In 1984, it was not only raids that took lives, but also a devastating famine made worse by the political tragedy.[2] By some counts, up to a million people died during the disaster.[3]

Yodit and her three friends rode the train northeast to a town near the Djiboutian border. Once there, they paid some traders to take them to an unguarded area where they could cross into Djibouti and find a refugee camp. Yodit and her friends, dressed like nomads, moved in step with their guides' camels. They only travelled during the night, hoping to evade government patrols. They knew capture would mean return to an Addis Ababa jail—or for the women, rape and return.

For three nights, the group walked through windblown country until they found a refugee camp run by the UN High Commissioner for Refugees (UNHCR) on the Djiboutian side. It was not a refuge. Yodit counts her stay there among the worst times of her life.

Each night in the camp, her male friends took shifts standing guard outside their tent. They were watching for Djiboutian soldiers. If all went well, they could warn the women before the soldiers arrived. A warning told Yodit to crawl out on her stomach and slip into the next tent, again and again, a nightly round of hide-and-seek until the soldiers gave up or found what they were looking for: a woman. Whoever was found was taken to the barracks, repeatedly raped, and dumped back at the camp. It happened to one woman Yodit befriended during her near three-month stay. They found her outside bleeding and unable to walk.

In daylight, Yodit and the others walked to the UNHCR office to report the crimes, but only Djiboutian staff were there. They listened, but wouldn't confront their countrymen. Yodit's nights were sleepless. She spent most days waiting in line for one kilogram of rice in heat that climbed to 45 degrees. After three months, Yodit and a small group of Ethiopians bet they could find better shelter in Djibouti City.

In the capital, Yodit learned how to live as an undocumented migrant. Someone who knew someone else who knew a landlord could rent a house without an ID card. The housemates who could find jobs pooled their money for rent and food. Yodit worked as a babysitter, then a cleaner. For the most part, city police left Ethiopians alone. After all, the illegal population was a reliable source of income. Police could always extract bribes and sometimes, with the right threats, the company of an Ethiopian woman.

Yodit coexisted with a fantasy. "Ethiopian women are beautiful, they're perfect," she mimicked. This made it dangerous to be outside, especially at night. But in Djibouti City during the day, temperatures averaged over 40 degrees so when it cooled slightly during the evening, the women linked arms and strolled. That's how the police picked her up one night with three other women. They were taken to a concrete prison, to be raped, Yodit believes. So they latched onto each other. The police tried to pry the women apart, but they resisted, arms locked. Finally, they were left alone in their cell. It was a windowless room lined with bunks pushed back against the walls, away from the pit toilet in the centre. The women lay listless in the thick heat and stench for four days until an acquaintance, another Ethiopian woman, paid for their release.

Yodit didn't want to stay in Djibouti, and didn't bother adding the Arabic language to her native Amharic. She had cousins in Italy and asked them to send money. When it arrived by wire transfer to Addis Ababa and courier across the border, she used part to bribe an official at the Ethiopian embassy in Djibouti City to forge her a passport. The Italian embassy then stamped it with a tourist visa in September 1986, but they must have known she wasn't coming back.

September 1986, Rome, Italy

In Italy, Yodit wasted no time. The day after she arrived in Rome she submitted an asylum application through a Catholic group working with the UNHCR. She would get refugee status, and during the processing period, she worked.

Yodit kept her first job in Italy for less than a month and she understood her dismissal perfectly. She didn't know Italian. In the end, it was one of the best things that could have happened. Disappointed, her pride hurt, twenty-year old Yodit vowed she would never be fired from another job in her life. She sat down in her cousins' small apartment in front of the television and began soaking up the language.

She found a second job as a live-in caregiver for an elderly couple. Their daughter visited the large, ornate apartment every afternoon and soon began preparing Italian lessons for Yodit. "Italians are such good people. They are very open, they tell you what they think, there's no

politics. If they like you—you know; if they don't like you—you know."
Yodit added, "Which I like, that's how Ethiopians are."

Rome was dazzling, teeming with people and Yodit found a place
for herself in it, although she knew she wasn't home. She had to immigrate and her options, she learned, were Canada and the United States.
Yodit had heard immigrants to the United States wound up with isolated, outsider lives. But Canada had a reputation as somewhere new
people could belong. The choice was easy because she had spent her
youth in hiding in Ethiopia and another six years stateless in Italy, even
though four of those years were much happier with her Italian family.
Next, she wanted a home.

February 1990, Ottawa, Canada

Yodit chose Ottawa because it was not like Rome, charming but overwhelming. She had never experienced anything as cold as Canada's capital, but it was calmer. Once she was dressed for a bone-chilling winter,
her next challenge was choosing a career. As a government-assisted
refugee, she could get subsidized job training. She was twenty-five and
wanted to attend university but settled instead for something technical.
She had family to support in Addis Ababa and arrival loans to repay
her new government. Listening to her job counsellor list options, Yodit
stopped her at "hairdresser."

"I said 'oh, I could do hair,'" Yodit laughed. "So it was an accidental career."

Her first years passed in a whirl of sixteen-hour workdays between
three jobs. Scissors, a boutique hair salon in Ottawa's ByWard Market,
hired Yodit, and she added part-time jobs at McDonald's and a bakery
to her salon paycheque. Meanwhile, shortly after her own arrival, a man
she had dated in Rome, also a refugee from Ethiopia, landed in Toronto.
Yodit visited him one weekend and he returned with her to Ottawa, and
never left.

Yodit is now married, has three daughters, and lives in the Ottawa
suburb of Kanata, close to the Quickie Mart franchise owned by her husband, and to the good schools she wanted their children to attend. She
commutes downtown to a job she adores, still at Scissors. That lost job
in Rome had driven Yodit ever since. "I'm a very hardworking person.

You tell me to do something, I do it the way you want." After ten years with Scissors, the owners asked her to buy in and become a co-owner.

Yodit became a Canadian citizen in 1994 and first returned to visit Ethiopia in 1996. She wouldn't have gone back if not for her sister, who still lives in Addis Ababa. Yodit applied to privately sponsor her sister as a refugee but the application was rejected, a sign Ethiopian politics had changed. Mengistu fled for Zimbabwe in 1991, where he remains in exile, with impunity. That fact is hard to face, when Yodit feels punished, wanting so badly to have her sister close.

Since her trip back to a more stable, peaceful Ethiopia, Yodit's nightmares about armed militias and abandoned bodies have visited her less and less. It's strange remembering the city under Mengistu.

"It's very hard to explain to someone who's never lived that," she said. "For me, too, it's shocking. I think now: 'How the heck they got away with that?'" It was so easy to become a suspect in Addis Ababa ruled by the communist junta. Anyone walking the streets with more than two people was sure to be scooped up in a dragnet and killed or at least tortured. Yodit was always ready to start running. "Even now when I see a police car, I know—my intelligent mind knows—okay, they're there for us. But my first instinct is to look twice."

Her new normal is a quiet boulevard in the ByWard Market where she works, in the shadow of Parliament Hill, or a bright coffee shop boxed in by family cars in suburban Kanata. Ottawa was a radical change. "I didn't have to lie, I didn't have to hide, I didn't have to fear anybody. The rest was up to me to make it work."

14 Chairuth (Chai) Bouphaphanh

Laos

Chai Bouphaphanh in Drake.
Photograph by Chai Bouphaphanh.

1977, Vientiane, Laos

Chai Bouphaphanh was going on a family vacation, travelling to a relative's farm in the countryside. That's what they told him.

Ten-year-old Chai and his two younger brothers hugged their father goodbye and boarded a southbound bus in Vientiane, the Laotian capital, in August 1977, with their mother, aunt, and five cousins. They were heading to Ban Thouay and, following the strict rule of domestic travel in Laos, one parent stayed behind. A measure to make families think twice about trying to escape the country.

Chai watched out the bus window as Vientiane fell away. The city had been a French outpost with wide boulevards framed by rows of full trees that shaded the cafés scattered along the way. The wealth left in 1954 with independence from France. Then came civil war between royalists (supporters of the monarchy) and communists, the Pathet Lao. The war next door in Vietnam became the "American War," and Laos became an even more popular bombsite. To avoid American planes, the Viet Cong had begun using the Ho Chi Minh Trail as a supply line, and the part that ran over the border into Laos caught the Americans' attention. Beginning in 1964, estimates say more tonnage of bombs was dropped over Laos than in Europe and the Pacific combined during the Second World War,[1] averaging one sortie every eight minutes for nine years.[2] It was—in the words of the CIA—"the largest paramilitary operations ever undertaken by the CIA."[3]

But the statistics came later. If there was ever a "secret theatre," Laos was it.

A ceasefire ended the bombing and the war next door ended in 1975. In Laos, the Pathet Lao took over, and influenced by the Vietnamese communist government, began re-educating, purging, killing.

And that was the reason Chai's family had decided to take a vacation. Chai would learn later that for two years before 1978, his parents had been planning this trip. They used their evening walks together without the boys to figure out when and how to leave. Also later Chai would remember his mother's nervousness aboard the bus, especially whenever it stopped at checkpoints. The passengers police pulled off would never climb back on. Unlike his mother, Khem, Chai watched these purges with only a vague sense of unease. He was aware of the recent war, to be sure; the family lived alongside the Vientiane airport, so he was used to the sight of military aircraft, and the noise and tremors made by exploded bombs. But in the elastic way of children, Chai and his brothers just copied the war in their play.

He was more alarmed when he awoke around midnight after a few nights in the country to find his mother and aunt announcing another "trip." No speaking and especially no crying, Khem warned. It was a moonless night, and the children followed their mothers in near pitch darkness toward the Mekong River. They carried no flashlight, barely able to make out a wooden boat at the river's edge. They climbed in: eight children, two women, and one man, the hired rower. The river stretched at least a kilometre, and around them all Chai heard was the splashing ink-black water.

Again, Chai only realized later his mother's terror on that crossing. She didn't know that Chai and his brothers had taught themselves to swim back in Vientiane. On the river, she believed that if the boat pitched hard enough to throw them off, her boys would drown.

After what seemed like a very long time, the boat ran onto mud on the opposite bank, in Thailand. Chai's uncle lived in a village about a kilometre away and, after first attempting to report to a nearby but empty patrol base of the Thai military, the family travelled there on foot.

At almost any point leaving Vientiane, things could have gone terribly wrong, but they managed to go right. Soldiers didn't single them out on the bus ride. Although it was an uncommonly dark night, they made it to the Mekong River, which was smooth, not choppy. And most importantly, Chai thinks the Laotian guards stationed along the river were midway through changing shifts, so it's possible no one was on the bank to spot a boatful of refugees. "Normally on this kind of trip, if you even step on the Mekong at night, you would get shot," Chai said. "We were lucky." They were even lucky to have lived in Vientiane. It had been left in relative peace during the American bombing campaign, compared to the countryside.

Once settled in, Chai's mother told him the real purpose for the trip. To leave Laos for good. The family's ultimate destination was the Nong Khai refugee camp on the northeastern edge of Thailand, but Khem refused to go farther without her husband, who planned to escape

Laos at a later time and by a different route. And so, time passed at his grandmother's house on the Mekong more or less like a familiar, leisurely summer. Except that now, when Chai played with his brothers and cousins along the river, they could spot bodies floating by, some swelled up like balloons. They understood then how many people were trying to escape just like them, from the dozens they saw who didn't make it.

Completely cut off, Chai's father, Samlane, remained in Vientiane not knowing if his family was safe in Thailand. Contacting them by mail or phone was too dangerous. Months passed without any news. "Thinking back, it was just terrible," Chai said. "Mom and Dad had no communication, it was: 'You go do this, and I'll wait until the time's right, and then I'll go.'"

Samlane worked as a technical advisor with an American oil company, Caltex, and had often taken business trips to the Bangkok office, so leaving Laos would not be out of the ordinary. In communist Laos, working for an American company was its own risk, and a few months after his wife and children left home, Caltex closed operations. With his boss, who also decided it was time to go, Samlane drove to a border crossing (an official one), pretending business as usual, and passed without a hitch into Thailand.

Because he left as a businessman, Samlane had a briefcase, and in it, he carried a photo album. At the time, it was an afterthought, but the album became sacred. No other Laotians who Chai met in the refugee camp, or later in the diaspora, had escaped with their photographed past. Flight had to be decisive, minimalist, and if undercover, unceremonious.

Reunited, the Bouphaphanh family moved into a one-room hut in Nong Khai. Chai and his brothers went to school in the camp, while Samlane met with visa officers of every country present, and Khem turned the hut into a daytime shop for hairdressing and sewing. She grew vegetables in the small patch of soil curled around their home—resourcefulness that earned more than one double take from visiting foreigners. Canadian visa officers were among those stationed at Nong Khai, and in November 1979, after Samlane's lobbying, the family learned they were in. Chai only knew the country was cold, and on a map it looked like Siberia. "During those times, who can have time to explain to you what Canada is—or was—or how big?"

His grandmother came to the camp to say what felt like a permanent goodbye. "As a refugee, you never think of coming back home," Chai said.

After adding their suitcases—boxes wrapped in orange and green tarp—to a rooftop heap, the family boarded a bus to Bangkok as the sun went down. It was too hot to travel in daytime, and even at night, they wore T-shirts and sandals. That's how they boarded a plane for Edmonton on January 31, 1980.

February 1980 and December 2013, Drake, Canada

When the plane flew down over the tarmac in Edmonton, Chai saw a ground of sparkling diamonds. He had never before seen snow. Flight attendants on the Air Canada plane passed around red blankets, and there were jackets and boots waiting in the military barracks near Edmonton. All of it enchanted Chai and his brothers. Having never before wrapped in these layers, they couldn't believe their luck, getting to dress like astronauts.

His parents saw things differently.

From Edmonton, the family flew to Saskatoon, where a Canadian couple from the Mennonite Church congregation—their sponsor—was waiting to drive them to a new home in Drake, Saskatchewan. "The drive was very long, and when you look at the landscape, it does look like Siberia. There's nobody," Chai said. "My parents probably thought this is the wrong place to bring a family."

The Canadians, Claire and Wally Ewert, cooked them dinner on their first night, and Chai and his brothers made a new friend in the couple's five-year-old son, Matt, born and adopted in Vietnam. Claire made rice, guessing the family needed something familiar. Then the Canadians left and the family found themselves alone in a small country house surrounded by infinite lengths of snow-covered fields. That night, from the bedroom he shared with his brothers, Chai heard his mother's crying.

A week later, at his first Mennonite church service, Chai discovered that Drake was not like Siberia because it had people, hundreds of them, at church. They had a new community. Before long, Samlane began to work painting farm machinery and Khem, who had only worked at home in Laos, got her driver's license and a job in a restaurant.

Resisting the pull of Saskatoon, the family stayed in Drake. "My mom and dad loved this town and loved the people," he explained. And so did the brothers. Years later, Chai's nephew would be named Drake.

Chai practised English reading Wally's collection of *National Geographic* magazines. An old edition from May 1979 carried a feature on Saskatchewan, and Chai learned his family wasn't the first to arrive as refugees. Ukrainians, Russians, and others had come before. The glossy landscape images of Saskatchewan in the magazine made their mark. Chai developed a love for photography and when he bought his own camera, his first passion was capturing the cityscape of the prairie: grain elevators against cold blue sky. Chai jokes that he knows he's Canadian because he also fell in love with sub-zero weather.

As they grew older, the boys stayed in Saskatchewan. His brothers Phonesak and Bounport became IT professionals living in Saskatoon and Regina. Chai lives in Drake and works in the IT department at Drake Meats, doing freelance photography on the side.

When Chai first returned to Southeast Asia in 1993, it was to Thailand to visit and document his grandmother. That last goodbye hadn't been permanent after all. She passed away a few years after his visit, and the smiling woman in his photos is exactly how Chai wanted to remember her. On the same trip, he visited Laos, by then a peaceful if still poor country. Laos was politically open enough for him to tour and see the scars of war, like the pond-sized craters all over the countryside. He keeps going back, sometimes to shoot weddings for friends and relatives. One image taken in Laos won his personal gold standard when *National Geographic* grabbed it for its online photo archive.

At this part of his story, Chai comes back to Claire and Wally. It's like they're onstage with his family, sometimes bit players, sometimes leading ones, as good friends are over the years. Claire and Wally and their son Matt became like extended family. Claire was interviewed once by the Mennonite Central Committee about her congregation's sponsorship. She described how her relationship with the Bouphaphanh family grew. "They received support when they needed it, and over the years, they have supported us in ways we would not have imagined."[4] Wally died unexpectedly in 1991, and Chai and his family grieved alongside Claire and Matt.

Wally continued to influence Chai after he passed away. While helping Claire and Matt to sort through a lifetime of his things, Chai found his photographs and held onto one that Wally shot on a trip to wartime Vietnam, of a rose blooming behind barbed wire. "If you look close, everything's beautiful if you want to see it," Chai said. "That's how I trained myself to see the world. That's how I want to see it."

15 Zafar Iravan

Iran

Zafar Iravan at home in Richmond Hill.

Photograph by Ryan Walker.

March 1982, Tehran, Iran

When he was discharged in 1980, Zafar Iravan had served the Iranian Navy for fifteen years, was the commander of a minesweeper, and was training to head the beast of the Iranian fleet, a destroyer. His dismissal papers named his religion. *You are relieved of duty because you are Baha'i.*

Both Zafar and his wife, Mahnaz, are Baha'i and both were engineers in the Iranian Navy. Zafar had studied in Italy to become a naval officer and rose quickly through the ranks until Ayatollah Ruhollah Khomeini took power in 1979. New laws did not recognize the minority Baha'i religion, and adherents of the Ayatollah's brand of Islam treated Baha'is like heretics. They were barred from schools and government jobs, and had their property and holy sites trashed. In the early years of the Islamic Republic, Baha'is also began to disappear, some imprisoned and others executed.[1]

Zafar's dismissal was a simple case. But Mahnaz was fired in late 1981 when Iran was locked in fratricidal war with Iraq. She was accused of spying for the United States and Israel, a serious offence during wartime. Not long after, a friend in the public service alerted Zafar that officials were preparing a subpoena for his wife to appear before the Revolutionary Court, where those accused of crimes like espionage or blasphemy were secretly and swiftly found guilty. Trials here were a formality before prison or worse.

With the impending subpoena, in March 1982, the couple began planning to escape. Put simply, "There was no future for my daughter and son," Zafar said. Ellie was six years old and his son, AJ, was two.

Zafar and Mahnaz paid $23,000 US to a smuggling ring and had two weeks to quietly close down their affairs and prepare their young family. To prevent rumours about their plan, they said goodbye only to Mahnaz's mother and an uncle. But it's hard to keep secrets from neighbours and that's how one Baha'i man came to their door, pleading for them to take his sixteen-year-old son along. It didn't matter where they took him, only that it was out of the Islamic Republic.

Their money carried them by plane from the capital, Tehran, to the eastern Sistan-Baluchistan province and the border city Zahedan. From there, smugglers chaperoned the family from the airport to a village at the base of a shared mountain with Pakistan. The deal included a guided hike over the caramel slopes and would end once Zafar's family reached the first Pakistani town with a rail connection to Karachi. Zafar speaks well of the smugglers, and calls them professional and friendly. It was a family business—their wives and children joined Zafar's family in the back of the pickup truck leaving Zahedan. The women and children were useful cover. They made a less threatening appearance and answered questions from Iranian guards at the scattered checkpoints, since Zafar and Mahnaz didn't speak the dialect.

It was early evening but already dark when Zafar's family, the neighbour's son, and three smugglers walked quietly down a dirt alley to the edge of the frontier village, lit only by a handful of street lights. Ahead was blackness that in daylight was the outline of a mountain. They wore the clothing of Baloch villagers, but the disguise would only fool authorities. Locals would recognize the family as strangers regardless of their clothing, and they would know exactly why strangers had come.

Children playing nearby stopped to watch the group approach. They began to laugh, and then sing and clap. One of the smugglers translated their excited words for Zafar: "These people are going to escape!" They hurried past the children, eager for the end of the light posts. The smugglers had at least as much to fear as Zafar. Since the fall of the Shah in January 1979, Iranian borders were sealed and carefully patrolled. Revolutionary Guard soldiers arrested those trying to escape Iran, but shot smugglers on sight.

Zafar held his son, Mahnaz had the family's single suitcase, and the neighbour's son carried Ellie on his shoulders. One guide stayed with the family while the other two fanned out ahead. There was no moon that night and Zafar could not see the two men in front or even the ground at his feet. It was complicated terrain, all gravel and stones, and Zafar was carrying a sleeping toddler. At steep sections, Mahnaz had to crouch and use her hands to guide her husband's feet.

The smugglers communicated only by whistling, the coded language brief but clear: stop, start, or shut up. When the signal came to shut up, they stood like statues. Once they spotted figures moving behind them and hurried softly from the path into prickly shrubs. Zafar could hear the even breathing of his son, still asleep. The group of strangers approached and passed, talking as they went, oblivious to any shadows off the path. When the sound faded completely, the guides signalled to keep moving.

Just once on the climb up the mountain, AJ woke in Zafar's arms and began to cry. Footfalls and breathing already seemed like crashing noise—crying was like a siren that echoed off the rocks. Zafar spoke soothing words to the toddler, even put a hand over his mouth. But he kept on crying and the guides became frantic, motioning to do something. Mahnaz took her son, held him close, put her face against his, and whispered. AJ gave a final cry and fell back asleep. After handing him again to Zafar, from stress or from fear, Mahnaz collapsed. They had to move on within minutes, as soon as she could stand.

The climb took five hours. Zafar turned back on the mountain peak to see a silhouette of home. He remembers thinking, *I haven't done anything wrong. I have been faithful to my country, to my people, to my family and friends, everybody.* "I looked at Iran with a feeling of sorrow."

Their descent was smoother, but there were snags in the calm. Like the headlights they saw far below: *Our guys or the Pakistani police?* And driving away from the mountain to customs, they saw a car tailing them: *Civilian or military?* "It's all up and down in your mind," Zafar says of each long, panicked moment.

At the border, they easily cleared customs with bribes to the Pakistani officials and boarded a train the next day for Karachi. Zafar said goodbye to their guides, who had kept their word, getting his family onto a train.

One more incident nearly upended them. As was routine, police boarded and wound through the train, checking passports. The family had paid for fake Iranian exit stamps at Pakistani customs, so everything was in order, but Zafar didn't know the neighbour's son was travelling on a false passport and the picture actually belonged to his sister. Scenarios of deportation after making it this far flickered in his mind. But the solution to false papers was much simpler. More money changed hands, and they were on their way.

Hours later, Zafar stepped off the train into Karachi. It was hot. They were hungry and tired and his son had diarrhea. Yet, "At this moment, suddenly I felt that we are free now. This was the best feeling that I ever had in my life."

The elation was unmovable during three days in Karachi and on the flight to Madrid, where Iranians could land without a visa. His son's diarrhea had worsened so Zafar and Mahnaz went together to change his diaper during the flight, into a cabinet-sized washroom with a dripping tap. The toddler chose the worst time to go. The moment his parents took off his diaper. And it went everywhere in the tiny room. Mahnaz began to cry, Zafar began to laugh.

February 1983, Ajax, and August 2013, Richmond Hill, Canada

They spent eleven months in Spain while Canada examined their papers, and arrived in Toronto in February 1983 as refugees. The National Spiritual Assembly, a governing council of Canadian Baha'is, sponsored their arrival and helped them find a new home in Ajax, east of Toronto. From Spain, the neighbour's son continued to Austria.

In their first year, Zafar got a job doing repairs and maintenance at Toronto's Canadian National Exhibition Stadium, and Mahnaz began work as a technician with the Ajax firm Bayly Engineering.

Canadian weather took getting used to. One winter afternoon, Mahnaz was half an hour late picking Ellie up from school. The seven-year-old was waiting alone outside. Her lips were a bluish colour Mahnaz had never seen. She still feels guilty, though Ellie smiles, "Mommy, I don't remember."

Zafar and Mahnaz met other Baha'is in Canada who escaped like they did, although everyone had a unique exit plan—Istanbul to Lisbon to Toronto, went another. They exchanged news from home and they raised awareness. The *Oshawa This Weekend* ran a story in May 1983 about the families of local Baha'is still in Iran.[2] It featured Zafar and Mahnaz, but not their real names. Zafar's sister was in prison at the time and they feared reprisal against her and the rest of the family. The article urged "anyone concerned about the persecution to write to the minister of external affairs in Ottawa."

By 1989, ten years after the revolution, Canada had accepted around 2,300 Baha'i refugees, and had a hand in resettling thousands more through diplomatic cajoling.[3] Senior Canadian diplomats made dozens of visits, from the mid-1980s on, with officials from potential host countries like Brazil, Ireland, Luxembourg, and Uruguay to explain the Baha'i situation in Iran and to share Canada's resettlement program as a model.[4]

The Canadian Baha'i community, through its private refugee office, was the mind and muscle of the resettlement. The office moved incoming refugees to over 220 Canadian towns and cities after a short stay in Toronto or another airport city, hoping to avoid isolating them in their own cultural group.[5] Supported by a satellite Baha'i community and their non-Baha'i neighbours, Zafar and Mahnaz quickly found their feet.

The family now lives in Richmond Hill, a town north of Toronto. Zafar is the head of repairs and maintenance at Univar Canada, and Mahnaz is retired. AJ is an engineer, Ellie is an entrepreneur and new mother. Zafar and Mahnaz became grandparents on October 14, 2013, thirty years after arriving in Canada.

They speak often with relatives in Iran. There is good news, like underground movements by Baha'is to educate each other and, of course, bad: stories of punishments, homes confiscated, a friend's body hung for show from a crane in Tehran, the two years Zafar's sister spent in jail.

Around the dinner table in Richmond Hill, the family remembers the beautiful parts of Iran, like the cities not yet explored that they still hope to see. Zafar recalls seeing his wife for the first time, working in Tehran. She was lovely and he asked around to see if she was single. Mahnaz describes his white Navy officer uniform, sending Ellie into laughter.

"Should I change my shirt, Ellie?" Zafar asks at the beginning of our interview. Ellie, still pregnant, would be filming us, the footage heading to a school project. When she learned she was pregnant, Ellie took a break from work and enrolled in a documentary media program; a natural time to capture her family's story for the next generation, she said. Ellie teases her father, "You don't listen to me anyway. I took the pen out of your shirt and you put it back in." Zafar looks resigned and shrugs.

Mahnaz listens from the kitchen, Ellie from the living room couch as Zafar speaks. He describes their heavy breathing up an invisible slope, turning on the mountain for a last sweep of the Iranian countryside, and daily routines today. The house is silent when Zafar finishes. "Everything is beautiful here."

16 Samnang Eam

Cambodia

Samnang Eam at home in Ottawa.
Photograph by David Kawai.

May 1979, Cardamom Mountains, Cambodia

Rain dripped down the face of the nearly new father, bent in front of his wife's swollen belly, also veined with tiny streams of water. The baby would not wait for them to finish their journey. She would enter the world in a valley between the mountains that divide Cambodia and Thailand, surrounded by only her parents and siblings. Her father eased her out with bare hands, and held the infant while her mother cut the umbilical cord with the sharp edge of a palm leaf. Sam An wiped her clean as best as he could, and put his daughter in his wife's arms. He reached for the watch in his pocket, his last real possession, and saw that the baby was born at 7 p.m. They called her Samnang, "lucky" in Khmer.

———————

Sam An Eam and a pregnant Kim Lang Ting began their escape from Cambodia with their five healthy, young children—two girls and three boys—on April 15, 1979, through the western Cardamom Mountains. They didn't know it, but this was the last year of the Khmer Rouge regime, to end when the Vietnamese Army invaded in December. The Khmer Rouge had controlled Cambodia since marching into the capital, Phnom Penh, four years before. Then, Sam An, a teacher, and Kim Lang lived with their children in Siem Reap, site of the famous temples at Angkor Wat, those ancient symbols of Khmer greatness. They had a comfortable life, even during the years of civil war, before Khmer Rouge rule.

"Year Zero" changed everything because, as the proclamation suggested, time had just begun. All remnants of the past would be destroyed, except for the Khmer Empire treasures. A retraction of time, of art and science, of history. The Khmer Rouge killed anyone who betrayed signs of an education or literacy, like wearing glasses. Soldiers emptied cities and forced Cambodians into the fields and hard labour as part of a vision of low-tech self-sufficiency that, instead, brought famine, starvation, and untreated disease. Over two million people lost their lives in the small Southeast Asian country from 1975 to 1979.[1]

Surrounded by death, but still together, Sam An and Kim Lang finally left for the border with their five children, even though Kim Lang was eight months pregnant with their sixth. That's how she ended up giving birth in the jungle in the rain.

Samnang was born on May 7, 1979. She didn't cry, and it was a good thing. Khmer Rouge soldiers were patrolling the jungle near the border, searching for runaways. Earlier, along their escape route, the family had passed dead infants left abandoned and unburied at the edge of jungle trails. Soldiers had no use for the babies of their prisoners.

The birth of Samnang was a brief repose. Two hours later, the family was moving again, terrified of staying too long in one place. Kim Lang had been walking or running for the past twenty-two days, the better part of the final month of her pregnancy. Now, she was malnourished, exhausted, and had no milk in her shrunken breasts. The baby's diet consisted only of sap from palm trees, and the other children were equally starved, eating whatever they could scavenge from branches or the earth. Stretches of the trek took them away from rivers, and when there was no rain, they drank each other's urine.

The day after Samnang's birth, at dusk, the family reached a river bordering Thailand. With branches and vines, Sam An roped together a makeshift raft. He pulled the wooden float into the water, and rolled on top beside the others, holding his baby in his arms. One son swam behind to propel them forward. Trailing them was a ribbon of red, the birth blood still draining from Kim Lang.

They landed downriver on the Thai side of the bank. *Safe now*, they thought.

Thailand had a deluge of refugees from almost all sides and the government occasionally rounded up groups of them to deport.[2] Three days after arriving in Thailand, the Eams were picked up in just such a sweep. The last month from their lives meant nothing. Eight hours on a bumping bus, and they were deposited back in Cambodia. But Thailand's deportation efforts were largely in vain, as the Eams, and others like them, turned on their heels and headed back for Thailand. The Khmer Rouge would be aware of their disappearance, and they had no choice but to go again.

On the second march through the jungle towards Thailand, under a forest canopy so dense it blocked the sun, the children began to fall sick. On the first journey, Sam An had carried his two youngest, but now he cradled his second eldest son, ten years old and too weak to walk. At one point his son looked up to Sam An and said in a small voice, "Just leave me here." Sam An held his son in his arms that night on the jungle floor and when he woke, his son was dead.

Over the course of the next month, Sam An and Kim Lang lost three more children. Their eight-year-old, six-year-old, and four-year-old. By mid-June, only baby Samnang and their eldest son, Yong, remained. Yong helped his father dig four small holes to bury his two brothers and two of his sisters, while Kim Lang cradled Samnang. They wanted to die themselves, but Sam An and Kim Lang kept moving, pushed by their surviving son and baby daughter.

They were in shock from grief and hunger when they crossed into Thailand for the last time in September 1979. This time, the United Nations High Commissioner for Refugees (UNHCR) met and escorted the family by bus to a refugee camp in the eastern province of Sa Kaeo. Buses continued to loop from the border to the camp, depositing refugees, as if Cambodia had tipped to empty them. For days, Sam An and Kim Lang waited by the main road, watching the new faces filing off each bus. They were looking for their children. Delirious, their minds had blocked burying the missing children, and it would be a week before they remembered.

The family lived long enough at the Khao-I-Dang camp for Samnang to become old enough to have memories, one of a yellow and royal blue tracksuit laid out in a street market. She begged her mother for it. *No*, she was told, *too expensive*—the price of a few meals. But Kim Lang found a way to pay for it, and a few days later, Samnang got the tracksuit she still remembers.

After regaining their health, the Eams found work. Sam An began teaching, Kim Lang sewing, and Yong doing odd jobs for Canadian visa officials. The months ticked by and the camp became full of friends, fellow escapees from the humanitarian disaster zone that was Cambodia under the Khmer Rouge. But still no extended family arrived. They later learned that surviving relatives had been dispersed among other camps or else were eking out a living in Cambodia, under Vietnam's control after December 1979. Cambodia remained a bad place to be in the 1980s. Former Khmer Rouge mingled with civilians, and the puppet government presided over a closed economy, modelled on communist Vietnam.

Using any connection they could, the Eams applied for resettlement to Canada and several other countries. This was the era of the "boat people," when the international community placed Cambodians, along with Laotians and Vietnamese, in a rare group category, so that nationals living outside of these three countries were assumed to be refugees. Still, foreign governments selectively gave out visas, and their deputies on the ground screened candidates for assets like education and good health. Turned down twice by Canada, their third application was successful, and in November 1984 the Eams left Khao-I-Dang for the Thai capital, and flew from Bangkok to Ottawa.

"We came with nothing in our hands but each other," Samnang said. She was five years old in 1984 and had all she needed: her older brother, her parents, and a new baby brother, Tola, born stateless in Khao-I-Dang.

January 2014, Ottawa, Canada

Samnang spreads photographs from a brown envelope on the kitchen table in her home, while pet birds in cages twitter away behind her. The shots show her family in their first years in Canada. Her father with fellow English language students. Samnang, the five-year-old, with her teenaged brother. There's one from the refugee camp too, of her mother in a long red skirt and matching T-shirt, with dark hair cropped at her shoulders. Kim Lang is holding Samnang, then a toddler, and gazing at the camera without a smile.

Her parents worked hard from the start of their new lives in Canada. After months of English language classes, they both took jobs as cleaners, working all the hours they could get, and next switched to sewing. Samnang remembers piles of clothing at home and her parents working in the living room until late into the night. She used to help after her homework by threading wire into dress sleeves for a puffed effect (then the style) but she stopped in protest, indignant at their low wages. Her parents eventually quit those jobs and moved into separate fields. When they retired, Sam An was an electrician with a switchboard manufacturer, and Kim Lang a nurse's aide at a retirement home. The family became Canadian citizens in 1990.

The two continue working long hours in retirement, but it's all volunteer work. Like them, Samnang volunteers around the clock. Today, her day job is correspondence assistant at Health Canada and her in-between, voluntary job is president of the Cambodian Association of

Ottawa-Valley. She answers emails at late hours and holds board meetings on Saturdays.

Samnang had her first and only child, a baby girl, at a young age, while she was still in high school. But she stayed in school as a single mother and went on to earn a degree in Police Foundations at Algonquin College. In 2013, Samnang took a part-time mediation course with the Canadian International Institute of Applied Negotiation and plans to take more courses like it. She's vivacious and warm, and discovered she's a natural negotiator.

Her daughter is now sixteen years old, and to balance all the different elements, Samnang has the help of her parents, supports throughout her life.

Sam An and Kim Lang sometimes speak about their four lost children to their three surviving ones, so Samnang knows how closely she resembles one of her two sisters, in looks and personality. "My mom says I remind her of my sister, the only difference is she was very light-skinned, like my mother." Samnang has her father's dark skin. She and her brothers, all born in different places, are also perpetual reminders of each stage of her parents' escape. Her older brother of Khmer Rouge Cambodia, Samnang of the mountain crossings, and her younger brother of Khao-I-Dang refugee camp.

Samnang calls her parents "heroes." By this time, she's crying at the kitchen table. Her father can learn to do anything—build a raft or repair a switchboard. And her mother, Samnang shakes her head, "She's a strong woman. For someone to go through that and be able to come out of it, and to have that outlook where you're not angry at people, what they did ... how do you do it?"

Sam An and Kim Lang first returned to Cambodia in 1992 and shortly after, decided to build a house just outside Phnom Penh. They're snowbirds, spending Canadian winters in the Cambodian countryside. They fly home after the Cambodian New Year in April, to a house in Ottawa's Central Park that they share with their granddaughter and Samnang, who laughs through tears to say, "I miss them when they're not here."

Samnang has not yet travelled back to Cambodia. Her schedule always seems too full, but she wants to visit and bring her daughter. Cambodian culture is part of her Canadian life, sustained in a big way through the Cambodian Association. She and her team of volunteers organize events to celebrate Cambodian holidays, while other projects simply keep the community close. They're planning a trip to Ottawa's feted sugar bush after realizing many Cambodian Canadian seniors had never been, and they hold Khmer language classes at Ottawa's Buddhist temples.

Samnang especially wants the generation born in Canada, like her daughter, to feel attached to their Cambodian roots. Like other child refugees who arrived in Canada at a young age, Samnang also has a tenuous link to Cambodian culture and knows that holding onto it, just like re-learning Khmer, takes effort. "This is where our parents came from," Samnang said. "And we don't want to ever lose this."

17 Marko

Bosnia and Herzegovina

Anonymous portrait of Marko on Gamble Avenue
in Toronto.
Photograph by Christopher Manson.

1992, Sarajevo, Bosnia and Herzegovina

When Sarajevo was pockmarked with shellfire, in the slow stages of collapse, people began to believe in fate.

Marko did.[1] One day a bullet missed him by no more than a foot and grazed the forehead of the man in step beside him. Then an artillery shell ripped into his apartment, ricocheted around the room and spun to a stop, unexploded. Another time, a rocket-propelled grenade crashed into the south side of the apartment building and did explode, but it was one wall behind his family's north-facing rooms. By the time he escaped in 1994, Marko counted six times he nearly lost his life.

He was a third-year mechanical engineering student at the University of Sarajevo when war broke out in Bosnia and Herzegovina in 1992. Yugoslavia was a melting pot of ethnic groups, religions, political philosophies, tension, and memories of past indignities—where the melting had never really happened. The country's breakup was followed by vicious fighting and atrocities, which only later came to light. In the Sarajevo region, the struggle pitted Bosnian government forces against the new militaries of Republika Srpska and Herzeg-Bosnia, these two supplied by Serbia and Croatia.

Sarajevo, a multicultural, cosmopolitan city, surrounded by mountains, was under siege by Serb forces who controlled the heights and looked down on the residents below. The siege, at the time, became the longest military blockade of a city in the modern age. For four years, from April 1992 until February 1996, the citizens of Sarajevo were shelled and shot down in the streets by snipers. Grey clouds blossomed when shells hit high-rise apartments. Rubble littered streets. Sarajevans counted their dead and injured while watching their city crumble. Over ten thousand civilians were killed and many more wounded.[2]

Like thousands of others, the siege had cut Marco off from loved ones on the outside. His wife was in Belgrade. She had been a student there when the hostilities broke out. On his side of the blockade, the university had closed and Marko's days filled with other tasks, like hauling water.

In 1992, familiar living stopped and survival began. If the morning air was not filled with echoing gunfire, Marko, taking turns with his younger brother, mother, or father, would walk three kilometres to fill as many plastic jugs with water as he could carry back to the sixth-floor apartment. For heat, he brought home anything that could burn: chairs from the destroyed cinema or tires from stranded cars, useless without fuel. On charmed days, when fog from the southern mountains settled down over Sarajevo, Marko could reach the trees near the city's edge for firewood, out of sight of Serb positions and, from the other side, government—mostly Bosniak—patrols.

Marko avoided both sides of belligerents, Serb/Croat and Bosniak. He and his family were (Orthodox) Serbs living in a majority (Muslim) Bosniak city, besieged by a Serb army. As Sarajevans, they were targets of the enemy snipers, who steadied their crosshairs on anything that moved below. Bosniak neighbours viewed Marko's family as "one of us," victims in a mad war. But the foreign fighters who had come to defend the city did not. That meant civilian Serbs like Marko were targets of the pro-government, pro-Bosniak paramilitaries too.

Identity was everything in Sarajevo. Life depended on the guy with a gun determining if he was on your side. Faced with an armed man in Sarajevo banging on the window and demanding, "Whose army are you?" the right answer, it turned out, was, "Yours!"

"It saved my life. You have to tell them 'yours,'" Marko said. But when you call that out enough times, "You don't know who you are." He found it strange that when identity means everything, it can be reduced to nothing.

For many Sarajevans, Serbia was a safe haven and people fled at immense personal risk, quietly smuggled out or traded in the thriving exchange in human beings between the militaries and their thugs. *Hold your fire for my sister, we'll hold ours for your cousin.* People in Sarajevo would simply vanish. "How did he disappear?" Marko remembers the conversations. "I don't know. He disappeared." Stories of escape were only learned later, on the outside. The storytellers were not always proud about it because leaving usually meant leaving someone behind. Marko escaped, but his family remained.

For 2,000 Deutschmarks a UN contact hid him in a UN cargo truck bound for Belgrade. The bone-shaking ride lasted five, maybe eight hours. It was hard to tell in the back of a truck. In those hours, he couldn't stop thinking what would happen if anyone, Serb or Bosniak, decided to check the cargo.

1994, Serbia

Marko found an uneasy haven in Serbia. The Serbian government of Slobodan Milosevic, who would later die in The Hague during prosecution on charges of crimes against humanity, needed muscle during the violent breakup of Yugoslavia. As a result, refugees faced conscription once they reached the eastern republic.

A Slovenian-Bosnian Serb, Marko's wife had been living in the Serbian capital during the war, and contacts of hers shuttled Marko from the unloaded cargo truck to a village south of Belgrade where an uncle had a farm. He registered as a student, thereby avoiding the Serbian draft, and worked on the farm on weekends. He lived as a dual student and farmhand for six months, preparing his second escape.

The Bosnian War caused a mass migration within and from the former Yugoslavia. The United Nations High Commissioner for Refugees (UNHCR) reports that over 218,000 people in the region still remain internally displaced.[3] Others, an estimated 650,000 people, moved overseas.[4] A large number chose Canada. In the late 1990s, roughly 25 per cent of refugees resettled in Canada came from the Balkans.[5]

Marko applied for asylum at the Canadian embassy in Belgrade. He and his wife picked Canada on the strength of two sheets of paper covered in handwritten advice. They were cheat sheets passed from one nervous Serb asylum seeker to the next on how to answer the Canadians' questions. In the self-taught English of a BBC listener, Marko gave his rehearsed answers. Why are you leaving? *Scared, stateless, mixed ethnicity, opposed to the draft.* Marko adds, "Everything's true, it's just exaggerated." Where in Canada do you want to go? *Anywhere, really, but Vancouver since it rolls off the tongue better than Toronto.* "That's how little we knew," Marko says now. "Just leave, you know? Just leave. That's it."

One more harrowing trip then. Alone, because his wife would risk passage to Canada at a later date. The Canadian embassy, which accepted the couple as refugees, organized a bus to take Marko and others across the Serbian border into Hungary. Until they crossed, they were at the mercy of the whims of Serb officials. "That was terrible, passing that border," Marko remembers. "Even if you have a Canadian visa, everything, they can just remove you."

February 1995 and July 2014, Toronto, Canada

Real estate guides promise that, even today, passersby will hear Serbo-Croatian in and around the old apartment buildings on Gamble Avenue in Toronto's Broadview North neighbourhood. In February 1995, Marko joined the new and fast-growing group of former Balkan residents there. His wife followed two months later.

Marko had already taken a crash course in Canadian living back in Serbia. He was told anecdotes by a young woman who had briefly lived in Toronto. Before meeting her in Belgrade, Marko wrote a list of his questions in a small blue notebook that he still owns, and shows now. Travelling to Canada would take him on his first plane ride. In faded handwriting: *Will everyone on the plane be a refugee? How are dishes and clothes cleaned in Canada? Is there freedom of movement?*

The typewriter print on his old visa reads "Stateless." Marko can laugh at it now, and maybe he did then too. Marko has that curious ability to laugh with nearly every sentence and still be infectious. One of his first possessions in Canada was a pair of big, ugly rubber shoes handed to him by a government official at Pearson International Airport. "What the hell are these?" he thought. But it was February and Marko plunged out into slushy, grey Toronto. "After a time, I figured out these shoes are excellent."

Although a trained mechanical engineer, he didn't have the English to show his knowledge, but Marko noticed all the newspaper ads for jobs in information technology, clearly a growth industry. Using a large chunk of the little money he had, Marko bought a copy of Scott Mueller's anthology *Upgrading and Repairing PCs* (today in its twenty-first edition) and began reading, highlighting every English word he didn't understand. At about page 30, the highlighting stops.

He adapted quickly in his new career and today Marko is a senior consultant with an IT firm. If he won the lottery, he says, he would keep working. "It's my hobby." He's good with software and with people, calming tempers and handling the complex drama of the office. "Maybe because I'm from Sarajevo," he says. "You get used to the different people there."

His two teenaged boys savour visits to Sarajevo. Each year growing up, they visited their grandmother and, in Marko's words, toughened up on playgrounds built with a more fend-for-yourself attitude than in Canada. Like Marko once had to do in very different circumstances, his boys can easily transition from one world to another. It still amazes him to hear the two speak in fluent English, and Serbo-Croatian in the next breath.

18 Iren Hessami Koltermann

Iran

Iren Hessami Koltermann at home in Mississauga.
Photograph by Ryan Walker.

January 1979, Tehran, Iran

Iren Hessami was old enough to know it was a deadly serious game, but young enough to feel comforted anyway, when her father picked her up from high school and told her to mimic the passions outside. She and her brother, Farshid, older by one year at fourteen, rolled down the car windows and smiled. People were jubilant. A few blocks later, her father motioned to roll the windows up and they became, to anyone in the crowd outside their slow-rolling car, as sullen as any Shah supporter.

Back and forth, grinning, frowning, Iren swung her mood by neighbourhood on the drive home through Tehran in January 1979. It was the day Mohammad Reza Pahlavi, the Shah, left for exile, ending decades of pro-Western rule. Joy and dismay seemed to erupt equally as their car parted crowds across the capital. Iren didn't panic because her father kept his head. Play along, he told them.

Iren describes these events over lunch in a cafeteria below Toronto's Royal York Hotel, during a spare few hours between her meetings. Her story, she says, is about her parents.

———

At first, Iren didn't form an opinion about the Shah's successor, revolutionary leader Ayatollah Ruhollah Khomeini, who returned to Iran from exile on February 1, 1979. Iren is Baha'i and her religion taught her to be neutral in the kind of divisive politics that had settled over the country. When the monarchy fell in January 1979, it was not the snap end to an era that it appeared to outsiders. Change had been coming slowly. Iren's first memory of the revolution was before 1979 and, again, experienced from her father's car. "Is that a tank?" she asked, wide-eyed, gazing at, yes, a tank, perched like a monument in one of Tehran's public squares. Demonstrations began to grow in 1977 at the bidding of Khomeini, then still in exile. Strikes and marches filled the tree-lined backbone of the city, what is now Vali Asr Street.

"In that boiling water that slowly boils over, you actually get used to this," Iren explains. By contrast, idolization was swift. In the weeks after the revolution, she heard her classmates parrot the new state propaganda. *The Ayatollah's image was in the moon last night*, they gushed. People were changing in front of her eyes.

Iren and her brother finished their semesters at British private school in June 1979, as scheduled, but their mother, Iran (named after her country), doubted the school would reopen come fall. She was right. International companies including schools were quickly, ominously, leaving. Iran began searching for one that would take her children, thirteen and fourteen years old. She was repeatedly turned down and finally, the principal at a Jewish school confided, "I have to tell you, I have been told not to allow your kids to enrol." In short, Baha'i children were not welcome.

Long before 1979, some of the country's Muslim leaders including Khomeini had denounced the Baha'i faith, a young religion founded in Iran in 1863. However, their contempt was not yet state policy. Only after the revolution did Baha'is become outright public enemies, blocked from schools, work, worship, and government.[1] Those who condemned Baha'is did so passionately. For one, Baha'is are not considered "people of the book," as Jews and Christians are. A more fatal flaw is that the faith emerged from the teaching of a man who called himself a messenger of God, and that's heresy to some who believe Muhammad was the last prophet.[2]

Baha'i teaching presented another problem. Values like universal education and equality of men and women were denounced as "Western." And their neutrality in politics—another tenet of the Baha'i faith—was taken as proof of an absence of fealty to the new regime.

Violence against the minority took its cue, as it often does, from the leadership. Homes and businesses owned by Baha'is were targets of arson, and demonstrators gathered across the country to demand that Baha'is convert to Islam.[3] Summary arrests soon followed, and then executions. After mob attacks in the southern city of Shiraz, Iren's relatives from the south moved quietly to Tehran into the spare rooms of friends and family.

Iren felt safe at home in Tehran, until soldiers of the Revolutionary Guard occupied a nearby television station, taken with gunfire she could hear from her living room. Events had so far taught her that if the right people—her parents—were there, then she was safe. Now, "I knew nobody had the power to protect me." It hit her just as suddenly that her parents were not safe either.

The same summer that Tehran schools refused Iren and Farshid, their mother quit her job as the director of nursing in the coronary care unit of the National Oil Company hospital. She left on the pretense of early retirement, but she really quit on the strong advice of hospital management. Baha'is across the country were dismissed or else, as with Iran, pressured to leave. The family worried that Iren's father, Farhang, would soon be without work too. Like his wife, Farhang had been rising in his career. He owned an electrical contracting firm that had won several lucrative contracts for public works. But no matter their success and possibly because of it, Baha'is were being shouldered out of a living.

When it became clear to Iran that her children would not get back into school, she switched tactics. She would have to get them out of the country, and she began canvassing embassies, not local schools.

Most mornings in the summer of 1979, Iren and Farshid wore their best clothes and followed their mother through the security grilles of the country of the day. Iren remembers China and South Korea because they were more like houses, slight and tucked away. At embassies large and small, however, they were not alone. Weeks passed in stretching lines of Iranians outside each embassy. At popular destinations like the United States and United Kingdom, the three sat outside for hours in a queue that barely inched forward.

For weeks, nothing happened. Not until they found a crack in the unmoving queue. A family friend supplied a contact in Canada, a sister who lived in Port Moody, British Columbia, with her Canadian husband. The couple was Baha'i and had been feeling helpless, hearing stories about the community in Iran. They immediately agreed to sponsor Iren and Farshid to study in Canada.

Armed with a sponsorship letter, Iren's mother jumped the long line at the Canadian embassy and had an interview with none other than the ambassador. His name was Ken Taylor, and he would later be celebrated for his role in the escape of eight Americans during the 1979–81 hostage crisis, dramatized in the film *Argo*. Summoned alone from the waiting room, Iran paused to warn her children: "Don't even breathe." Inside, the ambassador stared across his office at the young mother and asked her why Port Moody? She admitted she didn't know much, only that Port Moody was not on the French side of Canada and it was probably cold. But in that corner of the world was a school that would take her children.

Three new visas to Canada were approved, and Iren, Farshid, and their mother left Tehran for Vancouver International Airport on October 10, 1979. Farhang stayed behind, where Iran planned to rejoin him after her children were settled in Canada. They still believed the anti-Baha'i zeal would end, as it had before.

With winter on her mind on a layover in London, UK, Iren picked out her first parka and snow boots—items on her mother's checklist of Canadian essentials. She arrived cocooned, overheated, and feeling ridiculous for a warm Vancouver fall.

October 1979, Port Moody, Canada

In the eyes of a teenager, life in Canada was more difficult than back home. Iren and Farshid saved their quarters by walking instead of taking the public bus to school, and as a small reward at the end of the week, they bought ice cream. For the first time in their lives, having pocket change was a treat. They couldn't get money out of Tehran so everything had to be saved. They got used to uncertainty, like how much money there would be next month, when they would see their father, and how long they would live in Canada. They grew up fast in other ways too. More than once, they walked into the rented apartment to find their mother waiting beside her packed luggage, ready to fly back to Farhang. Each time they talked her down. From Tehran, they argued, she couldn't help their father or any other family member or friend.

School was its own struggle, but Iren's English quickly improved. She could even spar with classmates, as occasionally needed. Fifty-two American hostages were taken by students in Tehran the month after Iren got on a plane and the major global news story was on the lips of Canadian high school students. They fired questions at Iren and Farshid, likely the only Iranians they knew. Tired of accusatory questions about a situation she had no way to understand, let alone control, Iren once hissed, "Last night, we decided not to feed the hostages." Teachers sensed the tension and intervened, as they did until Iren and Farshid graduated with honours from Port Moody Senior Secondary School. One teacher asked the two to give a presentation on Iran, and another used Iren's near-perfect grammar score to show her peers that halting English said nothing about intelligence.

"The staff and the principals, my mom talks about it to this day, they were amazing," Iren says.

Meanwhile, Farhang had gone into hiding in Tehran. He was a link in a chain of help for Baha'is fleeing other parts of Iran for the capital. He knew he had to be cautious, but the deciding moment was in the stairwell of his office building. One day on his way down, Farhang met a few men, climbing, carrying machine guns. They asked for directions to Farhang Hessami, and Farhang pointed them up to his office. He never returned to the building.

Canada was not an exit option for Farhang. The embassy had closed—the ambassador and his staff left swiftly after smuggling their secret guests, the American diplomats, from Mehrabad Airport on January 27, 1980. Other doors were closing fast. Most embassies sealed outbound travel in inadvertent step with the Islamic Republic. But Germany remained open long enough for Farhang to fly to Frankfurt in September 1980. He spent nearly a year in Germany while he and his wife planned their next steps. Iran hired a lawyer with the diminishing family savings, and they decided that Farhang would buy a ticket to South America with a layover in Vancouver. The lawyer would fly with him to intervene only if Farhang was stopped at Canadian customs. The fear was that if Canada rejected Farhang, Germany had no duty to let him re-enter and he would be forced onto the next plane back to Tehran.

Farhang entered Canada without incident on November 6, 1981, and at last together, the family applied to stay in Canada as refugees. While waiting for a hearing, they received temporary Canadian documents that marked them "Stateless." The label was abstract to Iren until she took a solo trip after high school graduation to see Baha'i holy sites in Haifa, Israel. On her layover in the United Kingdom, Iren planned to leave London's Heathrow Airport to sightsee. This was not allowed. She was stopped by a British immigration official, who told her the Canadian travel document was not valid. She stayed in the airport, and although Israel did let her in, she *felt* stateless. A powerful, lonely thing. Worse still, a Canadian immigration official stopped her again on return to Vancouver, suspicious of her statelessness. "I broke down, I remember I sat down—I really understood the awfulness of not belonging anywhere."

The trouble was temporary and Iren re-entered Canada after a few hours, but her belief in one human community, core to the Baha'i faith, felt more idealistic than ever.

The family's refugee hearing was in February 1982, and they became citizens three years later, on December 11, 1985. Years after, Iren can still see the imprint on herself of being a refugee. Sometimes in surprising ways, like during the first year of her marriage.

Iren married a born-Canadian in 1990, and they spent their first year together in Haifa, which coincided with the First Gulf War between Saddam Hussein's Iraq and a US-led coalition. Some nights, air raid sirens sounded two, three, four times; a call to jump from sleep to a fly-faced gas mask and a safe room that few ignored, from fear that Iraqi missiles showering Israel held nerve gas. One night as sirens wailed for the fourth time, Iren saw her husband sitting still on the bed. Stunned, he said, "Damnit, I'm a Canadian, nobody bombs a Canadian."

"I remember thinking at that moment: that's the difference between being a refugee and not being a refugee, I never think nobody has the right," Iren said. Her husband had something like a default belief in security, but if she had one, hers was switched off. "I don't have that same assumption and need to remind myself of it," she said. Still, under the sirens in Haifa, Iren's belief in universalism was somewhat ironic-ally reinforced. Anyone can become a target, and anyone can be killed by a missile.

December 2013, Mississauga, Canada

Iren and her husband now live in Mississauga, where they moved from Israel in 1994. Ten years ago, Iren left a job at consulting firm KPMG to start her own business, a consultancy that helps companies address barriers to hiring, keeping, and promoting immigrants and diverse employees. It's family inspired.

There was her mother, for one. Before Iran got a job in Canada, she was asked for original transcripts like everyone else. No exceptions, even if they were locked up in a country now hostile to Canada. Against the odds, she obtained her records by mail from friends in high places. Even so, when Iran did get a job, as a care aide, it was a distance below her former position in Tehran. What she lacked was "Canadian experience."

If Iren knew struggle by her mother's example, she also knew potential. Her mother wanted to be a nurse again. It was a calling and Iren explained it also as a form of worship for her mother. In the Baha'i faith, working for the common good is doing service. So Iran first worked at Seton Villa, an assisted living facility in Burnaby, British Columbia, and, after successive promotions and stints back at school, she not only qualified as a registered nurse, but retired as the director of nursing, her last position in Tehran. She continues nursing in Burnaby in retirement.

Iren shares her mother's determination. She began a second venture a few years after launching her consulting firm, and managed to earn her master's degree in between, in international and intercultural communications. Iren is the founder of a Canadian non-profit named Musonda that works on the other end of human resources, with the people who can't find jobs. The work is all about inclusion, "a concept that is as real as gravity," she explained, a nod to her belief in oneness that was once tested at the Vancouver airport. She has felt what it's like to not belong and wants to help others get past that, as she has. For some of her clients, a foreign job history spoils their resume. For others, past trauma creates a personal, psychological barrier as real as any external one. Iren understands the power of the latter, because she confronted it in herself.

"I owe this to my parents," she says. They are unique, she explains, using the present tense although Farhang recently passed away. They taught Iren to see her story differently. The important part is not to be a victim, it's about how she moved on, who she helped, what she did next. "They did not accept a victim narrative, and they never, ever allowed my brother and me to feel that way."

19 Anwar Arkani

Myanmar

Anwar Arkani at language school in Waterloo.
Photograph by Scott McQuarrie.

1978, Buthidaung, Myanmar

When Anwar first fled his village, all he understood were his mother's words: "We have to run."

Anwar's family was running from Operation Dragon King. The Arkanis were Rohingya, an ethnic minority—Muslims in a Buddhist country—who were concentrated in large numbers in the western prov-ince of Rakhine in Burma (renamed Myanmar in 1989).[1]

This was the spring of 1978. Burmese soldiers were roaming through Rakhine, checking the status of its residents: citizen or illegal immigrant? Operation Dragon King was launched to oust those con-sidered illegal, and that meant soldiers indiscriminately targeted all Rohingya Muslims. They were then subject to mass arrests, mixed with torture, summary executions, and for those who survived, eviction.[2]

Anwar, his siblings, and his mother ran, but his father—a farmer—was arrested and then killed.

Anwar's mother knew what she was doing. Already, she had sur-vived a 1942 massacre when she was four years old and had never for-gotten. Now with her husband dead, she fled with her five children. They marched for days, more than twenty-five kilometres on swollen feet, to the Naf River. She loaded her children aboard a frail boat and crossed to the shore of Bangladesh.

Their time in Buthidaung had been a good period in the family's life. The heavy rains helped the Arkanis and their neighbours grow vege-tables year round next to bamboo-frame homes. There was one annual crop of rice, and fish could always be caught in the river. Anwar would get up in the morning and walk an hour to school.

Dragon King was the latest trouble between the Buddhist popula-tion and Rohingya. Since General Ne Win took power in a 1962 coup, about fifteen years after independence from Britain, Burma had been controlled by a military dictatorship. The coup was a turning point. It was the beginning of a campaign by the Burmese leadership to erase the Rohingya's place in the history and future of Myanmar.

Rohingya, according to the government's rewriting of history, were really foreigners from Bangladesh staying illegally on Burmese land. But Rohingya had lived in Burma/Myanmar for at least a century and pos-sibly longer.[3] Maybe the junta needed the us-versus-them myth to unite the people behind their dictator. Or maybe the story was told to distract the population from its growing impoverishment. Whatever the motive, for years the brutal truth became that the state wanted Rohingya gone. And it was brutal.

After the march to Bangladesh in 1978, Anwar's family and over two hundred thousand others lived for nearly two years as refugees in border camps, in conditions that saw around ten thousand people die.[4] They then returned to Rakhine, and shortly after, his mother fell ill and died.

The Burmese government had treated Rohingya Muslims like stateless people before, but they made it official in 1982. They officially stripped them of citizenship. Anwar was thirteen when the citizenship law arrived. With no ID card, there would be no high school. "The future was shattered," he says.

Violence against Rohingya by Burmese authorities and vigilantes among the Buddhist population became more common. The public hostility was real, but hand-wringing by the state—*What can we do? The people are angry*—was a farce. Vilifying Rohingya began at the top.

Their mother gone, Anwar and two of his younger siblings lived with their grandmother and uncle. Anwar wanted to leave Myanmar, but hesitated. Should he leave his siblings behind? Should he take them along? Where?

"Bangladesh was the only option we had," he says. "But I didn't know where to take them, or what to do. Everything was unknown."

Two years later, now fifteen, Anwar made a decision. He left Myanmar for Bangladesh alone, this time skipping the refugee camp and joining a Muslim rebel group stationed in the eastern hills at the border. He stayed in their ranks for one year, inactive, before moving on for a better living in the city. His next three years centred on finding food and shelter. "Whatever I did, I did to survive," Anwar says, describing exhausted days spent hauling stone and mortar on construction sites, selling clothes, and even tutoring students with his self-taught Bengali.

In his late teens, Anwar returned to Myanmar amid talk of political openness in Yangon (formerly Rangoon), but swiftly left again. He saw nothing had changed after a few encounters with police who always had their hand out for a bribe. He moved on to Thailand in 1989, where he would sell fried flatbread called paratha from a push cart, learn three

more languages, and find a refugee agency that helped stateless people
get a passport.

1989, Bangkok, Thailand

For the second time, Anwar was alone in a new country. People said
there were better jobs in Thailand, but as a resident with no permit,
Anwar became an indentured worker to the owner of his paratha cart.
He once escaped a police chase and the shot they fired at him. And he
paid his dues, the innumerable bribes handed over by illegal migrants.

Still, he could always find work because he spoke Bengali and could
pass for a Bangladeshi. In other words, he could pretend not to be Rohingya. No one knew his real identity apart from fellow Rohingya and,
finally, the United Nations High Commissioner for Refugees (UNHCR).
It was during the process of applying to be a refugee that Anwar discovered, "Learning a language is the most crucial part of survival."

By the time the UN Refugee Agency in Bangkok called for an interview on his refugee application, Anwar spoke Thai, Malay, and halting
English in addition to the languages he knew before arriving in Thailand—Bengali, Burmese, and Rohingya. He told the UNHCR caseworker,
"I don't know English very well, but I will try my best to answer your questions." Hearing these words, the interpreter in the interview room looked
surprised, then furious. He was Burmese but not Rohingya, and Anwar
believes he was deliberately mistranslating Rohingya stories. Anwar and
fifteen other Rohingya men filed asylum claims in unison, and one by one,
had their interviews. They shared extraordinary histories, but only Anwar
told his story without an interpreter, and only he received refugee status.

Back in Myanmar, Rohingya were still up against round after
round of horror. By word of mouth, Rohingya living in Thailand spread
news of houses burning, murder, rape, and always, people fleeing. In the
early 1990s, Bangladesh received another major influx of Rohingya.[5]
UN agencies would later describe the decades-long violence as "systematic" and sometimes state policy.[6]

Anwar now had international recognition as a refugee. Which
didn't count for much when the police arrested him in a regular roundup
of illegal workers. Thailand is not a signatory to the Refugee Convention
and does not observe international standards of treatment of refugees.

Anwar was taken to a cell shared by over two hundred others. But he remembers it as decent, clean, and everyone had a mattress. There was no torture, no harassment. It was far better than the stories of Burmese jails. He learned to read and write Thai there, and was soon appointed to teach fellow inmates English. After two years and three months, in 1994, Anwar was released. That's when he first met a young Canadian man who asked, "How would you like to teach?"

The Canadian, born in Elora and raised in Guelph, Ontario, taught English in Bangkok. He believed Anwar's lie about having completed grade ten (Anwar later admitted to his friend that he'd quit after eighth grade), and he persuaded Anwar to write an English test to become a certified language teacher. Anwar sat the tests and earned the highest certificate, even though speaking to the Canadian was "the first time I really spoke to a native English speaker in my whole life." Anwar soon wrote—in English—to the Australian and Canadian embassies asking for asylum. In the meantime, he had a good job.

But one morning in 1995, at his desk preparing a lesson, Anwar looked up to see the police there to arrest him for the second time. They wanted money. He had none so they brought him to an immigration detention centre and, among other things, accused him of working illegally. During his second term in detention, his Canadian friend visited often. He also chased Anwar's refugee application at the Canadian embassy, so when Anwar was released ten months later, embassy staff were waiting for him.

His interviewer, a Canadian visa officer, wanted to know what Anwar would do for a living in Canada. "I vividly remember, I said 'anything.'"

September 1998 and July 2013, Kitchener-Waterloo, Canada

When Anwar heard an immigration official at Pearson Airport say "Welcome to Canada," he cried. A few hours later, he was in the back of a taxi heading for Kitchener, trying to keep his eyes open as the sky turned dark. He arrived at Reception House, a temporary home for government-assisted refugees at the edge of Victoria Park. Already there were three refugees from the former Yugoslavia, including two Muslims, so his first meal in Canada was cooked halal.

Anwar returned to Thailand in 2006 to marry Zainab, a Rohingya raised in Yangon. It took eighteen months to process her Canadian papers, and during that time, the couple waited in Thailand, meeting countless refugees from Myanmar. Some had left on boats and were telling stories of being arrested, jailed, deported, trafficked, released on ransom, and on their second or third escape. Everyone needed information and translation.

Anwar thinks he was the first Rohingya in Waterloo Region, but there is now a community of hundreds. Like him, many arrived as refugees. In between Anwar's switchboard job with the IT firm Descartes and raising their three boys, Anwar and Zainab work as translators for the growing Rohingya community. They find the greatest need is often between Rohingya parents and their children's teachers. The children, especially those born outside Canada, are not doing well. That's how Anwar and Zainab began teaching courses to both children and adults in a friend's basement.

In the spring of 2013, the Rohingya Language School opened in Waterloo. The improvised classroom set up by Anwar and Zainab evolved into a program at the International Languages school of the Waterloo Catholic District School Board, and Anwar says it's not done growing. Neither is the community. "Education is the main thing that we can use to improve this community and help them move forward," he says.

Anwar is an advocate for Rohingya beyond Kitchener-Waterloo. He is founder and president of the Rohingya Association of Canada and organized the Canada arm of Burma Task Force, an international coalition. He twice addressed special sessions of the United Nations about crimes in Rakhine state, which have continued into this decade. Mobs killed over two hundred people (a low estimate) in 2012 in yet more violence between Buddhists and Muslims, who remain officially stateless inside Myanmar.[7] Rohingya are now described by the United Nations as among the most persecuted minorities in the world.[8]

Anwar speaks with passion and calls Burmese acts against his people "genocide." These actions claimed his parents—the mother who told him to run—and they still haven't stopped.

20 Elvis

Namibia

Elvis at home in Toronto.
Photograph by Ryan Walker.

2011, Windhoek, Namibia

By the time he was twenty-one, Elvis[1] knew that he saw men differently. If he glanced sideways in the locker room before ball hockey practice, he might think, *Wow, he's cute.* Above the others, though, was his best friend. But Elvis said nothing out loud. He allowed himself only careful looks at the handsome face he had known for years—like in the rearview mirror, driving a car full of friends. Why was this happening now? Could a person have his attractions so suddenly flipped? Or was being gay a trait by birth, like the shape of a nose?

He didn't know how to explore any of this complexity. "Even asking someone a question, that person will turn your words around," Elvis says. So he did everything he could to keep his feelings and questions hidden. Homosexuality is illegal in Namibia, the western neighbour of South Africa, as well as in over seventy countries worldwide, half of them in Africa.[2] Officially, offenders in Namibia face jail, but police have been incited to do worse. In 2000, the minister of Home Affairs told police to "eliminate" homosexuals "from the face of Namibia."[3]

Elvis feared that if anyone grew suspicious—the community, even his family—someone would tell the authorities. He was right. Elvis thinks his uncle was the one who went to police in the end. It was vile and ironic, considering what had happened at home.

Elvis always had a difficult relationship with his family, one as torn in several directions by apartheid as any in the former colony of both Germany and South Africa. His mother, who raised Elvis alone, was the product of a German father and Herero mother. Elvis's grandmother knew there would be raised eyebrows when she took her light-skinned daughter out by the hand in Windhoek's streets. Apartheid also kept Elvis's mother out of a good school. There were plenty of ugly ways to classify a girl of mixed colour and being white enough for the superior education system wasn't one of them.

So his mother stayed home to help raise her younger siblings. But she got a good job, first house cleaning for a South African doctor, then raising his children, and eventually working in his business, a pharmacy. She also sent Elvis and his older sister to a school that taught in Afrikaans, the spinoff Dutch widely spoken in Namibia. Elvis also learned English, Namibia's official language. To the extended family, that was two strikes against Elvis's mother. Strike three—and it was a big one—Elvis wasn't taught Herero.

It was unthinkable not to learn the language of genocide survivors. The attempted extermination happened under colonial-era Germany, when an estimated 65,000 Herero were ordered killed.[4]

Aunts, uncles, and cousins sniffed their noses at the family's modest wealth too. Here was a single mother whose children not only spoke the language of colonizers, but who also had a big glass aquarium in their big brick house. *Mm, okay, now they're having cell phones.* Family remarks like that were jealousy, Elvis says. And yet, the big house enabled them to take in Elvis's uncle when he was divorced and temporarily discharged from his post in the Namibian military. It was sometime during that stay that his uncle became suspicious.

Maybe his uncle saw Elvis hanging around with men rumoured to be gay, because Elvis did begin moving in different circles. Whatever way he caught on, he didn't immediately report his nephew. One day when the two were home alone, Elvis heard his uncle call from a bedroom. He walked in, and everything happened quickly—his uncle gripping and kissing and trying to pull off his clothes. It ended by Elvis using his fists and running from the room, outside, and away from the house.

They both knew Elvis would stay quiet. "If I go to the police and say I'm gay, my uncle tried raping me, they're just going to laugh and do nothing about it. That's how it is," Elvis says. So the molesting and beating, by his uncle's fists or his belt, persisted. Elvis feared being alone at home and he was desperate to keep the situation above the heads of his mother and sister. They didn't know about his sexual orientation and he wasn't ready to change that. The bruises and scratches he passed off as fights in school hallways or sport fields; his mother knew Elvis had a critical mind and no qualms about confrontation.

As long as his sister and mother knew nothing of his sexuality, Elvis couldn't speak about his uncle's abuse. But his uncle could spread one truth without revealing the other. Slowly, extended family and then neighbours began treating Elvis differently, threateningly. His mother was upset and confused, "Why do they want to hurt you?" He would never tell.

Something was going to break, though, if he did nothing. So in his last year of high school, in January 2010, Elvis quit his classes. He had dreams of law school but shelved them. He needed a new environment and a new schedule, so he took a job with an IT company where he had worked before, during school breaks. His shifts ended much later than class had, and even later than his mother's work day. Elvis was now rarely alone with his uncle. Life was better—not good, but bearable.

Then one night, on October 4, 2011, just before leaving home to walk to a party, his cell phone rang. The friend hosting the party, who knew Elvis's secret, told him to stay away because the police were outside, almost certainly waiting for Elvis. He knew without having to ask that his uncle had finally reported him. It was the only plausible reason for officers to be there, ignoring the rest of a city notorious for its crime rate.

Elvis went to his mother. He still kept her on the fringe of the whole mess, but she understood enough to see a serious threat. They consulted another uncle, one who was kind to his nephew but, equally important, worked as a travel consultant and had the right contacts to book a last-minute flight. He suggested South Africa. Elvis shook his head—he wanted more distance. "I wanted to go far, far from South Africa because I knew my uncle would find me there." The next idea was Canada. It was peaceful and in 2011, Namibians didn't need a visa. His mother gave him her savings for a seat on an Air Namibia flight that the trio purchased that night. Elvis left the following day, on October 5, with only a backpack slung over his shoulder.

October 6, 2011, Toronto, Canada

Elvis walked toward an immigration desk after landing at Toronto's Pearson airport. Behind the desk sat a man in what looked like a police uniform and Elvis wondered if Canada had been the right decision. It was supposed to be free, but he knew nothing about the country's LGBT rights; it would be much later, even, before he first heard the term "LGBT" to describe lesbian, gay, bisexual, and transgender people. In Namibian slang, Elvis would have been called *mofie*, a severe insult for a man who acts like a woman.

He asked the desk officer to speak to someone who could tell him what to do next—he was from Namibia and couldn't go home. The man pointed down a hallway to a separate office. Inside, a uniformed woman asked Elvis to read a passage in English. When he finished, she said, "You need to tell us where you really got your passport." For the next four hours, Elvis tried to convince various immigration officials that what they thought was his British accent, and thus a betrayal of his claim to Namibian nationality, was really a product of Afrikaans and English. They didn't believe him and threatened to send him back to Windhoek on the next flight. He hadn't prepared for this. He didn't panic, but Elvis didn't relent either. So they told him to come back the following morning when the refugee desk reopened. When Elvis asked where he would sleep, the Canadians shrugged.

He wandered out and found the baggage carousel, still looping around, and picked up his backpack. He saw an empty table against a wall, and that's where he spent his first night in Canada, on a tabletop beside the carousels. He was outside the refugee office when the doors opened on October 7.

Not believing Elvis's identity, it's likely the immigration officials were searching for evidence of passport fraud, which is a legal basis for detaining someone. After Elvis made a refugee claim, he could not be sent back to Namibia before his claim was heard, but he could be detained if he had used a fake or altered passport. A strange accent on its own cannot disprove a nationality, so the Canadian government would have to prove his passport was invalid.

After another full day of repetitive questions, and although it seemed to Elvis as if they made no progress at all, Elvis heard that he could stay in Toronto and apply for asylum. The officials handed him a few sheets of paper with the names of shelters and numbers of refugee lawyers, then wished him well.

Elvis wandered downstairs for a second time to the baggage carousel but stopped short of the arrivals gate. He must have looked stunned because a woman in a cleaner's uniform walked over. She had seen him sleeping there on her shift the previous night and wondered if he was okay; if he knew where to go next. He held out the papers and she scanned the list of shelters, before tapping her finger on Covenant House in downtown Toronto. She'd heard it was good.

Next, she took his arm and led him outside into the cool October evening to the bus stop. She drew a small map showing the bus route he would take to the subway, and marked where he would transfer and finally emerge at College station. She put two transit tokens in his hand and chatted until the bus arrived. Kindness after two long, lonely days; he hasn't forgotten her.

October 2012 and February 2014, Toronto, Canada

His refugee hearing finished in less than one hour on a Monday morning in October 2012, a year after he arrived in Toronto, and Elvis walked out smiling. He called his mother first. She still didn't learn from him the details of his asylum claim or of his new refugee status, only that he was accepted. Elvis left behind a rift in his extended family: his mother now knew his uncle had abused him, but the details, the why, she didn't know.

Although he is openly gay in Canada and recently told his sister, he isn't ready to face his mother. "I know if I have to go out to her and tell her the truth, she's going to be disappointed as a mother," Elvis says. Still, he thinks her response would follow an old adage of hers, "Love your life."

In different ways, he began to enjoy Toronto. Here, Elvis went to his first gay club and witnessed openness he had not ever imagined. Hesitating, he explains, "I felt—like I'm relieved. I felt so differently. Like I'm free." The feeling continued into his first Pride Parade in 2012.

Helping him experience it all were two mentors, a Canadian couple, who Elvis met through Supporting Our Youth (SOY), a non-profit with a mentorship program for LGBT youth. They helped him navigate a foreign culture, not just the LGBT community. Elvis calls them "life mentors" and close friends. He too volunteers with SOY and a few other non-profits. He became a volunteer counsellor thinking he can help people find their footing in Canada, like all those who have kept him balanced. He speaks his mind and prods others to do the same. When they do, he listens intently, his eyes soft and studying. You can tell him anything.

Elvis is on track once more to become a lawyer, that long-ago dream. Soon after his hearing, he sent three applications to one-year programs designed as a bridge to an undergraduate degree. He received three acceptance letters and chose York University. He graduates in the spring and returns to York in fall 2014, for a bachelor in sexuality studies. After that, he says, he heads to law school.

In his backpack for Canada, Elvis packed a Namibian flag. Though he doesn't miss the country, he can't disentangle himself from it. Elvis was born the year of independence, in 1990, so he and Namibia turn twenty-four together. And Namibia is still home to the two people at the centre of his world: "The only thing that will take me back is my mom and my sister." He's been in Canada for three years and says, "I still cry every day ... Everything I do, I don't do it for myself, I do it for them."

21 Humaira

Afghanistan

Anonymous portrait of Humaira at the Afghan
Women's Organization in Toronto.
Photograph by Christopher Manson.

May 2002, Northern Afghanistan

In the spring of 2002 in the northern part of Afghanistan, a middle-aged pharmacist from Kabul was accompanying his elderly father who was campaigning to win a seat in the countrywide elections. They were coming on the heels of a massive retreat to the east into Pakistan by Taliban forces. Foreign soldiers, sent in after 9/11 in the United States, found themselves in a post-invasion lull, although the war would come to draw troops from over forty-five countries, including Canada, and last for more than a decade. The Taliban had fled Kabul in November 2001. It was now time to elect people to carry on in the vacuum left behind.

The pharmacist was a father of two with another child on the way. Not interested in politics at all, but being the oldest son still in Afghanistan, he was there as a duty to his father. But the campaign ended suddenly. Someone from a rival political camp stepped out and shot this son in the chest.

Back in Kabul exactly three weeks later, Humaira,[1] his twenty-two-year-old widow, gave birth to their third child, a son. Her life was about to change.

This was not the first time. When Humaira was in her second semester studying law at Kabul University in 1996, the Taliban took control of the capital, her city since birth. The Kabul of Humaira's childhood was home to a cosmopolitan middle class that thronged lively shops and cafés long into the night. Under the Soviet-backed regimes and even the mujahedeen, who had ruled the city since 1992, women could study and walk the streets alone with only loose scarves wrapped over their hair.

The Taliban ended all such expressions of free women. Humaira had to quit university. Home, too, was suddenly unsafe. People whispered about armed men arriving during the night and abducting girls.

Soon enough, Humaira sat stricken at the kitchen table, listening to her parents explain that they had arranged a marriage for her protection, to get her out of the city. He was her second cousin, twice her age, a man Humaira had called "Uncle." Eighteen years old, she cried; "How could I get married to him?" But she did, and Humaira followed family custom and her new husband to her in-laws home in the north, where the Taliban influence was not so strong. Now it was her in-laws, not the Taliban, she obeyed when she put on the burqa. She couldn't wear her glasses beneath the garment and began to prefer staying inside over stumbling on her own hem outdoors. Her university days felt far behind.

"I was angry," Humaira says, but events were out of her hands. "It was Taliban time in Afghanistan. The situation was like that." While adjusting to a new way of life, she gave birth to a daughter, then a son, and became pregnant a third time in the fall of 2001. She discovered that her husband was a decent, kind man and a loving father. Without intending to, Humaira realized that she loved him. It was not only women trapped in time and circumstance, but good men too.

When he was killed, Humaira was in Kabul with her mother preparing to deliver the baby. By the time she returned north, her husband was already in the ground, in the Muslim custom of quickly burying the dead. She never saw his body.

Afghanistan under the Taliban was not a good place for a widow. These were men who dealt brutal punishments, like death by stoning, and who believed in the corrupting influence of women, a calculation that was not strictly religious, but political, something the male base could get behind. All women were to have keepers, their fathers or husbands, or, in the case of a widow, her in-laws.

And her in-laws had plans for Humaira. They presented her brother-in-law, two years her junior, to replace the deceased elder brother, her husband. Humaira refused, and continued to refuse for nearly a year. "He didn't need me or my three children," she explains. "They just wanted to keep me in their home." Men can have multiple wives in Afghanistan and Humaira would have been her brother-in-law's first wife, and almost certainly the oldest, as he married other, younger women. Plus she would be occupied with her own children, borne by another man. All this told her she would essentially be his servant. Humaira and her children also had no property rights, further enhancing the prospect of servitude. She could not sign on to this, for herself or her children.

Back in Kabul, Humaira's father knew that life was becoming miserable for his daughter and her children. Sure that it would only get worse, he came up with a plan to shepherd his daughter and grandchildren to Kabul and then east to Peshawar, to go into hiding with an aunt and uncle in the city of 3.6 million. He picked them up on the pretense of a short family visit to the capital, but instead of stopping, they drove nine hours eastward by one bus and two cars, attempting to lose anyone on their tail.

It didn't take long for her in-laws to discover she and the children were gone, and to use their government contacts to jail Humaira's father for kidnapping. He revealed nothing about their hiding spot. A friend paid for his release after twenty days, but he lost his job in the public service and his health crumbled as he awaited—and feared—news of his daughter and grandchildren.

Straddling Central and South Asia, Peshawar officially sits in Pakistan but is stubbornly claimed by Afghanistan. It is big, busy, and awash in the colourful noise of a frontier city. But a bustling city still sees shadows and hears whispers. Informants bring news by jewelled, rustic "jingle trucks" across the unfastened border with Afghanistan. Anyone could be someone sent to find Humaira and her children.

Humaira left her uncle's flat only for urgent errands, and the children emerged even less. They slept and spent their days in a single room, a rectangle roughly eight by eleven feet. For five years they stayed in that room and, in five years, the children walked Peshawar streets just a handful of times. Even peering over the balcony off the main room of the flat was forbidden. Hadia was five years old when she arrived at the apartment with her mother and younger brothers, and she remembers very little of the space in between then and her tenth birthday. She tries not to think about bad memories, she explains.

Shortly after the family left Afghanistan, Humaira's father contacted a distant relative living in Canada. Afghan by birth but now Canadian, she had an upcoming trip to Pakistan and agreed to stop in Peshawar during her stay to visit Humaira. The woman visited once, and then again the next day, returning to the apartment. She had seen them and having seen them, had to do something. It was their cell-like room, the lack of a future, and the big personalities inside, that drew her back. She asked Humaira if she could bring them to Canada as refugees. "Yes, of course, thank you," Humaira replied.

"She felt so sorry for me and for my children. She was like an angel."

While she waited on her angel, Humaira worried. Her father was unemployed and unhealthy. She had little contact since it could take two months for a letter to travel one way, and first required finding a courier to trust. She spent her days teaching all she could as Hadia, Ibrahim, and Bahram grew. She feared they would be illiterate and punished along with her, when they were eventually found. She also feared the costs and consequence if any of them, undocumented foreigners, needed a hospital.

Three years after the private sponsorship process began, Humaira had an interview at the Canadian High Commission in Islamabad. Two weeks later, she received notice that her request for asylum had been denied. She was devastated, and feeling the weight of her family on someone else's conscience, she reluctantly phoned her would-be sponsor. "I felt so ashamed to get in contact with her again. I didn't want to force her. I felt so ashamed, I lost my hope." The Canadian promised she would find a lawyer and an appeal, but Humaira had no news for a long time.

Almost a full year later, in 2009, Humaira received a remarkable phone call: Humaira and her children were refugees. Her sponsor said a judge had reversed the first decision. They would soon be on a plane from Islamabad to Toronto. She explained the journey to ten-year-old Hadia but not to her boys, aged nine and seven, who could accidentally spill a big secret before they got out.

May 2009 and September 2013, Toronto, Canada

The family arrived in Canada in May 2009, and spent their first four months at the home of their sponsor in Toronto. In September, they moved into their own flat in a high-rise apartment across the city. It was brilliantly spacious. A large living room window let the daylight stream inside. For a time, rent money came from their sponsor, who was frequently at their door to help Humaira buy groceries and run errands.

Full independence was some way off, but Humaira tried to do all she could alone. The nearest grocery store was a twenty-five-minute walk away. *Nearby*, the neighbours had said. Distance, however, is measured differently in the steps of three children ten and under, too young to stay home alone. Humaira couldn't afford bus fare, or a stroller for Bahram, so they set out on foot. Four times the family tried to make it to the store, and four times they turned back, defeated by tired boys. The fifth time, they made it all the way.

Seven months after she arrived, Humaira got a job at a daycare. She wants to go back to school to study early childhood education, and maybe, in time, to study social work. During her first few years in Canada, she learned English through courses and, in 2013, earned a credit for grade twelve English. Today, Hadia corrects and translates for her mother only in short bursts here and there.

Humaira baked a cake and pastries for our interview, and she refills emptying plates without question. Like their mother, the children are gracious. They chat shyly and curiously, and give unprompted pleased-to-meet-yous.

Hadia, in grade ten, is worried about speaking in an upcoming mock trial in her extracurricular law class, but she thinks about becoming a lawyer even though public speaking makes her nervous. She thinks she would like arguing right and wrong. All three love math. Ibrahim likes how there's always an answer, and different ways to find it. Bahram, the youngest, is a writer—a great one, his older brother and sister brag. "He's really incredible." "When he writes, you can really see it, like you can touch it and taste it."

Humaira begins to cry recalling the phone call that told her to prepare for Canada. "I knew I will be able to rescue my children's lives. They will be able to get educated. They will feel free." Ibrahim leaves the couch to stand beside her, sensing her emotion before it is visible, and kisses her on the cheek. Hadia and Bahram stand too, uneasy, watching their mother in tears.

Their closeness is palpable. A bond forced in Peshawar in an eight-by-eleven room is steadying them in Toronto.

22 Joseph

Sierra Leone

Anonymous portrait of Joseph in Toronto.
Photograph by Christopher Manson.

May 1997, Freetown, Sierra Leone

On a Sunday in May 1997, Joseph[1] was shaken awake by his uncle. There had been a coup, his uncle said. *A coup.* There were the expected questions, like who did it? And are we safe? But Joseph's first thoughts were about his O-level exams. Writing his last one crowded everything out. Wide-eyed but still groggy, he breathed, "How am I going to do my French?" They stayed indoors listening to the radio.

A band of officers in the Sierra Leone Army had forced the elected president into exile. Over the airwaves on Sunday, May 25, the junta announced themselves the new leaders in Freetown, where Joseph lived. In the coming weeks, fighters ordered in by the rebel group Revolutionary United Front (RUF) would help seize control of the capital.

Unrest in Sierra Leone was not, by now, new. Civil war began in March 1991 when RUF rebels attacked from Liberia. They were fed and fuelled by Charles Taylor, then on his way to becoming the warlord president of Liberia and, today, a convicted war criminal. Almost exclusively one nepotistic party had ruled Sierra Leone since 1967, the decade of independence, and it ground the country into poverty. The rebels claimed their primary objective was to rid Freetown of its longtime corrupt leaders, but there was a second force at play. Control of resources like the diamond and bauxite mines seemed to drive fighting year after year.

In the middle, between the RUF and the Sierra Leone Army—both sides stacked with foreign mercenaries—were civilians caught in ambushes and facing immense pressure to join the fighting. Even boys and girls, who could barely wield them, got weapons in exchange for income, food, care of sorts, and probably, the opportunity to keep on living.

Life went on in Freetown after war began in 1991, but even the markets, the universal pulse of a city, emptied in May 1997. People knew how brutal the RUF rebels could be when they didn't hold power. Now that they had it, their next step was anyone's guess.

———

Because a coup had happened more than once since the start of the civil war six years earlier, Joseph went to school on Monday. Around noon is when residents of the capital started to run.

When they heard commotion outside, most of Joseph's classmates fled the building. He hid in a classroom for the first hours of panic, and then jogged through the empty hallways and outside. He saw cars had been deserted, a sign that road blocks were already up. It also meant the rebels were targeting people with money. They surrounded whatever and whoever glittered, so along with cars, people also hid or ditched other status symbols like their jewellery, watches, and sneakers. The rebels appeared young to Joseph. Some didn't even look his sixteen years. Their clothes looked shabby and none of the boys (they were mostly boys) wore fatigues.

The buses had stopped so Joseph set off walking the thirteen miles home from school. Along the way, he saw a group of teenagers push two men to the ground. Joseph kept moving, and went faster when he heard the moist thud of their machetes. He guessed the sound; didn't want to see a severed limb. These men weren't the first or last civilians to have their arms and legs cut off this way. Amputations were a popular tactic, a trademark of Sierra Leone's war.

Joseph had witnessed grim scenes in the street before (it could take hours for Freetown police to clean up traffic accidents) but this deliberate brutality and the closeness of it was new, and so were the strange effects of adrenaline. "I don't know how to explain it," he says. "I mean, you fear death, and you fear these things, but you don't really comprehend the magnitude of it. It was scary but it was kind of exciting."

Once home, Joseph and his uncle locked themselves in the backyard shed, and there they stayed for nearly two months. Joseph's parents and siblings lived several countries east of Sierra Leone, in central Africa. His mother left for a teaching job when Joseph was young, taking most of the family with her, but he stayed behind and was raised by his grandmother and uncle. The big house now stood empty because Joseph's grandmother had already fled the country for Guinea. She was visiting a friend across Freetown when news of the coup struck and she never returned home.

The shed was hot and small and ended up saving their lives. Nigerian troops had arrived to counter the rebels in Freetown but they sat bobbing in ships in the Atlantic, firing artillery, somewhat aimlessly, over the city.[2] One indiscriminate shell split the house apart, missing Joseph and his uncle by the space of a backyard.

While they hid, the two mostly ate rice mixed with pine nut oil, and waited for the city to grow quiet. Now and then, Joseph crawled out on his stomach across the yard to the crumpled house to search for anything they could use, like canned food and matches. Although mango trees dotted the yard, it was too risky to stand and reach for the fruit. Joseph could hear bullets overhead when they sliced the branches or pinged off the walls. Once, through a crack in the shed walls, Joseph saw a young girl gunned down in the field beside the house. She fell as if she had tripped.

When the gunfire finally subsided, Joseph's uncle chanced going into the streets. There had long been a market in human trafficking out of Freetown and without much difficulty, his uncle found an agent to lead Joseph to Guinea, promising to follow later. Joseph doesn't know what his uncle paid, but guessed it was around $50,000 US.

The agent planned the trip and named the conditions, such as Joseph keeping his ID card hidden. Their cover story was of a father and son, both Fula—an ethnic group in West Africa known as roaming tradespeople. The agent belonged to this group and like other Fula, had lighter skin than most Sierra Leoneans. So did Joseph, thanks to a jumbled ancestry from Central Africa, the United Kingdom, and Jamaica.[3]

When it was time to go, Joseph and his agent waited in a bustling depot in central Freetown to crowd onto a minibus, the kind that carries more people than seats plus an overflow of passengers on the roof. It was July, two months after the coup, and people were beginning to recover their former routines, like operating a bus and climbing into the back of one.

Radiating from the Waterloo region, about thirty kilometres outside Freetown's core, were checkpoints, some patrolled by the rebels and others by Nigerian soldiers. At stops controlled by the Nigerians, Joseph and his fellow passengers pooled money to bribe their way through. But beyond these zones, even the stability of corruption disappeared. Farther from Freetown, the Nigerian presence faded away. This was rebel territory once more. Civilians could find themselves in the small palm of someone wearing Adidas sneakers, red gym shorts, and a long white T-shirt; someone with his arm curled under an oversized rifle, the butt dragging on the ground.

A new and terrible scene appeared each time the minibus stopped. At the police station, Joseph could smell the stench of dozens of bodies piled faster than they could be buried. At another road block, the passengers lined up outside while rebels searched the bus. A young boy—a child soldier, the muscle of the RUF—stared at Joseph and then approached him. His face seemed blank, with no humour or curiosity. He could do anything. "I was just shaking, thinking I'm going to get killed, I'm going to get killed." But the boy only asked for money, and accepted Joseph's shoes instead.

The minibus pushed on until the sky turned dark, then pulled to a stop at the roadside. They slept outdoors in the bush, thick and green now from the wet season, and boarded again at sunrise. The next day and night passed in this way. Then, on the third day around noon, Joseph's agent signalled the driver to stop where a man with two bicycles stood near the road. His agent gave curt directions to the bicycle man, and then ordered Joseph out. It happened quickly: the minibus disappeared and Joseph found himself pedalling behind a new guide, not trusting this stranger, but not with options either. The pair biked for over two hours and arrived at the northwest border with Guinea at dusk, as low clouds rolled overhead.

Joseph spent the stormy night in limbo, in the no man's land between Sierra Leone and Guinea, sheltering from rain and buying food at a cluster of stalls. What had in peacetime been a bush path crossing used by a trickle of locals, was transformed by war into a busy border ripe for hawkers. After another full day had passed, Guinean soldiers waved Joseph across, and with the last of his money, he took a taxi toward his grandmother and several cousins at a refugee camp named Forécariah.

His uncle never did leave Sierra Leone. He was placed under house arrest by the new military government soon after Joseph escaped. His uncle worked in a skilled trade and the junta foresaw that valuable citizens like he would only stay by force.

The camp Joseph found in Guinea was squalid. For drinking water, residents used old oil drums to catch the rain. The United Nations provided some food, but Joseph said it made people sick. "They were giving people food you wouldn't want to feed to pigs." But it was all there was. Joseph's grandmother, who was sixty-five, broke her collarbone in a fight over the scarce stuff. She stayed in the camp because it seemed like the safest place for her younger grandchildren, but a day after arriving, Joseph and his teenaged cousin left for Conakry, the capital of Guinea.

Their grandmother had a contact there and the two boys managed to track him down.

From August to October, they slept at the man's house or, when it was crowded with other visitors, on a mat rolled over the gravel yard of the Sierra Leonean embassy, which was still staffed by the old guard. Joseph roamed Conakry unencumbered and mostly unthreatened. He made friends and learned to play basketball. It was "One of my freest times, I would say. I didn't have anybody saying anything. I was sixteen."

Meanwhile, his grandmother applied for UN refugee status for her family, but before that process ended, Joseph received an emergency travel certificate from the embassy. In October 1997, he boarded a plane departing Conakry for North Carolina, to stay in America with an uncle he had never before met.

October 1997, North Carolina, United States

Joseph lived with his uncle for less than a year. It was a cool relationship. From the beginning, Joseph was told, "You're old enough, you can take care of yourself," and when his uncle left town in 1998, Joseph did. He enrolled in high school, moved in with a friend, and lived on a cash income from mowing lawns and other odd jobs.

His immigration status in the United States was a question mark. Joseph could go to school, but he didn't test his rights further. Once, he was in a car accident bad enough to cause whiplash, and he recovered at home without seeing a doctor. "I didn't know the rules," he explains. "I just kept quiet." Incidentally, it was no different than in Freetown. "Back home, you have an accident, you just deal with it."

In North Carolina, Joseph began to look ahead to the blank page after high school. He needed a plan. He heard good things about Canada, especially the Ontario College of Art and Design (OCAD) in Toronto. He loved art, but had never taken his interest seriously.

In February 2000, Joseph took a bus to Buffalo just south of the Canadian border, then a taxi to the Peace Bridge border crossing where he asked for refugee protection. The Canadians explained a rough version of the inland refugee process and let him enter. Joseph was now twenty years old. Had he known about the Canadian system, he might have arrived sooner to benefit from a different set of rules that govern unaccompanied minors, those under eighteen. Joseph shrugs, "I didn't know anything."

February 2000 and October 2013, Toronto, Canada

While he waited for his hearing, Joseph went back to high school. If he could stay in Canada, he would apply to OCAD, and he thought a Canadian transcript would help. He lived with a man he knew from Freetown, and he soon met other Sierra Leoneans who helped orient him in Toronto.

Not until he was moving through the legal system of a safe country did anxiety catch up. What if his refugee claim got rejected? "When you're young, you don't care about these things. But when you get older, when you realize 'what am I going to do?' ... you get really scared." He grappled with that fear for more than a year until, three months after his Immigration and Refugee Board (IRB) hearing in March 2001, he received a positive decision. Joseph returned to his usual easygoing self in the following months, and his circle of friends grew. He "started seeing how you get from one day to another."

A year later, in 2002, civil war officially ended in Sierra Leone. British and Sierra Leonean troops had forced the RUF to retreat and mass disarmament was at last underway after a decade of war. Joseph followed the news but felt no pull to return. Peace or not in Freetown, Toronto was home.

He met Vera at a barbeque hosted in his basement apartment. She was friends with his friends. He served his specialty peanut chicken, and she liked it. She also liked the art on his walls, which was his own. Joseph and Vera married in 2007 and today, they have a four-year-old son who won't fall asleep without a bedtime phone call from Joseph, from his commute or an evening class. Joseph has a voice that carries his smile, and it's easy to hear his small son sending a crinkling laugh back over the phone line.

Joseph was accepted to OCAD and earned a bachelor's degree in design and illustration. He returned to the same school for a 3D art and animation program to finish in May 2014. Some of his work is political, some celebrates culture and life. In one sketch, a man, woman, and child form a single silhouette against layers of yellow, orange, red, and blue. His palette recalls Sierra Leone's wet season in sunlight, the plants dripping and ablaze.

"I see colours that way," Joseph says. "When you go outside, everything is just a bright shade of all these bold colours."

23 Christine

Rwanda

Anonymous portrait of Christine in Toronto.
Photograph by Christopher Manson.

April 1994, Nyamata, Rwanda

Their neighbour—she doesn't remember his name now—hid Christine's[1] family in his house. He gave his word he wouldn't tell, and Christine thinks he tried. But the bodies of her father and little brother were found in another part of the house, separate from the rest. Her parents had split up to hide, taking one child each.

Maybe Christine heard the muffled sounds of their deaths, but if she did, they would not have made sense to her. She just remembers learning from her mother that the other half of her family had been killed. Christine was five years old and her little brother, three.

Her mother guessed their best chance at survival was to flee the neighbour's house. They headed for the swamps surrounding them in Nyamata, a town south of Kigali where the famed rolling hills of the north smooth lazily down into lakes and ponds. Along with two of her uncles, Christine and her mother ran away from buildings, roads, people, trying desperately to become invisible.

Few outside Rwanda saw the blueprint for genocide taking shape before April 6, 1994, the day the Rwandan dictator, President Juvénal Habyarimana, fell to earth in a burning plane. The killing began within hours of his death. There had been local massacres leading up to April 6. They would be remembered as small compared to what now happened.

If outsiders missed seeing the preparations, even fewer foresaw the speed of the assailants, who murdered more than eight hundred thousand Tutsis and moderate Hutus by hacking them to death with household tools. They used machetes, saws, clubs. Some shots were fired, but for many, death did not come quickly. Before the physical attacks, came the running, the hunting, the sudden betrayals by neighbours and people known since childhood. Neighbourhoods echoed with triumphant shouts and terrified screams as another hiding place was uncovered—in a home, a church, a swamp.

The international community, and many Rwandans, were blindsided by the sheer energy of the murderers and by their astute command corps, a mix of political elites and community brass like church leaders and radio personalities. The political architects of the genocide knew foreigners believed that what they were seeing was a disturbing outbreak of "age-old" ethnic violence. Tribal fighting, a pity. They later realized what was happening was the absolute and unprecedented slaughter of a people.[2] Inside Rwanda, the elite *génocidaires* could play off another kind of weakness, using a simple ideology called Hutu Power. It said the minority Tutsis were enemies, and Hutu survival required Tutsi extermination. The Hutu Power radio station Radio Télévision Libre des Mille Collines clogged the airwaves with propaganda for nearly a year before the genocide, and climaxed in April 1994 with the message *cut down the tall trees*, or kill the Tutsis.[3]

From mid-April to the end of the genocide, around one hundred days later, Christine and her remaining family hid for their lives. They slept on high dryer ground and ate only raw food like cassava roots, tough and bitter tasting. But softening them over a cooking fire was unthinkable, for the time taken to linger in one place and for the rising smoke like a shooting flare.

Christine remembers the cold. April is rainy season in Rwanda, when the skies open like clockwork and soak the earth. The swamps were full and though the water wasn't deep, it was easy to sink into mud. There were no extra layers of clothing, nothing new and dry to change into on nights that dropped to 15 degrees, and of course there was no fire for warmth or scattering mosquitoes.

The swamp stank unnaturally. Decomposing bodies lay where they were slain or dragged by the current. But the living, if they were outdoors, couldn't stop moving. "Because you were trying to save your own life, we wouldn't pay attention to what was happening, we would just run." It took a good degree of numbness to *just run*. Christine says that even at five years old, "When you are scared, it's over being that scary. You don't feel like anything. You don't feel anything."

When news rippled through the country in the middle of July, 1994, that it was over, that the Tutsi rebels of the Rwandan Patriotic Front (RPF) had taken the capital and the guilty were streaming out of the country, Christine and her mother made their way back to Nyamata, moving cautiously after months of basic survival. Their brick home had become rubble, resembling buildings across Rwanda ruined in a final assault before the mass Hutu exodus to neighbouring Zaire. Like other surviving bits of families, the two moved into a still-standing, deserted house of the génocidaires.

Before April 1994, Hutu and Tutsi families lived not only in the same towns, but in side-by-side homes. They had for a long time. All the while, the colonizers, Germany and then Belgium, steadily engineered social differences among Rwanda's ethnic groups, weighted in favour of the Tutsi minority. Tutsis had better jobs, more money, more prestige. After Rwanda became independent in 1962 with a Hutu government in office, the resentment continued. Still, people settled in as neighbours, especially in the cities. The proximity of both households meant people could as swiftly kill as hide their neighbours.

When the genocide ended, the new RPF government was eager to keep the country moving, so Christine began school in September of 1994. She and her mother spent two years in their hollowed hometown before moving to Kigali.

Christine didn't ask questions about what had happened and her mother didn't talk much. "I was still a kid and maybe she was thinking, 'I'm going to hurt her.'" But her mother did tell Christine about letters that she sometimes found over the years, quietly left outside her home: *Although we didn't get a chance to kill you, we will still kill you.* The notes carried no signature but Christine guessed whoever had murdered her father and brother was behind them.

Despite the written threats, their lives moved forward along with the country, one with no Hutus or Tutsis, only Rwandans—the official line went. Her mother opened a small business. Christine wound her way through grade school, learning how to be alone without her shadow, her little brother. Grade school came and went, then high school, and in 2009, Christine began a degree in computer science at the National University of Rwanda in the southern city Butare. She boarded at university but often travelled back for breaks and holidays to the capital and her mother.

These outward signs of a society returning to normal reflected areas of genuine and healthy change, but they masked continuing divisions that ran deep, including a horrifying belief by some ex-génocidaires that there was unfinished business. Those who had earlier fled to Zaire were returning to Rwanda. While some sought forgiveness, others seethed, accepting a fallacy that the Tutsis, back in control in Kigali, had all along wanted to humiliate Hutus and deny them power.[4] That it had been a plot.

Christine was in Kigali in January 2011 when her mother's body was found in one of the sloping streets. She had been murdered, but no one was caught; there were no charges and no trial. Whoever left the notes had kept their word.

Somehow, Christine finished her second year of university before moving back to Kigali, into the home of one of her mother's good friends. Meanwhile, an aunt in Toronto took maternal control of Christine's future. She talked her niece through her next steps: a plane ticket to New York, a cheap hotel, a bus to Buffalo, then an asylum claim at the Canadian border.

The choice to leave her country was easy. Christine assumed that, as the sole survivor of her family, she would be the next to be killed. That, and she had no one left in Rwanda.

December 2011, Saint-Armand, and February 2014, Toronto, Canada

Twenty-one and alone on December 12, 2011, Christine explained to Canadian officials at the Saint-Armand border crossing who she was and why she had left. They spoke to her kindly, gave her food and a place to rest, and soon explained how to get to Montreal and then on to Toronto.

She had a hearing scheduled with the Immigration and Refugee Board (IRB) in March 2012. Christine had a lot to be nervous about. She faced a new city, a new language (she was raised in Kinyarwanda and French), and even a new family because Christine hadn't seen her aunt for seventeen years. With a lawyer and through a translator, she told her story in a little under one hour. A few weeks later, she opened a package with a positive decision.

"I was really happy, I said 'Okay, now no matter what happened in the past, I should keep going,'" Christine says. "Yes my parents died, but I think now it's time to be responsible for myself because I'm not the only one who lost parents."

She aimed to get back to university but had to start with English courses and adult high school to earn a Canadian transcript. Then Christine followed an acceptance letter to Mohawk College in Hamilton, for a chemical engineering program she began in September 2013. She loves chemistry, its recipes for controlled change, and being in a lab. She's getting used to the school system and her bulging schedule of endless assignments and social events, and she thinks university is next after her three-year degree.

It will be another three years until Christine can apply for citizenship. Still, she pauses with a smile and says, "All I need is a paper, but I'm Canadian."

Christine has purple hair woven into her long braids, pulled into a ponytail that she twirls now and then as she speaks. She talks about the annual genocide commemoration each April, observed in cities around the world beginning with Genocide Memorial Day on April 7. In her hometown, victims are remembered at the Nyamata Church, where around ten thousand people had gathered for protection before being killed on April 10, 1994.[5] Inside the brick walls are neat rows of bones and what once covered them, dirty clothing, all heaped in another room, like fresh piles of laundry. These reminders sit in the open, within arm's reach, as if to compress time along with space; to say, *look what just happened*. Outside, the church is draped in purple ribbons, a memorial colour that unites this site with hundreds like it across the country.

Her mother is there whenever Christine thinks about the genocide, though it claimed her years after officially ending. "When I remember my mom, I remember she was a strong person and passionate.... When I feel like I'm not doing the right thing, I try to remember how she used to find a solution. I believe my mom is my role model. I still learn from her."

Attending the annual ceremonies in Toronto is heart-breaking, but no matter the toll, it's important to Christine to honour the dead and to show how wrong people were. This duty is bigger than April 7. "Remembering is something you have to do every day, it's not just that day," she says. "We do that officially, but personally, I do remember every day."

24 Mie Tha Lah

Myanmar

Mie Tha Lah in Toronto.

Photograph by Christopher Manson.

March 1994, Near the Thai Border, Myanmar

The bus ride uphill from Myanmar to the Thailand border was twenty-eight hours with stops. There were hardly any security checkpoints where government soldiers might have grabbed Mie Thah Lah, his mother, older brother, and twin sisters.

But the country's border crossing checkpoint was coming up so, as their escort had warned them, *off the bus.* The last long leg of their departure would be a grueling four-day, eighty-kilometre trek. Having no time to second guess, they were pushing through the wet jungle on a muddy trail, escorted by twenty-five guerilla fighters. With their long hair, rough clothing, many wearing bandanas and carrying automatic weapons and food, they made Mie Tha nervous. Rebels like them had taken his father. But then, confused, he noticed the soldiers were also uneasy. Or maybe—shy? Of course. They were not used to chaperoning an educated family from the city. Yangon no less.

Not that Mie Tha could voice any of this. Long stretches of the muddy path were narrow and rocky. In places, Mie Tha could reach out on one side and touch the jungle wall and on the other, air. The hillside dropped off into a deep ravine. Mie Tha also feared that the dense jungle and crashing rain that kept pouring down would muffle the boot-falls of an approaching government patrol. His mother had her own fears. She had the rebels give her their word that if she collapsed, they wouldn't stop; they would throw her body into the ravine and press on with the children.

The family was trying to reach Mie Tha's father. Rebels took Ka Law Lah during the night in November 1989, the same year the military dictatorship declared martial law and changed the country's name from Burma to Myanmar. This abduction made the government suspect a connection between Mie Tha's father and the rebels—that the "taking" was a cover-up. Government men in uniform interrogated every family member, digging for stories, sympathies, anything that could tie the family to the rebels. "Where is Ka Law?" sounded like an order.

But the family had no information. Their only news source, they shared with the government: coworkers of Ka Law who reported him missing in the northern Maw Chi mining area. The family didn't know where he was taken, or if he was still alive.

That should have been the end of it. But several things nagged at the government. The family were Karen People, an ethnic minority, many of whom were Christian, not Buddhist.[1] Most troubling, the Karen National Liberation Army (KNLA) was feared inside Myanmar. Since fighting the Japanese with the Allies in the Second World War for their independence, Karen rebels had been resisting the Burmese military for sixty years in one of the world's longest running insurgencies.

So where did this family's sympathies really lie? True, both of Mie Tha's parents were civil servants working under the junta, his mother an accountant and his father a mining engineer. A family like theirs believed the official line that the Karen rebels were criminal and barbaric. Even believing this, however, did not make his parents supporters of the dictatorship. Ka Law, a year earlier and just before the martial law, had spoken about democracy before student crowds in Kan Bout. He was an articulate, intelligent man, known to colleagues for his thoughtful and prodemocracy views.

Ka Law was one of many, Burmese students, white collar workers, and monks, who cheered for democracy then. He survived what followed, what would be known as the 8888 uprising. On the eighth day of the eighth month, 1988, government soldiers killed thousands of civilians in the capital, still named Rangoon. They were tortured, jailed, or put under house arrest—the long fate of the peaceful resistor Aung San Suu Kyi. Older democracy sympathizers, though, could face a special punishment. Separation from family. After his public talk, Ka Law was forced to leave his family and move north.

The separation made it difficult to accuse the family of conspiring in Ka Law's disappearance, but officials nonetheless forced his wife, Nant Aye Myint, from her job of thirty-two years. The family was blacklisted, and a blacklisted woman couldn't work and her children couldn't get ID cards for university or jobs. Left without a household income, they moved to Yangon, to live with Mie Tha's grandmother. Money pooled by relatives kept them afloat.

His mother remained jobless and they heard nothing from his father. All that really changed as the months passed was that Mie Tha and his siblings crept closer to their high school graduations. Things looked bleak after that. What careers could they have? They had a missing prodemocracy father, a blacklisted mother and, setting them even lower in the social hierarchy, they were Karen Christians.

After more than three years with no news of Ka Law, one day in 1992, a black Mercedes with British and Burmese flags snapping over the fenders, pulled up in front of Mie Tha's home, followed by a small mob of curious neighbours. A foreign woman stepped out, and once inside, introduced herself as the British ambassador. She handed Nant Aye Myint a note and a photograph. It was Ka Law, and he was smiling.

The ambassador explained: New to her post and before moving to Yangon, she decided to visit a refugee camp in Thailand, where she met Mie Tha's father, heard his story—and was moved. She offered to bring word back, which she could do secretly by dint of her diplomatic immunity that prohibits the searching faced by everyone else. The note, in Ka Law's handwriting, said Karen rebels abducted him because they needed an educated teacher in the refugee camp. They treated him well and were planning to bring his family across the border next.

Mie Tha's mother burned both note and picture after the ambassador left. There would be more visitors to the house after this. In the following weeks, plainclothes informers showed up outside with greater frequency. They sometimes waved Mie Tha or his siblings across the street for questioning. *Do you miss your father? Yes. Is your father alive? I don't know.* Finally, the children could tell a lie.

His father's second letter arrived two years later in March 1994, this time in the pocket of an innocuous visitor who, inside the house, revealed he was a KNLA soldier. Ka Law's note asked them to leave everything behind and go with the man. There was a plan in place to get the family to Thailand, and Mie Tha, his mother, and siblings did not hesitate. They boarded a bus with the soldier the next morning before dawn. Mie Tha learned that his father had become a highly respected teacher. He did not fight with the rebels, but provided another service—literacy.

Mie Tha and his family—all five of them—made it to Mae Surin and collapsed into the arms of his father. "That was one of the happiest times of our life, when we were together," Mie Tha says. "At least we were together, even though we did not know what would happen next."

Along the Thai border with Myanmar in 1994 were at least ten refugee camps, home to mostly Karen, but also ethnic Karenni, Mon, and

Shan, other groups treated badly at home. The larger camps held over thirty thousand people.[2] Mae Surin camp was small by comparison, with about four thousand residents.

Mae Surin was at once a prison and place of transit. It was wrapped by a barbed wire fence because refugees in Thailand are not allowed freedom of movement. They couldn't leave, but they knew they couldn't stay. Signs posted around the camp warned *No permanent houses*, so instead of using bricks, people had to rebuild their homes each year after the wet season with wood, bamboo, and thatched roofs. Still, Mae Surin was breathtaking, with a skyline of limestone hills and mist, and a cool, bubbling stream that split the camp in two.

Foreign aid money supported a sanitation system, health clinic, school—where Mie Tha and his siblings spent their days. Then, in the late 1990s, came support for a handful of university scholarships. Mie Tha, at twenty-two years old, became the first pupil from Mae Surin selected to study abroad. He would go to Davao, Philippines, for four years of university on a forged passport. He would also fall in love.

May 1999, Davao, Philippines

Mie Tha wasn't sure he could pull it off.

Beginning each new class, he slipped his professors a note from the head of the humanities department who helped secure his spot at the Catholic university Ateneo de Davao. The note requested that Mie Tha, whose name did not appear on any class list, be allowed to attend the lecture. The note did not mention his immigration status. Burmese authorities would not have approved foreign study for a refugee camped out in Thailand, so Mie Tha was studying illegally in Davao. And illegal living required work. Each year when his tourist visa expired, he had to exit the Philippines for Thailand or India, wherever he stood the best chance of fooling security, and re-enter with a new visa in his counterfeit passport. To its credit, the organization funding his scholarship turned a blind eye.

Mie Tha's status was an unending source of anxiety, complicated by the feeling of isolation from living a secret. But there was someone in the Philippines, beside his department head, who knew: Jocelyn, a local Filipina, their class president, a girl whose short height only enlarged her energy and will. The beautiful Jocelyn became Mie Tha's friend, and then his strength when he shared his secret, and finally, his girlfriend.

She stayed his girlfriend even when the class graduated and Mie Tha returned to Mae Surin, wondering what to do next. Mie Tha graduated without a transcript. His only proof was a yearbook with his grainy head-and-shoulders shot in the rows of the graduating class of 2002. He spoke to Jocelyn once each month from the height of a jungle hilltop, where the camp's residents climbed for a precious few bars of cell phone reception. He told her about starting to teach, the curriculum he created for the camp's high school graduates, based on their university material. And always, he told her that he loved her. He said God would find a way to bring them together.

Students in Mae Surin lined up for Mie Tha's classes. Although he'd left four years before, conflict in Myanmar had continued. The camp just kept growing. Its size attracted donors and one of them, the Open Society Foundations, noticed his work and gave Mie Tha funding for his start-up university. Now he needed teachers. One day on the hilltop with his cell phone, he asked Jocelyn to come. She would make very little money, live there illegally, leave her parents behind, and descend to camp conditions, but she said yes.

Thai authorities banned non-refugees from living inside refugee camps so Jocelyn was illegal inside Mae Surin, and Mie Tha was illegal outside. Her round face and matching dark hair and eyes meant Jocelyn could pass as Karen, under the pseudonym Mie Mar. It's what the colourful banner said in 2006 when they got married in the camp, Mie Tha and Mie Mar. They had wanted a small wedding but every celebration in the camp was the business of everyone else, plus the couple were virtual stars among the Mae Surin students and their families. More than four hundred self-appointed guests showed up.

In 2007, Canada announced it would accept two thousand[3] Karen refugees who Thailand had agreed to help release in a deal with the United Nations High Commissioner for Refugees (UNHCR). The head of Canadian immigration in Bangkok made an official visit to Mae Surin to interview just one family before sending his deputies off for the real grunt work. UNHCR staff selected Mie Tha's family, one of the few English-speaking ones. The Canadian was awed by their story of escape and how they rebuilt their lives behind barbed wire, where most of the family had lived for thirteen years. He accepted all seven of them to Canada, including Jocelyn.

May 2007 and September 2013, Toronto, Canada

Mie Tha saw Toronto's CN Tower for the first time in the taxi from Pearson Airport, just after landing. It felt surreal. So did the news, about a year later, that Jocelyn was pregnant. They had tried to have a baby in the refugee camp but when nothing happened, they assumed there was a problem. Mie Tha says it's like God intervened, timing their baby for Toronto instead of Mae Surin. Their son Mehj was born a Canadian, not a stateless refugee. The rest of the family became Canadian citizens in 2012. Mehj became a big brother to two more babies.

Today, Mie Tha is a settlement program worker at the Jane and Finch Community and Family Centre in Toronto. He helps immigrant youth control the demands of multiple cultures and the more universal angst of teenaged years.

Mie Tha also clocks time as an accredited court interpreter in the Karen language. When Canada received its first parliamentary delegation from Myanmar in April 2013, the government of Canada invited Mie Tha to work as the official interpreter. He hesitated. Would the delegation resent him? Having a refugee facilitate their relationship with a foreign government was a strange and unusual power balance for Myanmar officials, even though the country had undergone a small democratic leavening in recent years. A civilian government now nominally ruled Myanmar, but the military still held tremendous power. As usual, Jocelyn gave him peace, by pointing out that the Canadian government needed him to interpret, not win the hearts of the dignitaries. But he did both. It's easy to become fused to a good interpreter and by the end of the week-long visit, Mie Tha was nodding politely to warm invitations to Yangon by the Burmese.

He hasn't been back to Myanmar but did return to Mae Surin camp in November 2010. "Nothing had changed, it was just the same. Every family wanted me to sleep in their house." That's how he wants to return to Myanmar if he ever does: as a visitor. "I find Canada my home," he says.

His son would agree. On a recent trip with his mother to visit family in the Philippines, Mehj badly wanted to go home to Toronto, to the bigger-than-king-sized bed he shares with his parents, younger sister, and baby brother. And to his grandparents, aunts, uncles, and cousins, who live upstairs. Mie Tha laughs on a tour of this arrangement, "It really surprises Canadians that we are all living here harmoniously." But this family treasures cramped quarters. For so long in Mae Surin, it meant being together and having survived.

25 Max Farber

Poland

As Told by His Son, Bernie Farber

Max Farber photograph, held by Bernie Farber.
Photograph by Christopher Manson.

September 1942, Sokolow Podlaski, Poland

The first years of the Second World War were relatively quiet for Max Farber, his family, and the other eighteen hundred residents of Botchki, a village with a large Jewish population south of Bialystok in Soviet-controlled Poland. After Russian troops withdrew in 1939, under a treaty with Germany, Wehrmacht troops had taken over in eastern Poland.

At first, a number of Jewish males in the region were sent to local work camps. But in 1941, German troops, Polish SS (Schutzstaffel), and collaborators began herding Jewish families into makeshift ghettoes.

Then the Jewish population, almost half of Botchki, was moved to a nearby larger town, Sokolow Podlaski, to a few fenced-in streets around the synagogue, an area of decrepit housing that lacked sewers and running water. In the summer of 1941, it became a closed ghetto with brick walls topped with barbed wire. Several thousand additional families were crowded in. Lack of food became a problem, then starvation. The death rate began rising quickly. To survive meant going beyond the barbed wire to search for food, a terrible risk. Jews caught outside the enclosure were shot on sight.

On a September evening in 1942, Max Farber and his nephew, Victor, crawled under the fence when it was their turn to find food. Undetected and unhurt, they crept back several hours later—into the midst of the camp's liquidation.[1] Sirens wailed, and dogs snarled above a din of human cries. Soldiers and police squads were forcing men, women, and children into cattle trucks. Max ran, shoving through the crowds, desperately searching for his wife and two young sons. No one knew what was happening and Max was forced toward the cars for men before he found his wife Zisela and his sons, Sholom and Yitzhak.

Max remembers the truck leaving and, sometime later, stopping so everyone could crowd aboard a train. It was most likely the junction where a special spur line veered off to the Treblinka camp. SS guards were silent about the destination. While Jews knew that other ghettoes in the region were being emptied, they had no idea the Treblinka II death camp even existed.

———

Max used to say it took a thousand miracles to survive the Holocaust— nine hundred and ninety-nine were not enough. Bernie Farber heard his father's story in bits and pieces during their time together up until Max died in 1990. A thousand miracles. Bernie still shakes his head thinking about it.

Max told Bernie, although the train was moving west, he and Victor and other men managed to rip out a floorboard and drop themselves onto the blur of gravel and railway ties passing below. They survived, and while Victor headed elsewhere for refuge, Max fled to a farm near Bialystok where Julian, a best friend, lived. Julian wasn't Jewish, but Max was sure he would help him hide. Julian did, becoming the kind of person Holocaust survivors today honour as the Righteous. It was a huge risk. Polish families caught hiding Jews were immediately shot. Max and Julian had to be careful, ingenious—and they had to make Max vanish.

Max called it a "grave." Early each morning he and Julian would cross the farm to a secluded site where they had dug a pit the length and width of a man's body. Placing a long straw in his mouth and pursing his lips around it tightly, Max would lie down in the trench, face up while Julian shoveled dirt over him, covering him, but careful to avoid the straw's tip. From before dawn until after dark every day, Max spent three months in his grave, and each night Julian would carefully dig him out. He would eat, exercise, and then lie down flat once more. Under the earth, Max would focus on taking even breaths. At the same time, he constantly thought about what could have happened to his wife and sons and what would happen if the SS ever literally unearthed him. And he agonized about what the discovery would mean for Julian and his family.

Then Julian heard a rumour. Botchki Jews had been taken to Treblinka that September night. It was still mistakenly believed to be a labour camp, but wild thoughts of what was happening there tormented Max. He left the farm and wandered the forest. Completely distraught he wedged his body between two trees and, because suicide is a sin, prayed to God to take his life. *Let me die,* he pleaded. He waited. Nothing. Max climbed out of the tree and decided to find another way to die.

Max joined Soviet partisans in the forest, hit-and-run guerilla fighters who attacked enemy troops—and he was especially good in noncombat missions. Another of the thousand miracles was that Max grew up in a milling family fluent in the business languages of Polish, Russian, and German. Using his flawless German, he once led an undercover team to release captured partisans. Max, blonde, blue-eyed, and dressed in a German uniform, convinced guards he was to take charge of a group of Jewish prisoners, and the guards unwittingly freed them.

In 1945, the war ended and Max returned to Botchki.

"He had this hope against hope that his family, somebody, would still be alive," says Bernie. But there was no one. With their arms in the air to save space, Treblinka prisoners had been herded into gas chambers. Years later, a West German court heard that three thousand people brought by freight train to Treblinka could be exterminated in three hours.[2] Max's wife and boys died the day they arrived, the day Max jumped from the train.

Now, still in Poland, Max and a former combat friend, Richard Small, were stuck behind the Soviet Iron Curtain, plotting how to get to Pocking, a US-run displaced persons camp in southern Bavaria in Germany. It was a doorway into the free world of the west, and Palestine, Max thought. Identification papers were no problem. As a partisan, Max had developed into a skilled forger. Arriving as Max and Richard Farber, according to their papers, they were just another two DPs in a camp that came to house almost eight thousand homeless Jews.

They spent two years at Pocking until Richard decided to join family in Ottawa, and asked Max to come along. Max now forged a new relationship. They became Max and Richard Small. Richard's Ottawa sponsor was his real brother; Max's saviour was an Ottawa man who signed up with the local Jewish Community Council as a sponsor.

1948, Ottawa, Canada

It's hard to tear your gaze from a photo of Max after the war. The hollow-cheeked face is emaciated and the sunken eyes look haunted. Bernie remembers his mother, Gert, saying it took five years to teach Max how to smile.

Max met Gert, a Ukrainian girl whose family immigrated to Canada before the war, at a social in Ottawa. She became his second wife. The surprise came a few years later, when they found out Max's Canadian sponsor had been none other than Gert's father. Their firstborn son arrived in 1951 and a second son soon after. It was an unnervingly accurate replica of an earlier family sent to Treblinka.

Bernie, his eldest, did not learn of his father's first family until he was twenty-two years old. Sitting at the kitchen table and watching his father unbury this history, Bernie realized Max was carrying the guilt of a survivor. He doesn't know how his father lived with the pain of always seeing in his second family the resemblance to his first, especially the second set of sons who, as young boys, were nearly identical to Sholom and Yitzhak.

Growing up without paternal grandparents, cousins, and the rest of a normal-sized family is what Bernie calls living "in the shadow of the Holocaust." Fellow survivors became family instead. They would gather and tell stories in the kitchen of the Farber home in Ottawa's Sandy Hill neighbourhood. There were, Bernie describes, "gradations of stories," like how Max knew the fabled battle heroes the Bielski brothers,[3] and how his nephews had visas from Sempo Sugihara, the Japanese diplomat-turned-lifeline for thousands of Jews.[4]

In time, the Max who Bernie knew as his father became, not the dour, introspective man who arrived in 1948, but a man who lit up a room with his sea-blue eyes and his smile. And he was a fervent Canadian. The Union Jack and the Red Ensign of Canada flags (before there was a Maple Leaf) flapped above the business owned by Max and Gert, the Osgoode Food Market on King Edward Street, and inside hung the face of Prime Minister Louis St. Laurent. The grocery shoppers of 1950s Sandy Hill were also greeted with a sign promising service in Yiddish, Polish, Russian, German, Ukrainian, English, or French. Theirs was an early polyglot store in a budding mosaic city. Max knew how to charm the younger customers, too. Bernie explains, "There's a group of French Canadian kids who grew up in Sandy Hill who can swear in Yiddish like troopers."

In his fifties, Max was a man who taught delicious expletives, and sailed down hilly streets on a bicycle with his sons.

August 2013, Toronto, Canada

Pictures of his three children line Bernie's office window. On the wall are newspaper stories on Max and Botchki. Gaps in his father's life continue to fill in as Bernie travels and writes. A stranger might email him, "I saw your column today. I knew your dad. Did you know ..." And on a visit to Poland, Bernie flipped through a history on Bialystok and found an old list of Jewish residents in Botchki, among them, Chaim Farber, his grandfather. They were no longer just *the Jews of Botchki.* "They had names. They were real people with real professions and real lives," Bernie says. "It just meant something completely different to me."

Bernie's family history of loss from anti-Semitism led to a career advocating for social and human rights. He worked at first with troubled youth in Ottawa, and then on sexual and child abuse files with the Children's Aid Society. In 1984, after meeting and marrying Karyn, he moved to Toronto and joined the Canadian Jewish Congress. He became interested in First Nations communities, struck that "Jews and First Nations had a lot of spiritual similarities, but hardly knew each other at all."

His career with the Congress moved quickly. Bernie became CEO. In recognition of his work, he was awarded the Queen's Diamond Jubilee Medal, among other honours. Bernie switched to full-time work with First Nations in 2012 with Gemini Power Corp, an investor in renewable energy on First Nations reserves. Friends voiced concern for something of a career jump and reminded Bernie he was nearing sixty. Yet, at age fifty, Max had arrived in Canada without money, his family, and even the language.

"I look at what he was able to do with his life and how he was able to change, completely. This is nothing," Bernie says. "He really became an inspiration to me."

26 Shabnam

Afghanistan

Anonymous portrait of Shabnam at the Afghan
Women's Organization in Toronto.
Photograph by Christopher Manson.

1985, Kabul, Afghanistan

Like many middle-class teenagers in 1980s Kabul, Shabnam[1] assumed she was heading for university. Her father was a prominent legal scholar, a progressive who worked at Afghanistan's Supreme Court and encouraged his daughter's education. He was in step with the times, ushered in by a Soviet-backed government that for all its repression and abuse of power, at least got women educated. Her fiancé, however, was just the opposite.

Four years older, he was from a conservative family and wanted Shabnam to quit school after their marriage, halfway through her degree in pharmacology at Kabul University. But with a formidable father like hers, Shabnam could brush aside her husband's complaints, dismissing his patriarchal side as mostly reflexive. She graduated in 1986 at age twenty-one, and got a job in a blood lab.

She had worked just over a year when, in 1988, her husband moved them to Herat City, his family home, to care for his sick father, he said. Shabnam suspected it was because he didn't want a working wife.

Leaving Kabul meant the end of a good job and the freedom of running errands between work and home, her brown hair loose around her shoulders. In Herat City, Shabnam spent her days mostly at home and beneath a burqa. Her husband had a different routine. He travelled back to Kabul, alone, sometimes for four to six months at a time, and with every return from the capital, it was clear that his drug addiction had worsened. Shabnam eventually learned he was taking hashish, opium, and heroin.

She didn't say a word to her father, whom she loved deeply and admired, a shade shy of fear. She saw it her duty to manage her marriage by herself. She didn't ask for her father's help when she had to leave Kabul, or when she learned about her husband's habit of disappearing to drink, use drugs, and see women. She kept silent even when her husband couldn't hold a job and then outright stopped looking for one, while still refusing Shabnam's desire to work.

What saved her sanity in Herat was her children: two daughters, Naz, born in 1986, followed by Asra in 1987, and two sons, Abdullah in 1990, and Hossin in 1997.

Outside her home, Afghanistan was changing. The views of its leadership became aligned more closely to her husband's than her father's. The mujahedeen moved into Kabul in the early 1990s followed by the Taliban in 1996.

Shabnam followed her husband's rules for ten years, raising her children in Herat City at home with her in-laws. She finally disobeyed in 1998 when the household finances began to fall apart, and she had to find money for food and school fees, fast. Rather than ask her father, Shabnam went back to work. She shrugs, "I wanted to be on my feet, I didn't want others to help me."

Few women still worked in the formal economy in Afghanistan. The Taliban regime had introduced a severe version of Sharia law. The rare jobs women were allowed to hold were almost exclusively in health care.

Shabnam first took a volunteer position at the pharmacy in the main Herat hospital, and as she hoped, it led to a paying job. The international aid group Pharmacists Without Borders (PSF) distributed drugs to the hospital and needed a supervisor for its inventory. She was on her feet for this job, doing rounds with a clipboard in one arm and her baby son, Hossin, propped against her chest in the other. Shabnam, with Hossin in tow, worked for PSF for eight months until the office closed in 1999 because of falling security.

Some aid groups remained, and Shabnam next worked for the World Health Organization teaching pharmacology at the same Herat hospital. Her pay was three bags of wheat a month, just enough to feed her family of six. After American and other foreign troops arrived in Afghanistan in 2001, the United Nations hired Shabnam. There were not many Afghan women with her skills—including English learned by reading drug labels and writing inventory reports, or with her courage—working for the enemy of the Taliban.[2]

As UN staff, Shabnam travelled to rural areas of Afghanistan and surrounding countries that held displaced Afghans in refugee camps, to teach workshops on health and women's rights. Her work should not have been dangerous, but the Taliban were ruthlessly intolerant of women's rights and those who promoted them.

Once in May 2002, returning from a workshop in the western Pakistani city Quetta, Taliban fighters arrested Shabnam and her team of seven other UN workers, all Afghan and mostly women, and accused them of spreading Jewish propaganda. The group was brought to the Herat City jail, controlled by the Taliban, to a mosque inside the brick building, where dozens of other women were already being held. On paper, Herat province was liberated from the Taliban, but they still held enormous influence and control beyond Kabul. Inside, Shabnam and her coworkers joined the noise of cries, prayers, and reading from the Koran. "You never could imagine our situation," Shabnam says. "It was very bad. I never thought that I would be in jail."

One by one, the UN workers were called to a separate room and it became clear the target of the arrest was the Herat City resident, manager for the United Nations, Shabnam. All were asked, "Who is Shabnam?" After a day and a half of questioning, they were released. Foreign UN staff intervened on their behalf (including a Canadian named Teresa Poppelwell, who smuggled a handwritten note into jail for Shabnam that urged courage, a note Shabnam would keep and one day bring with her to Canada). Or perhaps the more influential intervention was Shabnam's brother, who found an acquaintance among the Taliban jailers. The two men talked, her brother paid, and the group was freed.

If people in Herat City didn't know Shabnam before, they did now. She was among the first scattering of women to work under the Taliban, and she survived their jail. Shabnam began to receive handwritten notes delivered by anonymous men during work trips to remote villages. The notes warned her—by name—to stop working for women. She ignored them.

In 2008, Shabnam finally left her husband. He was a drunk, an addict, idle, and abusive. He never hit the children, but he regularly lashed out at her. Shabnam found it more unbearable as her profile as a campaigner for women's rights grew. She moved back to Kabul to work at Afghanistan's UN headquarters. Her sons came with her, but her daughters stayed in Herat. Several years earlier, when the girls were seventeen and sixteen, they were married. Explaining this, Shabnam turns her palms upward, as if to ask what else could she have done. She was always travelling and it was dangerous to keep daughters home alone, especially ones as beautiful as Naz and Asra. Once she learned that powerful people were heard speaking about her daughters, she began searching for good families—and she found good young men, one a doctor, the other a lawyer.

As far as Shabnam knew, her husband stayed in Herat but the anonymous threats followed her to Kabul. She received phone calls, men's voices saying, "This will be the last time we call you ... You will never see the sun ... I arrested you once, and now you are here in Kabul working."

Meanwhile, security in Afghanistan's cities had deteriorated. Suicide attacks jumped from two in all of 2002, to one every five days on average by 2006.[3] UN staff travel to remote regions had to be in armoured vehicles. Roadside bombings and ambushes were major threats outside the capital. But in 2010, the United Nations contracted a separate employer to hire Shabnam. Now she could move about without the conspicuous, and expensive, armoured vehicles.

A different set of rules applied to Afghan staff in Kabul too. On days without an emergency, UN drivers escorted them to their neighbourhoods at the end of the workday. But if there was a security threat, international workers were evacuated in the armoured vehicles. Local staff would slip into a burqa and out of the compound on foot.

When Shabnam reported to the head of UN staff security receiving threatening phone calls, the only added measure was to drop her off at different intersections, at different times of day, between 3:00 p.m. to 5:00 p.m.

Shabnam soon lived alone in Kabul because her eldest son won a university scholarship to study economics in India, and her youngest left for Canada on a scholarship to a private high school in Oakville, Ontario. Each time she walked in her front door, Shabnam thought how easy it would be for someone to kill her. It could be her husband, or the Taliban, or both in collusion. She imagined the Taliban or any group of provoked men from a village she had visited, using her husband against her. Shabnam worked for the "infidels," she had left her husband, and she had defied him by sending their sons abroad to study, something he was against. She feared revenge for all this, but was unapologetic, especially on one count: "It was an opportunity for my sons. I couldn't stop them."

In 2011, Shabnam applied for a Canadian visa at the High Commission in Islamabad, planning to visit her sons first in New Delhi and then in Oakville. A brother who lived in Germany booked her flight. She was afraid to do it herself in Kabul, in case the Taliban discovered her departure plan and intervened.

———————

December 2011 and November 2013, Toronto, Canada

Shabnam arrived in Toronto on December 24, 2011, and spent Christmas Day with the Canadian family hosting her son. During her stopover in New Delhi, Abdullah had pleaded for her to simply stay in Canada. Her daughters, both in Afghanistan, likewise wanted their mother out of the country. Hossin said the same thing in Oakville. Shabnam knew the danger but still planned to go home to Kabul. She had travelled abroad before, including to the United States four years earlier, and a one-way trip had never held appeal.

And yet, her children were right, the risks had increased now that she lived without a husband. Wanting reassurance, Shabnam emailed UN security in Kabul and asked what else could be done. They told her the situation was getting worse, that once she left the office there was no guarantee for her safety.

Shabnam applied for refugee protection on January 3, 2012, and included her youngest son in the application in June. A judge accepted their case within the year, on November 26.

Hossin is now in grade 11 and has a large photo of his smiling parents in a thin, gold-coloured frame. Shabnam packed the picture with him when he left for Canada in 2011, wanting him to remember his father as a good man and husband, because in the beginning, he was.

Her eyes fill with tears recalling her husband as a young man, before his spectacular fall amid the fall of Afghanistan. The couple had studied together in Kabul. He enjoyed writing poems. For most of her adult life, Shabnam tried to help him. "I tried my best. As a human, because of my children, I tried to rescue him, but he himself did not help." Shabnam lost that battle, but probably won another. "I always tried to be a mom and father, and support my children so they never feel like they don't have their father with them."

Her resilience was tested the first few years in Toronto. Her son almost lost his scholarship in 2012, when he became a refugee claimant and no longer qualified as an international student. Shabnam lobbied whomever she could at the school, and in the meantime, worried about losing their refugee case. She worried about going home, and about her family in Afghanistan; her mother, two daughters, and four grandchildren. On top of it all, her first apartment came with cockroaches and mice. (She scrubbed her unit clean, and then the hallway, the staircase, and all around the building). Her first job was at a Pizza Pizza and, to her horror, on her first day she learned how to clean the washrooms. And earlier in 2012, her father died.

She cried often. When she felt tears coming, she rushed down the apartment steps and stood on the street, out of sight of her son—or so she thought. He called Shabnam one day during her Pizza Pizza shift and said, "Mom, let's go to Afghanistan. Let them kill us." He said the risks of Kabul would be better than seeing his mother work as a cleaner (and, she suspected, seeing her cry). At home that night, she sat him down. "I told him: 'A job is a job, work is work. I'm not doing bad work, I'm doing work. It's good, you have to accept this. It's not our country.'" Shabnam knew some Afghans saw janitorial staff as lower-class, but she explained that Canadians did not think that way.

Privately, the switch from the United Nations to a restaurant felt bittersweet. "It was so sad for me, and still I was happy because I thought I am working, not taking from other people. I wanted to work, even if it is as a cleaner."

After eight months at the restaurant, Shabnam was hired by the Afghan Women's Organization, a non-profit that supports newcomer women and their families. Shabnam knows the clients' histories from her work with women across Afghanistan, and sometimes from first-hand experience. Her work is all about giving support, but Shabnam says the help is mutual. "It changed my way of thinking," she says about the organization and its executive director Adeena Niazi, one of the first Canadians who gave Shabnam the feeling she would not be alone in Toronto. Next, Shabnam is considering going back to school to upgrade her degree and work in Canadian health care. Hossin did keep his high school scholarship, and in a few years, he might study business or law at university.

Photos of Shabnam from the past decade show a radiant woman, smiling, with round brown eyes and thick brown, uncovered hair. In one, she smiles beside Laura Bush at the White House. In another, she laughs with her counterparts in Turkey on International Women's Day. She was heavier than she is now, but she says she is slowly getting back to her normal size, recovering from the effects of stress and likely trauma. But symptoms still bother her, and she's been occasionally hospitalized since arriving in Canada.

She says she's happy, and her son is too. She wants to return to Afghanistan with him, possibly to stay. "I never wanted to leave my country ... I wish that peace comes to Afghanistan and we can live together with our family." She misses her daughters and their husbands, her own elderly mother, and especially her grandchildren, one of whom asks Shabnam to send Barbie dolls.

Shabnam and Hossin are close and it's hard to picture one returning without the other. When she calls him her best friend, he nods in agreement, with only a hint of a teenaged smile.

27 Robi Botos

Hungary

Robi Botos in Toronto.
Photograph by Christopher Manson.

1998, Budapest, Hungary

In the early Budapest daylight, Robi Botos walked his stepdaughter to school and as he walked, he listened. His ear was trained for the sound of loudspeakers echoing from the city's public squares, which usually signalled a gathering of neo-Nazi demonstrators. *Jews are stealing Hungary, Gypsies are making it criminal.* If he heard the sound, and careful to keep chatting to his stepdaughter, Robi would veer away from the square and down another street, an indirect route, but clear of the men in black jackets with sewn-on swastikas.

He couldn't do much to keep his stepdaughter, Barbara, out of reach of racism at school. Teachers treated her differently, and students told her why. *Your skin is dirty*, they said, because she was Roma and had darker skin than other Hungarian children.

Robi's wife, Violet, heard the same things. She rented a space to sell hats and other goods at a downtown apartment building on a busy street, just inside large front gates like the archway of a church. She had a permit to be there but residents threw insults anyway. *Dirty Gypsy, you make our building look like you.*

Sometimes in subtle ways, racism shapes the behaviour of those on the receiving end. Robi and his brothers, all musicians, played late shows together and, depending on the neighbourhood or the crowd that night, they took a taxi home. Attacks by skinheads against Roma were too frequent. It wasn't fear, deciding to avoid confrontations. It was common sense.

"When you grow up like that, you don't really think of it as 'you're scared,'" you just get used to that," he explains. But in his twenties, with a wife and two young daughters and a stunted career, Robi thought more about these incidents. He realized things had stopped getting better for "Gypsies"—a pejorative for Roma.

The Botos family outgrew extreme poverty just one generation before. Robi's father was born in Rakamaz, northeastern Hungary, in a makeshift home near the water where the wealthier villagers piled their garbage. Only Roma lived on this edge of town. But in the evenings, when music from violins, clarinets, and elegant stringed instruments called cimbaloms transformed the waterside, even non-Roma came to listen. The musicians began receiving invitations to play elsewhere, and before long, Robi's father moved to a better part of the village.

His family were genocide survivors. Everyone knew the Jewish people were victims of the Holocaust, but alongside the Shoah was the lesser-known Porajmos, Romani for "devouring." Romani people (Roma and Sinti) and Jews were singled out as racial enemies by Hitler's Nuremberg Laws, and during the Roma Holocaust, some 25 per cent of European Roma were killed, or 220,000 people, although the estimates vary widely with some closer to half a million.[1] In a few countries, Roma were all but wiped out.[2] They were hunted in the Baltics, the Soviet Union, France, and countries allied with Germany, including Hungary. Although extermination orders did not terrorize that country on the same scale as others, by one estimate, at least 10,000 Hungarian Roma perished.[3]

After Hungary fell to the Soviet Union near the war's end in 1945, the politics of communism were in some ways an equalizer. Robi's father was a talented drummer and his popularity grew as racism diminished under the new paradigm of workers' unity. The family income kept improving. Robi was born in 1978 the youngest of three boys in Nyíregyháza, a richer village than the birthplace of his father, and the family next moved to Budapest when Robi was four years old.

The boys all learned to play their father's drums, and they were good. Good enough to become a trio, thought Robi's father, who brought home the two remaining pieces—a bass guitar and a piano—when Robi was seven. Robi took over the upright piano, learning from his father and two grandfathers whom he calls "self-taught masters." The Botos brothers first performed with their father and before long, became a standalone act. But although they had plenty of gigs, the continuous demand for favourite tunes was stifling. For the most part, Hungarian patrons wanted what was familiar. If the trio dipped into slower, irregular rhythms, stage managers shouted them back to traditional scores.

It was only at home during daily jam sessions with family where Robi could express himself. The music of his grandfathers had a thousand moods. It danced and dipped, following lives and moments in real time. It was, "things I can't talk about, but I can put into notes." And like the early jazz musicians in segregated United States, "being hated and pushed aside will make you play different ... It's part of the deal, to play jazz." Increasingly, it was the deal in Hungary.

Like other countries under the Soviet yoke until 1989, Hungary skipped from communism to a multiparty democracy almost overnight.

Some Hungarians wonder if missing out on the dialogue about shaping their society, and about multiculturalism, explains the backlash of nationalism and xenophobia that emerged in the early 1990s.[4]

Robi had the talent and ambition to know he was not growing into his music as he would if he was a non-Roma artist. But not until he was a father did persecution actually start to scare him. "When you walk around with your daughter who's got dark skin, you've got two options: you stay there and try to fight this whole thing which the majority of people believe in, or you just say, well, the world is big and it's going to be hard, but I don't want my kids to live like that."

Robi had two children, ages six and one-and-a-half, when he and his wife made the hardest decision of their lives. In 1998 they left their families and boarded a plane to Canada. They carried their daughters, a few hundred dollars, two suitcases with clothes, and an electric keyboard.

December 1998, Burlington, and October 2013, Toronto, Canada

Robi and Violet picked Canada because they didn't need a visa and they heard that anyone, regardless of race, could get a job. They weren't ready for how fundamentally different an inclusive country would feel.

They knew enough English to say "We're refugees" at Pearson International Airport on December 6, 1998, and miraculously, a process they didn't expect began to unfold. The immigration officials smiled and let them pass. Somehow, someone found a pair of shoes that fit Violet, whose own fell apart on the way from Budapest. "Who are these people?" they asked each other. Later, when Robi first stepped on a public bus and saw radically diverse people shoulder-to-shoulder, he had the same ethereal feeling. "When I was in Hungary, the only place that I could imagine like this was in heaven."

There was space in a refugee shelter near a highway in Burlington, west of Toronto, and that's where the family went. From there, two processes began at enormously different speeds: Robi almost immediately found a place within the Canadian music community. But it would take more than five years before he became a permanent resident of Canada.

Robi entered the music scene when a friend brought him to a club in Hamilton to hear David Braid on piano. Robi was introduced, and

David, a household name for Canadian jazz fans, invited him onstage to play. David recognized a fellow jazz pianist within a few bars.[5] Robi began joining jam sessions with musicians in David's network, and then he was getting phone calls for shows. Whenever David couldn't fill an invitation for a gig, he asked callers if they'd heard of the new musician in town, and gave Robi's number.

Robi felt part of the community. One day in his new apartment in Toronto, where the family moved after three months, he answered a call from David asking if he planned to be home all morning. Robi put on a pot of coffee and waited. The doorbell rang but instead of David, there were two movers with an upright piano. Robi could box up his keyboard.

Meanwhile, Robi and Violet had a hearing scheduled with the Immigration and Refugee Board (IRB). A letter in the mail several weeks later informed them their claim was rejected. They did not meet the legal criteria to count as refugees. They appealed but got the same decision.

On a Saturday morning in February 2002, Robi opened his door to a man and a woman in uniform. They were there to take the family to the airport and a plane back to Hungary. Robi walked back inside and time slowed down. He looked at the bedroom where his daughters were asleep and thought about their school, about his work, about their Canadian friends, and then he walked into his room to find his wife waking up. He told her who was outside. Violet was pregnant and near her due date. She asked him how she could travel—the pregnancy had been causing a lot of pain. They stared at each other. "All this stuff just comes to your head in a few minutes and you really fear ..." Robi leaves the sentence hanging.

One of the strangest moments was back outside when he told the officers that his wife was pregnant, and one of them radioed the information elsewhere, asking, "Are we still taking them?" The radio crackled into silence, and Robi remembers, "I'm just shaking. I'm praying and shaking." Another crackle and the radio voice replied "No." The family could stay in Canada to have the baby, but had orders to report themselves immediately after.

Canadian friends found Robi a lawyer and they decided to fight the deportation. Robi filed an application to remain in Canada on humanitarian grounds, usually a last resort for asylum claimants. His brother, Frank Botos, had arrived in Canada shortly after Robi and was likewise struggling to stay. The brothers weren't alone. David Braid and other friends helped rally the music community around Robi and Frank. They sent letters to parliamentarians, circulated petitions, and spoke to the media. All the while, Robi and Violet raised a newborn son and Robi played show after show.

In October 2003, five and a half years after they arrived, Robi and his family heard they could stay in Canada. One of the immediate benefits was that Robi could finally travel. In 2004, he won first prize in the solo piano competition at the Montreux International Jazz Festival in Switzerland. Part of the prize package was getting to open for Canadian legend Oscar Peterson. Like young jazz artists around the world, Robi was raised to the sound of Oscar on vinyl. He next won the best soloist prize at Belgium's Jazz Hoeilaart in 2005, Canada's National Jazz Award for keyboardist of the year in 2007, first prize in the Great American Jazz Piano Competition in Florida in 2008, and so forth, until he won the best of the best, the Grand Jazz Award at the Montreal International Jazz Festival in 2012. He added a 2014 Juno Award to the list, for the album *Ripple Effect* with trio mates Mike Downes and Ethan Ardelli.

To watch Robi play live is an experience. His fingers are a blur against the keys, but you pay more attention to his face, always working, moving easily from clamped concentration to a riotous grin.

Robi says he fell in love with Canada that first time he saw the world on a public bus. He still thanks God for being in a country where people accept differences and a stranger's reflex is to find good in another, not bad. He was shocked when he first heard refugees from Hungary and other countries with large Roma populations called "bogus" by Canadian politicians. It suggested a judgment against a whole people that was closer to attitudes he left behind in Budapest than anything he'd encountered in Toronto. So alongside Canada's Roma community, Robi became an advocate for fair treatment of Roma refugees, and in 2012, he told MPs on Parliament Hill about the persecution his people still face in Hungary.

Robi was right in 1998 when he guessed that treatment of Roma was worsening. But not even he predicted how ugly things would get. From 2008 to 2009, Hungarian neo-Nazis carried out multiple identical attacks that went something like this: A Molotov cocktail is pitched through the window of a Roma home and as people run outside to escape the flames, they are sprayed with bullets. The murderers escape arrest for an absurd length of time.[6] Such attacks aren't isolated. The third largest political party in Hungary is the xenophobic Jobbik, whose supporters have stoned Roma houses chanting, "You are going to die here!"[7]

Partly by following these events, Robi is more acutely aware of Canadians' humanity and also finds it the worthier of protection. He recalls a dinnertime shortly after his daughters began school in Toronto. While telling a story to his wife, he jogged her memory with "That black guy, that singer I worked with" and the girls interrupted sharply, "Dad, you're not about to say something wrong, right?"

The question, to Robi, embodies all the right attitudes trickling down from Canadian officialdom, through the education system, to his children. Racism cannot be tolerated. And better, it has to be prevented. "That was the most shocking and beautiful experience to me."

28 Karim Teja

Uganda

Karim Teja in Calgary.
Photograph by Leah Hennel.

October 1972, Kampala, Uganda

Before the hijacking, Karim Teja's father, Sultan, said violence in Uganda ebbs and flows. When Idi Amin deposed the president and installed himself in 1971, promising more for black Ugandans, Sultan said, "Don't worry." Then rumours began about what could happen to the property and bank accounts of the Asian minority, but Sultan said, "This will pass."

It didn't. On August 4, 1972, Idi Amin announced that Asians had ninety days to leave the country. They would lose title to homes and businesses, and could take only what they could carry. One month later, the tortured bodies of two family friends were found in a nearby field. Soldiers behaved unpredictably under their new boss. Asians were recast as foreign saboteurs of the Ugandan economy, although families like Karim's had been in Uganda and East Africa for generations, back to a time when their ancestors had first sailed from India.

Sultan still saw a future in Uganda, but friends persuaded him to hedge. Canada and a handful of other Western countries opened immigration to Ugandan Asians after the expulsion order, and more applications than open spots spilled onto the Canadian visa desk in an improvised office in Kampala.[1] The Canadians drew applicant numbers by lottery and posted them each morning in the office window beside an interview time.

Karim was eight years old in 1972 and remembers the day ticket number 2231 appeared in the window. What did the number mean? Was his family one of thousands? What was Canada, anyway, and why was its door open?

On Friday, October 13, 1972, Karim and his family arrived for their interview where two things would be determined: their potential and their desperation. The Ugandan Asians were screened using the new immigration point system introduced by Ottawa in 1967 that rewarded people for things like education and language, but Kampala visa officers also had discretion to side step the rules if persuaded by a "particular plight."

Karim recited letters from an eye chart and reported his age, school grade, and English ability. He sensed that the Canadian official liked them. His family had potential and they were certainly desperate. Karim's father would soon be stripped of his Ugandan citizenship, and his mother's status was equally insecure. His mother, Khatun, was born in Kenya but her citizenship expired when she married Sultan, a Ugandan. She and the boys were not citizens of either country.

The interview for a life in Canada took one hour. Applicants knew their future before leaving the office because it was nearly impossible for the Canadians to reach them otherwise. Few owned a telephone and the post office was unreliable as well as dangerous, because of the paper trail it created leading to Asian families. At the end of their interview, Karim heard that his family was accepted. Sultan still had doubts about the need to leave Uganda, but having the option deserved a drive to the toy store.

———————

In the back of the family's car, a box-shaped Peugeot, Karim tore the packaging off his Chitty Chitty Bang Bang car and his brother assembled a viewfinder. In front, his father had on his three-piece suit and his mother wore a sari, their dress clothes from the immigration interview.

The chatter inside came to a stop when three soldiers spilled out of a roadside bar in front of the car, forcing it to halt. One soldier carried a rifle and he ordered Karim's father to play chauffeur. The men piled in the back of the five-seat car, moving the older boy to his mother's lap but leaving Karim squeezed in the backseat. Just hours after leaving the Canadian office, the new toys were forgotten and a gun-toting soldier sat behind the driver's seat. Sultan began to drive.

The soldier gave directions and Sultan followed until the Peugeot approached a roundabout with four offshoots, and he was told to take Masaka Road. Sultan knew the roads because he worked as a travelling salesman filling shelves across Uganda. Masaka Road led to Makindye, a Kampala suburb that became a mass grave under Idi Amin. Their dead friends had been found in Makindye. Sultan refused. "Not with my family," he said.

The soldier grunted agreement to another exit, Entebbe Road, but his face darkened. He began to load his weapon, narrating the clicks and snaps. "This is how you load a rifle," he told Karim, though really speaking to the adults. *Do not disobey me again.*

A way down Entebbe Road, Sultan realized there was an upcoming left turn that wound back to Makindye, and it hit him that they were driving in a circle to get there. He said nothing. Instead, he put his foot down and the Peugeot lurched forward, fast, on the dirt road. The soldiers shouted to slow but they flew past the turn. The armed man shoved his rifle into Sultan's neck with one arm and grabbed the wheel with the other. The move sent the car into a 180-degree spin, which Karim only realized when they stopped, facing the wrong direction. Doors clicked open and family and soldiers regrouped separately, staring at each other across the soundless car.

The curious scene landed in a stretch of road lined by huts. Storekeepers and shoppers began to edge in. What the crowd saw was a soldier with a gun berating an Asian man, repeating, "I'm going to kill you." A woman in a sari stood crying, and two boys were sobbing and possibly praying too. An engine growled nearby and the crowd turned to see a grey pickup truck pull over on the dirt shoulder. Another soldier got out.

Through tears, Karim watched the new soldier move toward them. He wore army fatigues, with one pant leg clipped below the knee, crutches under his arms. He asked what was going on. The soldier with the rifle was livid. "This man is not following my orders." Sultan interjected, explaining that he knew about Makindye and would not be taken there, and he offered his wallet, keys, and car instead. The soldier on crutches nodded—a reasonable exchange, he said.

The two soldiers seemed to size each other up. Sultan couldn't tell who had the higher rank but sensed they were not on good terms. He noticed the one on crutches had begun moving from the scene, walking and talking and leading away the three hijackers, like he was taking the argument aside for appearances. Was the man on crutches offering them a chance to escape? Sultan moved on his instincts and nudged his family toward the Peugeot. Within seconds, car doors slamming, Sultan had the car in gear.

Before the soldiers were four hundred metres behind them, another soldier stepped into sight and slapped a spike belt on the road. Sultan slammed on the brakes. The new gatekeeper asked about their speed. Running from something? Without a beat, Sultan explained he was speeding because curfew was at 6 p.m., and it was now 5 p.m. He was out late, he said, because they had just given the soldiers down the road a lift. The soldier smiled and dragged back the belt.

Sultan didn't stop again until they were outside the Ismaili worship house. It was prayer time inside the Jama'at Khana. Slowly, heads turned to see the faces of Khatun and the boys streaked with tears and Sultan, in a three-piece suit, his jacket dripping sweat. Friends and neighbours closed in a worried huddle around the family and Karim watched his father cry for the first time. Much later, Sultan would tell Karim that it wasn't until the moment the head of the congregation held his hand that he realized he was still alive.

The next day, Saturday, Karim's family heard soldiers in a truck were winding through the neighbourhood, looking for a family of four Asians with a Peugeot. The Tejas spent two nights in hiding with friends and on Monday, Sultan risked a visit to the Canadian visa office. He skipped the queue, walked straight to reception and asked for the official who had interviewed his family. The receptionist took him seriously. Sultan told the visa official about the hijacking and manhunt. He knew by now his bank account would be monitored so he had no money to pay for the flight to Canada, which Ugandan Asians were expected to do. The Canadian told him there were four seats on a departing flight tomorrow, a Tuesday, and not to worry about cost.

A friend drove the family to a loading point organized by the Canadians early Tuesday morning where buses waited to form a convoy to the airport. Customs teemed with soldiers, any one of whom might recognize the family. Sultan was again drenched in sweat, even after they had crossed customs, and even when they were on the tarmac seated in an Air Canada plane brimming with nearly new Canadians. Their flight attendant must have guessed something extra was happening to this family because when they left Ugandan airspace, she stopped to put a hand on Sultan's damp shoulder. She said, "Sir, there's nothing the Ugandan Army can do now." For the second time, Karim watched his father cry.

October 1972, Vancouver, and September 2013, Calgary, Canada

Karim's first Canadian home was the Mayfair Hotel on Robson Street in Vancouver. The government paid rent for two months. Sultan worked night shifts sorting Christmas mail at the post office and, later, moving furniture. Khatun became a bank teller at CIBC. Karim's parents barely saw each other, working opposite shifts to stretch out a living. They taught him and his brother that, in Canada, the ladder up was education.

At that time, Karim's father had to decide between a cup of coffee and his bus fare home. Some thirty-four years later, Sultan and Khatun sat in their finery at a gala dinner in Calgary, Karim's new home. Karim had flown his parents from Vancouver for the Ernst and Young Entrepreneur of the Year awards. He and two colleagues were nominees for the entrepreneurs in health-care category. His company was one of the first to capture x-ray images digitally, and Karim was chief financial officer and co-manager of the Chinese and European business units. When he heard his name called out as winner, Karim looked at his mother and father. "It meant a lot to me, but it meant more to my parents."

When Karim turned thirty-nine, around ten years ago, he began seeing his parents' journey differently. His father was thirty-nine when they left Kampala. "I can't imagine having to leave Canada, leave my comfortable life, and have no money in my pocket."

He sits back, reflecting on how the Canadians got them out. "It was their primary objective: we need to get this family to safety," Karim says. "I tell my kids, what country does that? Even today, it brings tears to my eyes. I was a proud Canadian before I was even a Canadian."

Between September and November 1972, 4,420 refugees were evacuated on charter flights to Canada, and another 1,278 would later follow.[2]

When Karim's plane landed in Montreal on October 19, 1972, Canada again amazed him. Through the plane window, eight-year-old Karim saw men in berets walking below on the tarmac. Snow fell lazily from the dark sky, but inside the plane, Karim and other children panicked because it looked like the Ugandan Army was outside. But the Canadians were friendly, smiling. Some were even doctors. And when the family arrived at the Longue Pointe base, military cooks had a surprise for them. They had consulted Montreal's Indian Canadian community about the food requirements of Sikhs, Muslims, and Hindus.[3] They had learned how to make chapati.[4]

This early experience is partly why Karim doesn't work on November 11. His family observes a day of thanks to the Canadians who made their arrival, and everything after, possible.

In 2007, Karim returned to Uganda with his wife and their teen-aged children, two boys and one girl. They saw glimpses of their father's childhood, and they saw poverty. For the first time, his children wondered about the randomness of birth and the luck of opening their eyes in a safe country. A good experience, Karim says. "I think the harder time they have reconciling that, the more they appreciate what Canada has."

29 Avtar Sandhu

India

Avtar Sandhu at home in Caledon.

Photograph by Christopher Manson.

June 1987, The Hague, Netherlands

Avtar Sandhu watched the shapes of strangers slip onto the deck of a cargo ship, a far smaller one than he had expected. It was a warm June evening in 1987 in The Hague and the dock was growing dark. Twilight kept the ship, overfilling with Indian travellers, obscured from the view of any passing Dutch authorities.

If Avtar stepped onboard, there would be 174 passengers, many, like himself, Sikhs who had fled India's Punjab region. Word of mouth helped fill these rust-streaked vessels. Friends muttering to friends how to find the agent. Avtar had covered his spot with a $3,000 US loan from a friend in New York.

His passage paid and a few belongings in hand, all Avtar had left to do was board the *Amelie*. But all the unknowns kept him still, and thinking. How long would the ship be at sea? Where in Canada would it anchor? Did the Indian crew know what it was doing? Would this worn freighter hold together in the wide Atlantic? Avtar couldn't swim and he saw from the dock there were no life boats. He gazed at the starry cobalt blue sky and prayed. He was among the last to board, after he decided to trust in God.

Avtar had wanted to leave India in 1975 at the age of twenty one but it wasn't until 1985 that he had enough money to reach Germany.

He was the youngest of six siblings on the family farm in Kandola Khurd, a village in India's majority Sikh Punjab state. He knew about the drive by Sikh parties for a separate Punjab, independent from India, but farm work held him and his family back from politics. They harvested year-round crops of sugarcane, wheat, rice, and potatoes. Even in good years, though, it was tough to make money. New Delhi set wholesale food prices. If the price of fertilizer rose, Avtar's family might not recoup their costs. They had food on the table, but no savings. They felt stuck.

Poverty inflamed competition among neighbours in Kandola Khurd. Between 1983 and 1984, Avtar was arrested three times on various counts of hiding illegal weapons and drugs. The police never had evidence, just neighbours' reports. Each time, the family had to scrape enough together to buy Avtar's release. One more reason to leave.

Another was the government's response out of all proportion to Sikh protests in 1975 supporting separation, when Indira Gandhi imposed "the Emergency" and suspended the constitution. Many innocents got swept up in the confusion, arrested on trumped-up charges. In the early 1980s, there were times of the day when it was foolish to be outside the home.

All this was only a prelude to the bloody pogroms by Hindus against Sikhs that erupted in 1984 when two Sikh bodyguards killed Indira Gandhi; payback for deadly government raids in Punjab that year. An estimated three thousand Sikhs were killed following Gandhi's death, and the new prime minister, her son, did nothing to stop the massacres. He declared, "Once a mighty tree falls, it is only natural that the earth around it shakes."[1] Kandola Khurd was spared the scale of slaughter elsewhere, but Avtar was now convinced his family's future lay outside India.

Avtar had married Mohinder in 1977. By 1984, they had a five-year-old daughter and a son, aged one. The next year, Avtar borrowed $2,000 in rupees from a relative for a flight to the Soviet Union and from there, a train to East Germany where, as other Indians knew, it was possible to get a visa and cross into West Germany as a refugee, find a job, and then bring your family.

Avtar used his twenty-four-hour visa to claim asylum at the border on May 6, 1985. He slept in a West German government shelter, began by picking cherries, then worked in a corn mill, getting paid under the table at five marks an hour (around $3.70). Although scraping by, he admired Germany. He thought Germans were honest, compassionate. "If you need help, within five minutes, somebody helps you," he says. But after fifteen months he had to leave to earn more money.

He tried the Netherlands, Belgium, and France, sometimes working a job for just a week. His unsuccessful attempt to enter the United Kingdom earned him his first ever boat rides: one across the English Channel in an overcrowded speedboat and one back from Dover, guided by immigration officials. Then in April 1987, Avtar learned of a planned voyage from the Netherlands to Canada. Two months later, on June 23, 1987, for the third time in his life, he got on a boat.

Below deck, it stank from day one. There were 174 passengers, including a sole woman, and five crewmembers up top. The floor of the hold was a swamp of vomit, but still Avtar, who was sick whenever he stood, mostly stayed horizontal as the boat swung up then dipped down in the rolling sea. He tried eating, but the vegetables and chapati just came back up. It was cold on the Atlantic. Avtar shivered beneath two blankets spread over four bodies. He joined others in prayers and sometimes songs. He stayed below deck for eight full days, in a mental haze from the stench, dehydration, and the unfamiliar roll of the ocean.

On the ninth day, the sea calmed and Avtar finally climbed a rung ladder into the open air and sunshine. All around him was blue, flashing ocean. Even so, the mood lightened. Occasionally, the captain would open his maps on deck to show their progress, plotting the ship closer and closer to Canada. It was reassuring, until the loud metallic bang.

It turned their heads, and the motion of the ship changed, distinctly slower, more rocking. A gasket had spun loose from the single engine in the ship's stern, and there were no spare parts. A crewmember, a mechanic, bent over the dead engine, the passengers crowded around. Avtar prayed until, four hours later, he heard pistons wheezing to life.

A second shock came when the captain announced he would be anchoring in sixteen metres of water off the Canadian shore. He needed the passengers to swim ashore so the ship could avoid rocks and Canadian vessels. Avtar and the others protested in disbelief. No one aboard the *Amelie* was a confident swimmer. And several had heard about other disastrous incidents, stories of migrants in lifeboats cast off early. History seemed near to repeating itself, but this time without the lifeboats.

Avtar never did have to experience the surf. A thick fog rolled in as they neared land and the captain decided to steer right for the shore. The anchor dropped just before 10:00 p.m. on July 11, 1987, after nineteen days at sea. Avtar walked down a plank from the deck to the beach and stepped onto sand, without ever touching the water.

July 1987, Charlesville, and January 2014, Caledon, Canada

The *Amelie* disappeared into fog as the group moved forward. Trudging through the sand, Avtar wondered what they would find. He didn't know where on the American continent they had landed, or if the beach would lead into jungle or city.

They stayed close to the shore for five hours, a promise to the crew to let them get away, and then walked for some two kilometres before reaching a stretch of road called Highway 3. Out of the fog, Avtar saw the headlights of a truck. The group parted off the road and waved at the driver, hoping for directions, but the man sped by, alarmed at the scores of foreigners who materialized from the fog in his headlights. It was now well after midnight, and they walked on until they spotted another set of lights, this time from a house.

At that moment, a police cruiser appeared out of the mist, lights flashing, followed by a fire truck and several more RCMP vehicles. It was all lights, noise, and confusion, and into the crowd walked Vernon Malone, the owner of the nearest home. Avtar saw him speak to the police and motion toward the house. Vernon was trying to get the people onto his property and off the highway, which would soon be filled with cars and trucks of fishermen heading for work.

A few Indian passengers could speak broken English, and someone asked for a taxi to Toronto. Someone else asked for a glass of water. Others nodded. Everyone was thirsty and exhausted and many were sick. Avtar had lost forty pounds during nearly three weeks at sea. Most of the men had on the same collared shirts and blue or orange turbans they had worn for nineteen days.

Vernon turned on the hose and passed around cups, and then he guided the only woman to the toilet indoors. Vernon's wife handed out slices of white bread and his son telephoned the neighbours with a plea for more food. By 8:00 a.m., the group was at the community centre with a breakfast spread of peanut butter and jam sandwiches and coffee, supplied by folks from Charlesville.

Their next stop was the Stadacona Barracks at Canadian Forces Base Halifax, where Avtar and the others would be detained until Ottawa assembled a response. They wore numbers around their necks instead of name tags. Avtar was number 73. Twice a day, they lined up outside to be counted.

Their welcome to Canada was mixed. Invariably, when an unexpected boat washes up in Canada, shore residents respond like the dozens of Charlesville families who instinctively jumped to supply food, first aid, and clothes. But elsewhere, the spotlight gravitates to security and its cousin, the "floodgates." In Ottawa in August 1987, Parliament met in an emergency session. The *Amelie* incident became "an issue of grave national importance."[2] There was the memory of 155 Sri Lankans drifting in lifeboats off Newfoundland and Labrador in 1986. Then there was the Air India flight 182 bombing in 1985, the worst terrorist attack against Canadians. Sikh extremists were immediately suspected and Sikh Canadians felt the chill of being blamed by association.[3]

The government dispatched a Canadian delegation to India to investigate the lives and dealings of the 173 men and one woman. Journalists repeated rumours about more ships full of women and children on the way, unable to otherwise explain a boatful of men.[4] The rumours proved to be absurd and background checks returned clean. "There is no particle of evidence you ever engaged in acts of violence anywhere," said immigration official Michael Sloan, releasing the last six passengers from detention in Halifax.[5] Even so, the government decided the arrivals would need a Canadian guarantor. And they would need to report to an immigration office once a week for five years.

Avtar left Halifax for Toronto when strangers in that city's Sikh community pooled their money and appointed themselves his guarantor. The number of Sikhs in Canada was strong and growing, notably in Surrey, British Columbia, and in pockets in Ontario like Malton and Brampton. Avtar moved into the basement of a Sikh family's home on Gerrard Street and found a restaurant job that paid three dollars an hour. He moved on to factory work and usually had two jobs, working fifteen-hour days, six days a week, and still found time to report himself to immigration at 136 Edward Street each week.

Avtar first paid down the loans he took to leave India in 1985, and then repaid his American friend the *Amelie* fare. When he became a permanent resident in 1992, he could finally sponsor his family, Mohinder and their two children, to Canada. Eight years had passed since he saw them. Even telephone calls were few over the years because of the cost—Avtar recalls paying $3.50 per minute—and the coordination. Avtar would place the first call to India to someone in the nearest city, who alerted his family in the village, who then came to the city to wait beside the phone for the ring of a second call from Toronto.

In a celebration he compares to a wedding, friends and members of his gurdwara, the Sikh place of worship, stood noisily around Avtar to welcome his family at Pearson International Airport on July 17, 1993.

He watched them walk in, his cheeks wet. His son was a boy, not a toddler, and his daughter was almost a teenager. Gurdeep asked his mother as they passed the arrivals gate, "Which one is my father?" His son only had memories of Avtar in a turban, which he no longer wore in Canada (although he would again, much later).

In January 2014, at his home on a big patch of frozen land in Caledon, Ontario, Avtar describes how he worked his way up to higher paying jobs, while Mohinder raised the children. His work was always labour intensive, like plastering drywall in the endless ring of new homes circling Toronto. He worked as a licensed plasterer until his health no longer allowed, and he now spends his days at home, filled with family including three young grandchildren, a fourth on the way. The gurdwara community remains a large part of his life. It's a source of strength he draws from and deposits into. He helps anyone who needs it. "It's a duty," he says.

Avtar first returned to Nova Scotia to visit Charlesville in 2000. He's gone back many times since to see Vernon Malone, and more than once, he has accepted a ride on his friend's fishing boat. Not everyone would be so willing to be back on open water, but Avtar shrugs and laughs. "Now, I'm not scared. It's my life."

30 Sabreen

Israel

Anonymous portrait of Sabreen.

Photograph by Christopher Manson.

2006, Negev Desert, Israel

"They're going to do it on Thursday," Sabreen's[1] brother-in-law quietly told her once the other men of the family had left, after their meeting.

It was a Monday afternoon, and in three days, Sabreen would be killed by her cousin. She had refused a marriage arranged by her father so there was no honour in the family while she lived.

"It will be better for everyone," Sabreen answered calmly. But her pulse had changed, and for the first time since this hell began, she did not want to die.

When Sabreen was born, her mother was killed. She had dishonoured the family by sleeping with a man who was not her husband and becoming pregnant with his child, Sabreen. The family delayed her execution until she gave birth in case it was a boy. Had they been able to see the shadows of a girl through ultrasound, the fetus would be gone with her mother. Her male relatives watched Sabreen closely as she grew up to see if she turned out the same way: a whore, in their minds. If she did, the evidence told her to expect death. Sabreen was thirteen when she watched her sister being strangled with a rope, her body then tossed in the water.

Tradition was above human life in the Bedouin family and village that raised Sabreen. Tradition meant total obedience by women, and the failure to answer the moods of men was an easy loss of honour. Tradition also required offering hospitality to strangers. A man might arrive at the family's tent and stay for three days before his hosts could ask why he came. He would eat their food, drink their coffee, make small talk, and then, on the fourth day, he would discuss his business, like trading camels or women.

Bedouins are an Arab ethnic group native to the Negev, and those who stayed put after the war that created Israel in 1948 became Israeli citizens. Sabreen's family was one of many belonging to Israel's inherited Bedouin who chose to remain living in the desert instead of resettling to towns designated for them by the state. They were nomads. They spent just a week or even a few days on one stretch of sand at a time, before disassembling their tent and harnessing the animals. The family migration always circled back to a rooted, stationary village. But as an "unrecognized settlement," their village had no electricity, water, or contact with paved roads.[2]

The minority Bedouins are vexing for Tel Aviv. Attempts by the government to improve living conditions are routinely vilified and likened to destroying Bedouin identity, culture, religion, and land—none of these easy issues in Israel.[3]

Sabreen was lucky to attend school. Other girls in the village were not so fortunate; family service was the only routine of their lives. Sabreen's father, who was not her biological one, allowed school for the most part, but she missed days now and then, according to his whims.

In high school in Beersheba—a donkey ride, a walk, and a bus ride from home—Sabreen read novels and discovered another world. There were people who were not Bedouin, not even Israeli, and there was romance. The world got bigger after graduating in 2004, when she began her Israeli military service and met people from the cities.

She learned about her fixed marriage during a visit home in June 2005. Her adoptive mother relayed the news. Sabreen was twenty, her suitor in his fifties, and she couldn't conceive of a crime he hadn't committed. He had murdered, run drugs through the desert and trafficked foreign women for sex. He had spent seven years in jail. Now he was paying Sabreen's father for her, and she said no.

"By that time, I was really done. I was really done with the abuse. I was really done with the mistreatment. I was really done with the fact that I'd always be labelled the 'whore daughter,'" Sabreen says. She knew exactly what her defiance meant. It had happened to her sister and biological mother, and she expected the same. Her adoptive mother knew too and cried, cradling Sabreen, pleading with her to accept. But she wouldn't, her mind was set. She recalls thinking, "Kill me, I don't care. End it."

They nearly did. Her father and brother beat her so severely she was hospitalized three times, twice arriving unconscious. After two of the attacks, she drank gasoline to kill herself. It didn't work and she recovered, again in hospital. The hospital staff knew about the suicide attempts, and they would have known about the beatings too, as the injuries didn't match being trampled by a horse. But Sabreen didn't dare

alter the facts of her father's story. If her superiors in the military suspected anything about her interrupted service, for "family problems,"
there was no hint of it.

Against her best efforts, Sabreen survived, and the villagers remained
scandalized that she did. As if connected by veins, the thinking went, the
same honour coursed through everyone. The village wanted her gone.

Sabreen doesn't defend her father, but speaks about the intense
pressure on him to do something about her. Most painful for Sabreen
was not the beatings she received or the glares from her shamed community, but was watching her mother and sisters repeatedly beaten too,
unfairly feeling the fury she had caused.

By 2006, Sabreen became aware that she was at the centre of a
plot she knew too well. To murder a woman with impunity in the Negev,
Bedouin men, she explains, needed a simple alibi. She noticed her father
began spending time away, attending the mosque. That was unusual for
a nomad but behaviour that would pass a police investigation. And her
uncle, the head of the family, she heard, was planning a trip to Jordan.
The killer would be a peripheral man, a cousin, the kind the police never
seemed to suspect. In what she guessed was another piece of the plot,
her father approved of Sabreen working at a nearby primary school,
while she recovered.

Two military friends were volunteers at the same school. They
knew someone was beating her, from her cuts and bruises, and they
told her to run away. *Where? Out of Israel. What's out of Israel? Other
places you can be safe. How do I get there? Planes, you fly there.* She
couldn't picture doing it.

But hearing her brother-in-law confirm the murder plans changed
that. On Tuesday, just two days before her scheduled death, she made
one phone call. "You have to help me, you have to do something," Sabreen
pleaded. She was in the school washroom on a borrowed cell phone. "You
have to get me out of here." On the other end of the line was her clos-
est friend, a young woman in the military, who promised to spearhead a
rescue. All Sabreen had to do was get herself to school the following day.

But when Wednesday morning arrived, her father told Sabreen to
stay home. She played indifferent. Heart beating but calm, she asked
for permission to visit the school to tell the staff she would miss the day.
He agreed.

Sabreen left barefoot because in the desert, shoes signal a journey. She left her identity card behind too, but on an impulse, slipped her high school transcript in her pocket. Stepping from the tent, Sabreen saw her mother's back a short distance away, stooped over to feed the animals. "I just looked at her and walked away, pretending everything was fine, but I was dying inside." She assumed she would never see her adoptive mother again. It was the hardest walk of her life.

Sabreen couldn't have known it as she forced her legs to take normal steps toward school, but the previous night, the friend who she had reached from the washroom had set a plan in motion with a small group of her own friends.

A man and woman sat waiting in a car near the school. They were strangers to the villagers (and to Sabreen), but a couple chatting together on the roadside was not that suspicious. When they got the signal—a phone call from Sabreen—the couple pulled into the school parking lot and paused just long enough for a skinny, dark-haired girl to dart out and climb into the back seat. They drove fast back onto the road and without stopping went straight to a nearby kibbutz, another desert village, where a second car sat empty. The man stayed behind the wheel of the first car, while Sabreen and the woman jumped out and switched to the waiting car. Before they each peeled away, the woman also switched her hair colour, removing a blonde wig to become a brunette. The first car took off in a different direction while the two women sped towards Tel Aviv, Sabreen lying flat on the back seat.

The strangers who saved her were two recent immigrants from Russia, and Sabreen's only connection to them was their mutual military friend. Sabreen spent less than seventy-two hours at their Tel Aviv apartment before going with the woman, now one of the central characters in her life, to the police station. Sabreen didn't trust the police, but her new friends persuaded her to report herself.

Back in her village, Sabreen's father had stormed the school, interrogating the staff and accusing anyone who knew his daughter of abduction. After seventy-two hours without word from Sabreen, the police would begin to search, so she went to the station and gave her story but not her coordinates—the apartment. "I'm staying in a kibbutz in the north," she lied. "I'm twenty-one years old and leaving home is my decision." The police officer on duty eyed her and said, "It doesn't matter, even if you're thirty-five, you're still under your parents' rules." That was his opinion, not the law. She thanked him and left.

Through the young serviceman posted in her village, whose cell phone she had used to escape, Sabreen learned that her father had hired private investigators and her head was worth one million shekels, over $300,000. She also learned that the private search team had moved north to the kibbutzim, justifying her distrust of police. Only one desk officer knew that false detail.

Back at the apartment in Tel Aviv, her new friends clothed and fed her, researched asylum countries, and, deciding on Canada, scrounged for a plane ticket. A major hitch was the matter of getting a passport. Sabreen had just one paper to prove her identity at the passport office, the high school transcript she pocketed on impulse in the desert. But it worked, and Sabreen walked out with her first passport.

Friends pulled together another $600 US in cash, and arranged transit to the airport. They also had in place a guardian among the airport staff, another friend of friends, who agreed not to give a young and likely petrified Bedouin woman any trouble at security. Sabreen knows the risks taken by these new friends and strangers. "They were doing all this to protect me from someone I knew for all my life."

She spent her last night in Israel sitting alone and awake, nerves overpowering sleep, until it was time to wake her friends and meet her early morning flight.

During her two months of hiding in Tel Aviv, and entrance to the bizarre limbo of an international airport, Sabreen was made of stone. She gave no expression of fear and nothing of her wild disorientation. Canada loomed as a blank place without buildings, streets, or cars. She assumed she would be homeless. She assumed everyone was evil, that in some way, people would hurt her, on the plane, during the layover in a cavernous Amsterdam airport, and in Canada. And yet, she could absorb all that, she told herself, as long as they didn't send her back.

October 2006 and September 2013, Canada

In the desert, Sabreen had never lived long in one place. Her family packed their things to move over a hundred times each year. Her longest period ever spent in one place would be at a women's shelter in Canada,[4] where, it turned out, she would not be homeless.

Through the shelter, Sabreen met a lawyer and within one month they filed a refugee claim. Her hearing before the Immigration and Refugee Board (IRB) was scheduled for December 2007. Sabreen still distrusted everyone and men in particular, so she asked her lawyer to request a female judge, which is typically granted by the IRB in cases involving gender-based claims and male violence. She secretly hoped for three things: she didn't want a dark man, she didn't want a tall man, and simply, she didn't want a man. She got all three.

Her lawyer had gathered evidence from women's organizations in Israel to detail a failure of Israeli police to protect against honour killing. And a psychologist reported that Sabreen was telling the truth. But the judge was not persuaded. After her hearing, Sabreen received a package by mail explaining the judge's decision that she was not a refugee. He wrote that Israel is a democratic country and that Israeli police protect their citizens.

She could appeal the decision, but the worst part of losing her case, Sabreen says, was waiting for a new hearing while not working or going to school.

Sabreen found a new lawyer who successfully appealed the first decision. Five months after winning the appeal, she had a second hearing scheduled. By now it was 2010. A woman sat at the bench in round two and decided on the same day that yes, the young Israeli woman was a refugee. Sabreen became a permanent resident of Canada the same year.

The hours and minutes of what she calls her personal hell, 2005 through 2006, seemed to drag. "The time was just too long," she says. Today, there's never enough time. Sabreen is a certified personal care worker and spends her days caring for elderly patients. Mid-afternoon is for volunteering and personal therapy sessions. The evenings are filled with courses in a two-year college nursing program she completes in the spring of 2014.

One of her goals is to be selfless, like her Israeli friends who smuggled her from the desert, and her Canadian friends who helped her stay and later adjust. She's curious about addiction and volunteers in homeless shelters in her in-between hours, in part because seven years ago, she readied herself for life on the street.

Recovery from her trauma has been slow but visible. Sabreen laughs as easily as she cries. She's blunt because she swore off pretending. It shows in the contradictions about herself she keeps uncovered. She doesn't think there's justice in Israel, but she loves where she came from—she has the diamond-shaped country tattooed in blue ink on her skin. And she's angry when she hears talk about refugees abusing the Canadian system. "Refugees do not go through hell, to come here, to stay on welfare. That's a joke." While she lived on welfare during her undecided-case years, she had a tooth pulled without anesthesia because it wasn't insured and she couldn't pay. But she shakes her head, "I will be thankful to this country for the rest of my life."

She misses her adoptive mother and sisters terribly. Sleep still feels empty without curling beside their warm bodies in a tent. There is no way to contact them, to get around the desert or the men. Her mother was a force, a tall woman with the will to raise orphans like her own and endure their disappearance. Sabreen speaks through tears when she describes her. And yet, she smiles, "I'm very happy. My life is wonderful."

Then and Now: Would They Get In Today?

Peter Showler

Canada's Generosity

As Canadians, it would be surprising not to feel some measure of pride while reading the stories in this book. And the feeling is not misplaced. The word most frequently used to describe Canada's refugee policy is "generous." The logic usually goes like this: "We are a nation of immigrants. We are a wealthy nation. We can afford to be generous and, accordingly, Canada's treatment of refugees has been generous." Fortunately and unfortunately, the statement is both true and not so true.

Let's begin with the positive side of the equation. The statement is resoundingly true and here is the evidence:

In 1986, the people of Canada were awarded the Nansen Medal by the United Nations High Commissioner for Refugees (UNHCR) "in recognition of their essential and constant contribution to the cause of refugees." It is the only occasion when the Nansen Refugee Award was given to an entire people. Yeah Canada.

From 1989 through to the early 2000s, Canada's Immigration and Refugee Board (IRB) set standards for fair decision making that were praised by the UNHCR as the model for other nations to emulate. As a result of its fair procedures, the IRB's acceptance rates were always in the highest ranges compared to other countries.

Canada has been one of three leading Western nations, along with the United States and Australia, to give new homes and lives to refugees trapped in refugee camps around the world. Since 1979, we have resettled nearly five hundred thousand refugees across Canada.

In its treatment of refugee claimants and refugees, Canada has been a straight shooter. Unlike the majority of host nations, we play by the rules of the Refugee Convention:

- we let the children go to school, primary or secondary;
- we let claimants work;
- we provide welfare for those who can't work;
- we offer medical care (until June 2012).

If refugee claimants are accepted, we let them apply to be permanent residents and then citizens. We don't park them in a demi-world of temporary status; we welcome them into the Canadian family.

In addition to regular resettlement, Canada is one of a handful of nations to consistently step forward to lend a helping hand in emergency situations when exceptionally vulnerable or disadvantaged refugees require immediate relocation to safety.

Some would say that should be good enough. Canada is generous, end of story. Unfortunately, it is not. It is half the story. Our use of the word "generous," especially out of the mouths of politicians and media, has often had a self-satisfied, back-patting quality that ignores the immense burdens of international refugee protection that have been primarily borne by the poorer nations of the world, countries like Tanzania, Kenya, Iran, Pakistan, Jordan, Ecuador, Lebanon, and a half dozen more, depending on the era. It is these countries, neighbours to major civil conflicts, that have received the great bulk of the more than 15 million refugees outside of their own countries, often for decades. At the time of writing, the tiny country of Lebanon, a country of 4 million, shelters more than 1.5 million Syrian refugees and 250,000 Palestinians, more than a third of their total population.

This is not to suggest that new refugees should be immediately distributed throughout the world, but, on the scale of generosity, it is important to recognize which nations are truly bearing the heavy end of the load when we speak of international burden sharing. When ministers of government say that Canada is the, or one of the, most generous nations toward refugees, they ignore the real heavy lifters.

There is also a darker side to the word "generosity." In recent years, the government has steered refugee policy in a very different direction.

It has diminished the inland refugee claim process, stripping away fair procedures in the guise of reform. In the worst cases, it has imposed undeniably harsh treatment on some refugees, denying them basic medical care and threatening some, including children, with long term imprisonment and family separation before their need for protection is even decided. Most recently, it has passed legislation to allow provinces to deny basic welfare to refugees.

Worse yet, it has conducted a public relations campaign against refugees who have made their claims in Canada, stigmatizing the very notion of a refugee, peppering the media with endless repetitions of *bogus, fraudulent, undocumented, queue-jumpers, associated with organized crime*. The campaign has successfully undermined the Canadian public's positive attitudes toward refugees. In the government's view, although contrary to international law and our commitments under the Refugee Convention, real refugees should remain in refugee camps, until they are called. They should not come directly to Canada.

In the House of Commons and the media, every draconian government measure has been introduced with the word "generous." Canada's past generosity becomes the justification for measures that are distinctly not generous. In the mouths of government spokespersons, the word has become a poison pill.

But before digging deeper, what follows is a brief history of Canada's refugee system and our global role as a country, which has, by and large, been a positive force for the international protection of refugees.

The Refugee Convention

The modern era of international refugee law begins with the 1951 UN Convention Relating to the Status of Refugees ("the Convention"). It was drafted after the Second World War in the shadow of the newly formed United Nations and the Universal Declaration of Human Rights. Article 14 of the Declaration grants every individual the right to asylum. The Convention spells out what that right means for refugees and host nations, although its global application beyond Europe was not confirmed until the Protocol of 1967.

The keystone provision of the Convention, article 33, requires that host nations shall not send a person back to a territory that threatens his or her life or freedom unless that person is in some way a threat to the host nation.

Canada did not sign the Convention and Protocol until 1969. Compared to many nations, we were a foot dragger. We were the fifty-third nation to sign. Prior to 1969, Canada often assisted refugees but only through its regular immigration programs, or specific overseas humanitarian programs targeted to specific groups of refugees.

All of these humanitarian programs were distinctly different from the role Canada would have to play as a signatory to the Convention. They were singular overseas programs dealing with defined groups of refugees and, more importantly, there was no legal obligation on Canada to accept any refugee, no matter how desperate or destitute. The Canadian governments of the day, since 1951, had been reluctant to surrender that loss of control, to accept the obligation to receive any refugee who arrived on Canada's shores. It was seen as a surrender of a small portion of Canada's sovereignty, of the absolute right to say which non-citizens can or cannot enter Canada.

By signing the Convention and Protocol in 1969, Canada took on a different role, which was and is to grant protection to refugees who arrive at our borders. Unlike the overseas resettlement programs, Canada cannot set limits or quotas on the number of refugees it will accept within its borders. If a country is a signatory to the Convention, an asylum seeker cannot be turned away until their refugee claim is legally assessed, and, if they do have a fear of persecution in their own country, they cannot be sent back unless they are a danger to Canada or have themselves committed serious human rights violations.

As with the other Western nations, the chronic tensions that arise in Canadian refugee policy are invariably linked to the perception that globally there is an overwhelming number of refugees, and the uncomfortable reality that the government has no legal means of limiting the number of arrivals other than with visa barriers and off-shore interception.

Who Is a Refugee?

Most nations, including Canada, have adopted some variant of the refugee definition in the UN Refugee Convention which states that a refugee is

any person who ... owing to a well-founded fear of being
persecuted for reasons of race, religion, nationality, mem-
bership of a particular social group or political opinion, is
outside the country of his nationality and is unable or, owing
to such fear, is unwilling to avail himself of the protection of
that country.[1]

If you look carefully, you will see that the definition has certain
basic elements:

- Location: The refugee must be outside his or her country
  of nationality.
- Inability to return: The refugee must be unable or unwilling to
  return to her home country.
- Fear: The refugee must fear persecution, implicit in the notion
  of fear is that it is a threat of future harm. Refugee protection is
  not granted for past persecution but to avoid future persecution
  if the person were to return to her country.
- Well-founded: There must be an objective basis to the claimant's fear. In Canada, that means there is a reasonable possibil-
  ity that the refugee would be persecuted.
- Persecution: This is not defined, but is generally taken to be
  serious physical or psychological harm or a loss of fundamen-
  tal freedoms.
- Motive for the persecution: There must be a motive for the
  persecution. This eliminates certain kinds of harm such as
  flood, drought, general civil conflict, or indiscriminate criminality. The five motives listed are threats to a person's core identity
  and basic individual rights:
  - race
  - religion
  - nationality
  - particular social group (interpreted to include persecu-
    tion because of a person's gender, family identity, or
    sexual orientation)
  - political opinion

In addition, Canada has expanded refugee protection to include
"persons in need of protection," a second definition, even more complex

than the refugee definition. It is intended to cover off certain gaps in the refugee definition. To a large degree, the two definitions overlap and most successful asylum seekers are granted protection under the basic refugee definition.

Two Refugee Systems

Canada has two refugee systems, not one. There are two ways for refugees to obtain protection in Canada, through overseas resettlement or through Canada's inland claim system. The two systems are complementary and historically have admitted comparable numbers of refugees annually, each allowing in the range of twelve thousand refugees per year.

For overseas resettlement, the person is recognized to be a refugee while outside of Canada, often in a refugee camp, and is then brought to Canada as a permanent resident.

For the inland system, refugees arrive in Canada as asylum seekers and must first prove their refugee claim before they are allowed to apply for permanent residence within Canada.

Canada's dual system reflects the United Nations' basic structure of international refugee protection which allows refugees two routes to protection: in a refugee camp or in a host country. The international system recognizes that refugee camps are not always available or appropriate for all refugees. It is also a means of sharing the international asylum burden more equitably since a few countries unavoidably host the great majority of refugee camps.

Many host countries only allow refugees temporary residence but Canada, in its wisdom and generosity, allows refugees to apply for permanent residence. The *generosity* lies in Canada's concern that refugees, like all human beings, should be able to reunite with their families and get on with their lives. The *wisdom* lies in the understanding that refugees can make more positive contributions to Canada as fully accepted members of Canadian society, rather than as temporary immigrants with limited opportunities to study, earn a living, or become engaged members of their community.

Consequently, refugees are seen as and treated as immigrants. Through the two refugee programs combined, resettlement and inland claims, Canada historically has granted permanent residence to approximately 25,000 refugees per year, about 12 per cent of the annual immigration flow.

1: Outside Canada

Canada's resettlement program was implemented in 1979 but refugee resettlement has been a part of Canada's immigration history from the beginning of our nation-building enterprise.

In the late 1800s and into the next century, the Canadian government was eager to settle the West. Immigrants with agricultural skills and the hardiness to withstand prairie winters were in high demand. Land reserves were set aside for Mennonites, Russian Jews, and Icelanders, and all were accepted as immigrants but all were also fleeing some form of harm or oppression in their home country. In this context, the Mennonites were the largest of the early group resettlement programs. In 1871, the Mennonite communities of southern Russia were seeking new homes where they could practise their religion free from Czarist threats. Canada opened its doors offering land, loans, and promises of religious freedom. Tens of thousands came and proved to be remarkably successful farmers and citizens.

Smaller programs of Russian Jews fleeing pogroms and Icelanders escaping from volcanic devastation were also granted land reserves. Later still, there were Hutterites and Doukhobors. But there can be no pretense that these were primarily refugee resettlement programs. They were immigration programs to bolster Canada's economic and social goals. Religious persecution was the motive for flight, not the motive for acceptance. Canada was in competition for good, hardy farmers, particularly with the United States, which offered warmer climes but no promises of religious and educational freedom. Regardless of the government's motives, we can look back more than a hundred years later to see the many ways in which each one of these groups has successfully woven its way into the Canadian tapestry.

After the Second World War, there was pressure on all of the Western nations to accept displaced people and refugees who were still adrift in the wake of the European war or were caught in the grip of the Cold War between the West and the Soviet Union. Between 1946 and 1962, Canada accepted almost 250,000 refugees or displaced people through a hodge-podge of humanitarian programs. Non-state groups, notably organized church groups and private businesses, were directly involved in the selection of individual refugees. Most of the refugee assistance programs were motivated by a combination of humanitarian impulse, international burden sharing, domestic pressures from church and business groups, labour needs, and finally, national self-interest. Refugees were accepted on a priority basis but were subject to the same screening criteria as immigrants, which meant assessing refugees for their ability to successfully establish in Canada, not just for their protection needs. Their age, education, religion, health, and occupation were all factors to be considered.

For example, within one Canadian humanitarian program, 23,000 stateless persons were brought from Europe in the early 1950s. The primary motives for the program were humanitarian and political. Several years after the war, displaced persons were still trapped within post-war Europe with no civil status and no place to go. European governments with exhausted economies were preoccupied with the needs of their own citizenry and the enormous task of recovering from the war. They asked other countries, particularly former allies from the war, to assist, and Canada did.

At the same time, Canada was selective. These were boom years for immigration to Canada, but the Immigration Branch often imposed strict standards for refugees, primarily selecting those who were young, healthy, and skilled, again mixing the humanitarian with national self-interest. By contrast, church groups, who had a formal role to play in the selection of refugees, publically lobbied for those in the most desperate circumstances, including orphans, with less attention to employability.

Sadly, it was also an era when ethnicity was still an overt selection factor. By regulation, citizens of Anglophone and other Western European countries received preferred immigrant status, while the eligibility of immigrants from other continents, notably Asia and Africa, was strictly limited. In the same vein, restrictions were placed on the number of Jewish refugees, particularly those accepted through contract labour programs.

The outpouring of Hungarians after the Soviet invasion of 1956 was a notable example of Canadian refugee policy. Canada did step into the breach to assist when several European nations were not able to do so. At the same time, the Hungarians were seen as ideal immigrants for Canada; they were young, well educated, European, Roman Catholic, and assertively anti-communist.

In the early 1960s, although still not a signatory to the Refugee Convention, Canada strengthened its support for international refugee protection. In 1962, it introduced its first non-European humanitarian program, bringing one hundred Chinese refugee families from Hong Kong. By 1965, Canada had become the fourth largest contributor to the UNHCR budget.

In June, 1969, Canada finally signed the 1951 Refugee Convention and the Protocol, taking on the legal obligation to accept all refugees who arrive on its shores with a well-founded fear of persecution.

There was one other very important group of refugees from the 1960s and early 1970s who had no special program and were not even classified as refugees. During the Vietnam War, thousands of young Americans, draft dodgers and deserters, crossed into Canada. Estimates of their total number vary between seventeen thousand and sixty thousand. The numbers are not exact because they entered Canada as individual immigrants, most of them already college graduates. However, it is generally recognized that these young Americans have had a more profound influence on Canadian society than any other single group of asylum seekers.

In the 1970s, two refugee crises caused adverse reactions in Canadian refugee policy, one becoming a source of national pride and one a cause for regret. In 1972, when the Ugandan dictator Idi Amin gave Asian citizens of Uganda ninety days to leave, the British asked for help. Canada dispatched an immigration team to Uganda and in little over a year, processed seven thousand refugees and brought them to Canada.

The efficiency and compassion of government officials and volunteers is still spoken of in immigration circles. One of those refugees, Nurjehan Mawani, became the chairperson of the IRB in 1992.

Canada's reaction to the refugee crisis in Chile was less salutary. Despite the evidence of wide spread torture and executions after the 1973 coup, the Canadian government was slow to issue visas to Chilean refugees, allowing fewer than a thousand. It was clear that Canada's policy was coloured by political sympathies for the US-backed Pinochet government. After vigorous objections from opposition parties, labour unions, and church groups, the government relented and eventually admitted more than six thousand Chilean refugees.

A New Era

The *Immigration Act* of 1976 dramatically changed refugee law and policy in Canada. The Act laid the groundwork for our dual inland and overseas refugee system. Refugees were formally recognized as one of three principal immigration sources along with economic migrants and family members of Canadians. Finally, the law created a resettlement program that was unique among nations. Canada became the only nation that had two parallel sponsorship tracks, government assisted and private sponsors.

The genius of the Canadian system is that it creates a legal framework to harness the generosity of Canadians who wish to assist refugees while sustaining a government program to bring a predetermined number of refugees to Canada on an organized and predictable basis. As well, the Act allows room for the old system of creating special programs, called "designated classes," to respond to specific refugee crises. The system was flexible.

The new system was barely off the drawing boards when a refugee crisis arose to test it severely. In turn, that crisis, the flight of hundreds of thousands of Indochinese refugees in small boats from Vietnam, Laos, and Cambodia, led to the most brilliant and proud moment in the history of Canadian refugee law.

The government designated the Indochinese as a specific class and originally pledged to accept five thousand refugees. Shortly thereafter, a new Conservative government increased the number to twelve thousand, including three thousand private sponsorships. International and Canadian sympathies for the refugees, the "boat people," continued to grow. The government announced that it would sponsor one additional refugee for every private sponsorship. To the shock of the government, Canadians opened their homes, hearts, and wallets in numbers that no one had dreamed possible. Sponsorship groups popped up like mushrooms. The mayor of Ottawa, Marion Dewar, committed Ottawa residents to take ten thousand refugees. The government had to acknowledge that it could not keep up with the people of Canada, it could not match the number of private sponsorships. By 1980, more than sixty thousand refugees were resettled in Canada.

It was an auspicious beginning for the new overseas resettlement program and, although the program has never matched the extraordinary numbers of the Indochinese program, it has served as a vehicle for a steady annual flow of resettled refugees to Canada. On any given year, Canada is usually the second largest resettlement country after the United States.

Here is how the program works:

In all instances, refugees are assessed overseas. There is no legal obligation on Canada to resettle any refugee. In that sense, it is purely voluntary. If selected, refugees are brought to Canada and granted permanent residence upon arrival. Government assisted refugees (GARs) are directed to particular communities where they receive living expenses and various government support services such as language training and medical care for one year while they adapt to their new country.

The unique aspect of Canada's system is the private sponsorship track. Groups like churches, humanitarian organizations, and other private citizen groups can sponsor resettled refugees and support them for one year. Members of the sponsorship group personally assist in the thousand small daily challenges and mysteries that confront new arrivals.

Lifelong friendships between sponsors and refugees are a common consequence of a year of shared struggle and learning. A refugee's lack of cultural knowledge can occasionally lead to humour as well as tension and frustration. A typical story is that of the Somali mother who, never having seen snow, faithfully bought boots and snow suits for her daughters and sent them to school well prepared on their first snowy day in Canada. At school, her children were surprised to see the other students remove their snow suits to reveal a second set of clothes.

The positive aspects of the private sponsorship program are admirable. It provides a vehicle for the generosity of Canadians, individuals and organizations, who have the time, energy, money, and aspiration to assist some of the world's most dispossessed and vulnerable people.

However, it is not all smooth sailing—there are tensions in the program, particularly in recent years. Long delays in processing files, on average five years, have sapped the morale of sponsorship groups. In concert with its criticisms of Canada's inland program, the government has touted overseas resettlement as the only legitimate form of refugee protection, a serious misrepresentation of the UN system of protection founded on the twin pillars of individual refugee claims in host countries and overseas resettlement. But the government has persisted in trading off one program against the other.

As part of its justification for reducing access to Canada's inland system, the government has promised increases in overseas resettlement. The government has portrayed itself as being more generous to "real refugees" who reside in refugee camps, but most of the announced increases have been made to the private sponsorship program. A notable example would be the resettlement of Syrian refugees. In 2014, the government set a resettlement target of 1,300 Syrian refugees, but 1,100 would be privately sponsored. Only 200 would be government sponsored. Using the resettlement program and private sponsorship as a misleading justification for the harsh treatment of in-Canada claimants has left many private sponsors with a bitter taste in their mouth.

From a more positive view, the framework of Canada's resettlement program is still in place. There are hundreds of potential sponsors across the country who are available to respond to the needs of millions of refugees trapped in camps or in vulnerable situations with little hope of safely returning to their countries.

2: Inside Canada
Deciding Refugee Claims: The Refugee Dilemma

In Canada, refugee claims are decided by a member of the IRB. The IRB hearing room is a crucible where life and death decisions are made every day. The challenge for the IRB is to make thousands of decisions—about 25,000 per year—that are consistent and accurate. The refugee has the obligation to prove her claim, to provide the evidence for why she is a refugee. The board member has a corresponding obligation to make an accurate and reasoned decision based on the evidence and the law.

In most instances, the gap between the experience of the refugee claimant and the perceptions of the decision maker, framed in the expectations of Canadian refugee law, is enormous. They both confront the same gap in understanding the perspective of the other, and there are many reasons why the gap is so wide:

- Persecution often occurs in remote or violent regions of the world. It is difficult to find the specific evidence to prove or disprove an individual claim.
- Refugees are not good witnesses. They are often frightened and confused and have trouble telling their own story.
- Extreme trauma causes testimony about violent events to be inherently unreliable.
- Most claimants testify in their own language. Imprecise interpretation easily leads to misunderstanding. It becomes a game of broken telephone.
- Cultural differences between the member and the claimant are often profound. It is difficult for the member to assess whether the claimant's conduct and motives are reasonable or credible, particularly during times of war or social collapse.

Inevitably narratives of refugees contain inconsistencies and incongruities. They can also contain daring falsehoods and shocking truths. Understanding the testimony of refugees takes great patience and skill. Most claims require articulate and sensitive questioning and excellent listening skills. Good decisions require clear legal reasoning and the ability to see the world from radically different cultural and individual perspectives. At end of the day, the refugee claimant must prove her claim but it is the decision maker, the board member, who must bridge the gap, who must find the means to ensure that the refugee has a fair opportunity to tell her story before a decision is made.

The Evolving Immigration and Refugee Board
The modern era of refugee law in Canada begins with the *Singh* decision in 1985, which stated that refugees, since their life, liberty, and security were at risk, were entitled to receive a fair evaluation of their claim consistent with the Canadian Charter of Rights and Freedoms.

In 1989, in response to that decision, the government established the Immigration and Refugee Board (IRB).

The new board set a high international standard for refugee decision making. The claimant had a right to a lawyer and an interpreter. The hearing was non-adversarial and emphasized fair procedures. Any negative decision had to be justified by written reasons that were subject to appeal before the Federal Court of Appeal.

Most importantly, two board members would hear and decide every claim. If there were a difference of opinion between the two members about the final outcome, the positive decision would prevail. It was a generous system that recognized the essential challenge of refugee decision making: that refugee claims were life or death decisions and refugee claimants needed time and help in proving their claims.

Canada was also generous in other aspects of refugee care and treatment. Eligible claimants could receive provincial social assistance, federal medical assistance, primary and secondary education, and could seek employment. In addition, rejected claimants were permitted to apply for permanent residence based on humanitarian reasons before being removed from Canada.

Within a few years, the IRB had established an international reputation for sound country research, fair procedures, and articulate decisions. The board developed the world's first guidelines on gender claims. The UNHCR frequently cited IRB procedures as a model for new refugee claim systems and used its excellent training materials throughout the world.

In turn, the Federal Court of Appeal developed a thoughtful and progressive jurisprudence that was widely quoted in other jurisdictions. A Canadian academic and occasional advisor to the board, James Hathaway, wrote a seminal text on refugee law that influenced a generation of refugee lawyers and judges throughout the world. By the mid-1990s, Canada was seen as a progressive and positive force for the international protection of refugees.

Although Canada's system was admired around the world, there were critics from both sides of the refugee debate within Canada. Conservative critics said the system was too generous, the board's acceptance rates were too high, refugees were given too many chances, the claim and removal processes were inefficient and too slow. The combination of high acceptance rates and slow removal attracted fraudulent refugees who took advantage of the system.

Refugee advocates said board decisions were too inconsistent due to the incompetence of some board members, the result of an appointment system where political patronage too often trumped merit. After 1993, there was no longer an appeal to catch board errors. A very limited judicial review by the Federal Court was deemed ineffective.

There were other problems too. Both sides of the debate agreed that the entire claim process was too slow: Claimants had to wait more than a year for a hearing. The removal of refused claimants could be delayed for years while they sought humanitarian relief. Some critics said long delays were a draw factor attracting fraudulent claimants from around the world. Refugee advocates said refugees needed prompt decisions to remove uncertainty and to get on with their lives. Delays resulted in years of family separation. Nobody was happy.

In 2001, the government introduced the *Immigration and Refugee Protection Act* (IRPA). The new law was intended to address all of the principal complaints: inefficiency, slow claim processes, lack of an appeal, delayed removal. From both sides of the equation, fast versus fair, the new system was considered to be either a partial success or a resounding failure.

In the first years of the new system, using one board member instead of two, the board was able to reduce the claim backlog, partially because claims had fallen to twenty thousand claims per year. Complaints about inconsistent decisions increased. There were extraordinary variances between the acceptance rates of individual board members that spoke of arbitrariness, incompetence, or bias. It is a terrifying notion for a claimant fearing persecution that her fate could be arbitrarily decided by the good or bad luck of which member would be assigned to the claim.

The new law also required a risk assessment before deporting a refused claimant who could also apply to remain in Canada for humanitarian reasons. With these additional steps, the removal process soon bogged down, causing three to four year delays before deportation. At the same time, anecdotally, many refugee lawyers will say that positive humanitarian decisions saved refugees who had been wrongfully denied years before.

The net result was a system that was not fast and not particularly fair.

Refugees and National Security

The IRPA passed through the House of Commons in May 2001. On September 11, 2001, a seismic event transformed global politics and radically shifted government attitudes toward refugees. Suddenly there was a third element to the fast/fair equation, namely, security.

False rumours about the World Trade Center terrorists coming from Canada drove the winds of hysteria around refugees and national security. The story of Ahmed Ressam, a refused refugee claimant from Canada who attempted to enter the United States in 1999 to commit terrorist acts, was endlessly repeated in the media on both sides of the US/Canada border. Long after the rumours were dispelled, refugees, especially undocumented refugees, were still seen as a potential danger to Canadian and US security even though they would be photographed, finger-printed, and interviewed, a far more intense level of scrutiny than foreign visitors or student visa holders. For refugees, borders tightened around the world, visa barriers were raised even higher, and refugee flows to Canada dropped precipitously.

Security provisions within the immigration law were also tightened. The government already had the power to deny access to Canada to claimants who committed serious crimes abroad, but the definition of serious crime was greatly expanded. As well, claimants with ludicrously remote associations with militant and terrorist groups were being labelled terrorists and deported with no opportunity to make a refugee claim.

In 2004, Canada closed another asylum door by signing the Safe Third Country Agreement (STCA) with the United States as part of a pact that both facilitated and tightened cross-border movements. Under the agreement, with some exceptions, refugee claimants arriving at a Canada-US border crossing would be turned back to have their claims decided in the United States.

In 2006, a newly elected Conservative government declined to reappoint many Liberal appointees to the board as their mandates expired, regardless of their evaluated work performance. Within eighteen months the productivity of the board dropped sharply, just as the number of refugee claims began to increase. A new backlog of refugee claims soon developed and, once again, there were delays in deciding claims as well as long delays in removing failed claimants.

The federal government's attitude toward refugees had clearly shifted and was expressed through a powerful new anti-refugee rhetoric. The themes were familiar: delays were caused by too many fraudulent claimants; Canada was flooded with bogus refugees here for jobs, welfare, and health benefits; fraudulent claimants were taking advantage of the Canadian taxpayer; real refugees went to refugee camps, they did not come halfway round the world to Canada.

The key messages were familiar but they were delivered in a new and focused manner, more typical of a public relations campaign than a government policy. Public statements were coded with negative colour words, repeated endlessly, and frequently distorted: *bogus refugee* was used in reference to any refused claim although many refused claimants, too, had come to Canada with a sincere desire for protection.

Refugees without legal identity documents were portrayed as implicitly fraudulent, even though refugees historically had often been forced to use false documents. The government ignored the obvious: the raising of visa barriers inevitably drove desperate refugees into the arms of smugglers as their only means of reaching distant countries of protection. Claimants arriving in boats were associated with terrorists, smugglers, and organized criminals regardless of circumstance.

Government leaders publicly alleged that claims from particular nationalities, notably Mexican and Hungarian Roma claimants, were without merit, even though a significant number of Mexican and Hungarian claims were being accepted by the board. This aggressive government posture vis-à-vis the legally independent IRB was unprecedented in Canadian legal history. Any third year law student could understand that a government minister responsible for the reappointment of independent board members should not publicly pronounce on the outcome of particular refugee decisions.

It must be said that the government's anti-refugee campaign was successful. Canadians by and large believed that there was a serious refugee problem and that the government had the solutions. Those solutions took the form of three different bills before Parliament. The *Preventing Human Smugglers from Abusing Canada's Immigration System Act*, was a draconian attempt to solve the manufactured "crisis" of two Sri Lankan refugee boat arrivals on the west coast of Canada in 2009 and 2010. In fact, the total number of arrivals, slightly more than six hundred, represented about 2 per cent of annual refugee claims. The bill included a shocking proposal to put all mass arrival refugees—man, woman, and child—in prison for one year. After creating a brief public storm, the bill was allowed to die a quiet death.

The *Balanced Refugee Reform Act* passed in 2009, after many of its harshest provisions were softened at the insistence of the opposition, which controlled the parliamentary majority. Most of the principal changes to the inland refugee system were never implemented. In the two year interim before implementation, the government won a majority at the polls and promptly introduced a much tougher law, Bill C-31, the *Protecting Canada's Immigration System Act*.

Using its parliamentary majority, the government reasserted its previous stance that Canada was being deluged by bogus claimants who abused our asylum system and cost Canadian taxpayers. They took their argument a few steps further:

- Refugees who came from secondary countries such as Sri Lankans from Thailand were "queue-jumpers" and should be deterred. Arguments that Thailand was not a signatory to the Convention, that no refugee camps were accessible, and they could be arbitrarily deported back to Sri Lanka fell on deaf ears.
- Long-term detention and family separation were deemed appropriate deterrents for refugees arriving in groups, even if they had suffered persecution.
- After being accepted as a refugee and becoming a permanent resident in Canada, any refugee who returned to their previous country for any reason, no matter how compelling, was assumed to be fraudulent.

Despite vigorous objections in the House of Commons and before parliamentary committees, the government steamrollered the bill through Parliament. The new refugee system was implemented in December 2012.

Canada's New Refugee System
At first glance, the structure of the new system appears reasonable. The basic stages of the claim process are as follows:

- Eligibility assessment by an immigration officer
- A hearing before the IRB
- An appeal to a new Refugee Appeal Division (only for some claimants)
- Leave for judicial review to the Federal Court
- Prompt removal if refused by the Federal Court

- No pre-removal risk assessment (for one year)
- No humanitarian application (for one year)

If the structure is reasonable, why are advocates so opposed to the new system? There are four principal reasons:

1. Claimants do not have enough time or resources to prove their claim within unreasonably short time limits or, for those refused, enough time to realistically mount an effective appeal.
2. Some claimants, about 40 per cent, are arbitrarily grouped into one of six categories that give them even less time to prove their claim and no opportunity to appeal a negative decision.
3. The removal process for failed claimants is too quick with little allowance for humanitarian exceptions.
4. Refugee protection is no longer reliable. Although granted refugee protection and permanent residence, refugees may still be threatened with deportation.

On point two, of the six categories of refugees who will be given even less time and opportunity to prove their claim there are two principal categories:

Designated Countries of Origin (DCO): These are countries the minister of Citizenship and Immigration, somewhat arbitrarily, decides are safe. So-called safe countries are not always safe for everyone. Many citizens may still be refugees. The criteria for designation are vague; there is no means to appeal a designation; there is no process for the minister to rescind a designation when country conditions have changed.

Designated Foreign Nationals (DFN): These are claimants the government arbitrarily decides have come to Canada as part of a group arrival. Members of the "group" may not know each other and may not even arrive at the same time. They can be automatically detained for two weeks, and potentially, for up to one year if over age fifteen. Their claim may be decided while in prison and they have no right of appeal. Even if accepted as a refugee, they cannot apply for permanent residence for five years, one consequence being they cannot sponsor family members for six to seven years. That is a very serious consequence since refugee families abroad are often in danger.

On point four, a new procedure—cessation—seriously undermines the stability of refugee protection. Even if a person is accepted as a refugee and then becomes a permanent resident of Canada, the government can strip that person of their permanent residence and refugee status if they return to their home country or even apply for a national passport of that country. Presumably the provision is intended to counter refugee fraud, but it takes no account of refugee realities, such as the willingness to risk travelling back home to help in situations of severe illness or death of a family member. Similarly, a refugee may need a passport to assist a family member in a third country. There is also no time limit; a refugee is vulnerable to cessation up until being granted Canadian citizenship many years later.

Would They Get In Today?

The government has not slammed the door shut on refugees but it has certainly wedged the door partly closed. The government's justifications for doing so always return to the same theme—fraudulent refugees, people who are scamming the asylum system. The government believes that using fraudulent travel documents, giving inaccurate or false information at border points, delaying escape from the homeland, delaying making a refugee claim, and returning to the homeland are all marks of a fraudulent claim. This is a fundamentally flawed understanding of the refugee experience. Refugees are driven by desperation, fear, and confusion about leaving their country that is dangerous, but still home. Seeking asylum is not a careful, rational process.

Refugees are often inconsistent in their motivations and actions. They love their homeland and are reluctant to leave. Once they do leave, they become vulnerable, fearful, and desperate to find safety. Much of the conduct that the government distrusts is exactly what the refugees in this book were compelled to do to reach safety in Canada. It invites the question, would they get into Canada today?

In 2013, for both its resettlement and inland programs combined, Canada accepted fewer refugees than at any other time in the past twenty-five years. Despite promises to increase numbers, the resettlement program has stagnated below its own limited goals, taking in approximately 12,400 refugees. The inland program declined more dramatically. The refugee acceptance rate at the IRB fell to 34 per cent, the lowest in the board's history, though it rose again in 2014. The number of annual refugee claims fell to just over 10,000 claims, by far the lowest number of claims since the formation of the IRB in 1989. The historical average has been about 25,000 claims per year.

There is no way of knowing how many legitimate refugees have already been deported or how many refugees went elsewhere, no longer confident of receiving protection in Canada. Many of the more unjust elements of the new system are being challenged in the courts, both on grounds of being a breach of the Canadian Charter as well as violations of basic principles of fairness, but it will be years before the higher courts will be able to sort out what is fair and what is not. Whatever the eventual outcome of those decisions, the courts will not be able to provide a solution for those refugees already deported or denied access to Canada. Nor will they be able to compensate refugees who have suffered years of unnecessary family separation. Individual lives will be lost or damaged and, in most instances, we will never hear about it.

So the title question is an important one: Among the people whose stories are told in this book, *who would get in today*? It is a hypothetical question and there are no definitive answers but educated guesses can be made.

Assuming similar conditions in their countries today, some of the refugees who came through emergency resettlement programs, such as the Vietnamese, Hungarian, and Ugandan programs, would not have made it to Canada under our current resettlement program. Those early programs were managed with a swift practicality and accepted many thousands of refugees within a very short period of time. By contrast, in 2014, during the world's largest humanitarian crisis surrounding Syria, Canada offered to resettle a paltry 1,300 Syrian refugees, and only 200 of those were government assisted refugees, the rest were passed on to private sponsors. (By comparison, the Swedes and Germans took 20,000 and 30,000 Syrian refugees respectively.) Worse yet, only about half of the 1,300 arrived in Canada by the end of the year. In 2015, the government announced it would resettle 10,000 Syrians over three years. Of this, 60 per cent would be privately sponsored and 40 per cent assisted by the government, or around 1,300 per year. On that standard, Andrew Hidi (Hungary), Karim Teja (Uganda), Ken Do (Vietnam), Chai Bouphaphanh (Laos), and Samnang Eam (Cambodia) would never have reached Canada or their arrival would have been delayed by years.

The fate of privately sponsored refugees is even less certain. A 50 per cent refusal rate by visa officers overseas would be a formidable hurdle. Even though their country may be in flames, their individual circumstances would now be scrutinized far more closely than before. Unless they are very fortunate like Humaira from Afghanistan, there will be no lawyer to challenge the visa officer's decision in Canadian courts. Even if accepted into the program, their arrival would be delayed for four or five years.

For refugees outside of their country but not in refugee camps, their situation would be even more desperate. Anwar Arkani (Myanmar), Loly Rico (El Salvador), and Marguerite Nyandwi (Burundi) would all confront the government's deep distrust of secondary asylum even though they were trapped in foreign countries without any legal protection.

Those seeking refuge in Canada will have even greater problems. The visa barriers around Canada are so impregnable that almost every one of the refugees in this book who claimed refugee protection within the country, would now have to use false or fraudulent documents to reach Canada. And for having done that, no matter how desperate their situation, they would be under suspicion. In both Canadian and international law, refugees are permitted to use false documents to flee their country. It is part and parcel of being a refugee, particularly where the persecutor is the claimant's own government. But in Canada, the government has turned that logic on its head. For coming to Canada with false documents, the claimant is under a cloud of suspicion.

At this point, the reasons for the lower acceptance rate at the IRB are unknown. The faster claim process may or may not be a cause. The system is too new for reliable data. The competence of the new board members does not appear to be a negative factor.

We do know that anyone from Hungary would be in serious trouble. Robi Botos is from a DCO country. Consequently, he would have only thirty days to prepare for his hearing after submitting his claim form. He would likely not qualify for a legal aid lawyer, he would have trouble collecting all the important evidence in time, and he would not have an appeal. Robi would have been deported before he was allowed to make a humanitarian application to remain in Canada. He may not even have attempted to come to Canada. Refugees will risk their lives and savings for a chance at protection for themselves and their families but they won't take the risk if they don't believe there is a reasonable chance of acceptance.

Sabreen, the young Bedouin woman, is from Israel, also a DCO country. She would not have had time to obtain and present the psychological reports that were so important for her claim. She would not have received medical care for her psychological trauma. She was initially refused and would not be allowed to appeal. She almost certainly would have been sent back to face death in Israel at the hands of her relatives.

None of the refugee claimants would receive basic medical care unless it was a medical emergency. For the refugees in the DCO category, no medical care would be provided by the federal government unless their illness, such as tuberculosis or HIV/AIDS, could harm Canadians. If they have cancer, diabetes, physical or psychological injuries from torture—too bad, no medical care. If they are fortunate enough to live in Ontario or Quebec, the provincial government will pay for some medical care but not necessarily medication or therapy. In other provinces, for very serious medical problems, volunteer clinics and medical staff may provide care.

Then there is Avtar Sandhu, who arrived by boat in 1987. He and everyone on the boat would be designated as a group arrival. He would be automatically detained for two weeks. If he did not have or could not get his identity documents within the two weeks, he would be imprisoned for another six months with no review of his detention, even if he did finally get his identity documents. He would be transferred to an overcrowded medium security prison. Canadian prisons are designed to manage criminals, and he would be treated in a similar manner. If he was at risk of physical harm because of his colour, race, religion, or inability to speak English, he would be placed in solitary confinement as a means of protection.

He would have to prove his refugee claim while in prison with limited access to a lawyer or interpreter. For his hearing, he would testify from prison to a board member via video-conference. If by some miracle, he was accepted as a refugee, he would not be allowed to apply for permanent residence for five years. His wife and two children were still in India. He could not begin to sponsor them for five years. It would be another six or seven years before he would actually see them.

For many of the other refugees, although the new system would not specifically limit their possibilities, their conduct would place them

246 FLIGHT AND FREEDOM

under greater scrutiny, for example, Elvis and Shabnam, who delayed their escapes from Namibia and Afghanistan. More than half the refugees in this book returned to their homeland, some to visit family, some to help with the recovery of their country. If any of them did so prior to receiving their Canadian citizenship, they would be at risk of a cessation application to remove their refugee status and permanent residence, and then be deported from Canada.

And lastly there is Max Farber, the Jewish man who needed a thousand miracles to survive the Holocaust, and then one additional lie to escape a camp in post-Holocaust Germany by posing as the brother of Richard Small, who had family in Canada. In the eyes of the government, a lie about family identity is totally unacceptable and grounds for a complete refusal, regardless of circumstances. Hundreds of sponsored refugees, such as Somali refugees in hellhole camps like Dadaab in Kenya, have been delayed for years because of their inability to prove the identity of some of their children. Often an expensive DNA test is demanded as a prerequisite. Sometimes a child is exposed as a niece or a nephew, someone still in need of protection but outside the family relation. In the eyes of the refugees, just as with Max, a meaningless distinction, in the face of unending destitution and the hope of a better life in Canada.

For each individual refugee in this book, the answer to the question "Would they get in now?" is "maybe." For the entire group of thirty, the answer is "some yes, some no." The doors have half closed. Today, some of these remarkable individuals would not make it to Canada. A tragedy for them and a loss for Canada.

The Bitter End

A chapter on Canadian refugee policy should not end with a bitter aftertaste. Canada and Canadians have been a positive voice for the protection of refugees in the world, partially because we remember that we are, apart from First Nations peoples, a country of immigrants. In contrast to polls in every other Western country, Canadians have traditionally held a positive view of refugees as well as immigrants. Those positive views have declined in the past few years in step with negative government messages, but Canadians still hold strong humanitarian views toward the dispossessed and disenfranchised.

One consequence of writing about refugee protection is the unavoidable emphasis on the refugees' persecution and need for protection. The full picture of refugees is inadvertently ignored, for refugees are far more than people in need of protection. They are also immigrants and form part of the national fabric. Approximately 12 per cent of all immigrants to Canada are refugees. As the stories in this book reaffirm, refugees are survivors. They are uprooted from homes, families, and countries but they survive through fortitude, resilience, and courage and they bring those qualities with them to their new country.

As well, many refugees have a deep and personal appreciation for the country that gave them protection, granting them freedoms and opportunities that were denied in their own countries.

Despite all the exceptions cited above, Canada has been a generous country toward refugees. At the same time, we have benefitted tremendously from the contributions of refugees to the Canadian story. As those who have worked in refugee programs will attest, and hopefully, all Canadians will come to understand, there are two general truths about refugees that are worth remembering:

Generosity is its own reward: the thankfulness of refugees who have received protection in Canada, through both resettlement and inland programs, is often palpable and profound.

Because of their deep appreciation for their adopted country and because of their own inner strengths, many refugees make exceptional contributions to their communities and to their fellow Canadians.

The people that you meet in this book are wonderful examples of both of these truths.

Notes

Introduction

1   Isabel Kaprielian-Churchill, "Armenian Refugees and Their Entry into Canada, 1919–30," *Canadian Historical Review* 71, no. 1 (1990): 85.

2   Citizenship and Immigration Canada, "Summative Evaluation of the Private Sponsorship of Refugees Program: Final Report," April 2007, www.cic.gc.ca/english/resources/evaluation/psrp/psrp-summary.asp.

1 Adeline Oliver, United States

1   Biographical information on Adeline Oliver and her husband, Moses Oliver, is drawn from two sources unless otherwise indicated: Monica MacDonald, "The Black Refugees of the War of 1812: Moses, Adeline, and Laura Oliver," Parks Canada, July 2, 2012; and "Archives of Maryland (Biographical Series): Adeline Oliver, MSA SC 5496-51390," Maryland State Archives, www.msa.maryland.gov/megafile/msa/speccol/sc5400/sc5496/051300/051390/html/51390bio.html.

2   Government of Nova Scotia, "Black Refugees, 1813–1834," http://novascotia.ca/archives/virtual/africanns/results.asp?Search=&SearchList1=4&Language=English.

3   Ibid.

4   Ibid.

5   Angella MacEwen with Christine Saulnier, "The Cost of Poverty in Nova Scotia," Canadian Centre for Policy Alternatives, October 2010, 21; Les Perreaux, "Racism's Long History in Quiet East Coast Towns," *Globe and Mail*, May 21, 2010.

2 Mampre Shirinian, Ottoman Empire

1   The Ottoman Empire became the Republic of Turkey in 1923.

2   John Kifner, "Armenian Genocide of 1915: An Overview," Times Topics, *New York Times*, http://www.nytimes.com/ref/timestopics/topics_armeniangenocide.html.

3   Samantha Power, *A Problem from Hell: America and the Age of Genocide* (New York: Perennial HarperCollins, 2003), 2.

4   Estimates vary widely. See, Martin Gilbert, *The First World War: A Complete History* (New York: Henry Holt, 1994), 167; or Robert E. Melson, *Revolution and Genocide: On the Origins of the Armenian Genocide and the Holocaust* (Chicago: University of Chicago Press, 1992), 147.

5   Jack Apramian, *The Georgetown Boys* (Toronto: Zoryan Institute, 2009), xxxiv.

6   Isabel Kaprielian-Churchill, "Armenian Refugees and Their Entry into Canada, 1919–30," *Canadian Historical Review* 71, no. 1 (1990): 85.

7   The Government of Canada contributed $25,000 to the project, while the majority of the funds needed to purchase the farm land and run the settlement program were raised by private donations from Canadians. The Armenian Relief Association of Canada was created in 1917 and led the effort to resettle Armenian orphans in Canada. Management of the farm transferred to the United Church at the end of 1927.

8   Mampre's proposed English name could not be found at the time of writing.

9   Apramian, *The Georgetown Boys*, 76.

10   Mehmet Ali Birand, "We Are Surrendering Ourselves to 'Genocide,'" *Hurriyet*, April 24, 2012.

3 Loly Rico, El Salvador

1   Carmen Diana Deere and Marin Diskin, "Rural Poverty in El Salvador: Dimensions, Trends and Causes," World Employment Programme Research, Working Paper, WEP 10-6/WP64, 8, www.ilo.org/public/libdoc/ilo/1984/84B09_41_engl.pdf.

2   "El Salvador Profile," BBC, March 18, 2014.

3   Julian Miglierini, "El Salvador Marks Archbishop Oscar Romero's Murder," BBC, March 24, 2010.

4   Mike Allison, "El Salvador's Brutal Civil War: What We Still Don't Know," *Al Jazeera*, March 1, 2012.

5   UN Human Rights Council, "Report of the Working Group on Enforced or Involuntary Disappearances: Addendum: Mission to El Salvador," October 26, 2007, A/HRC/7/2/Add.2, 9, www.refworld.org/docid/478788322.html.

4 Ken (Khanh) Do, Vietnam

1   United Nations High Commissioner for Refugees, *The State of the World's Refugees 2000: Fifty Years of Humanitarian Action* (New York: Oxford University Press, 2000), 82.

2   UNHCR, *The State of the World's Refugees*, 84.

3   Valerie Knowles, Forging Our Legacy: Canadian Citizenship and Immigration 1900–1977 (Ottawa: Public Works and Government Services Canada, 2000), www.cic.gc.ca/english/resources/publications/legacy/chap-6a.asp#chap6-16.

5 Hodan Ali, Somalia

1   World Health Organization, Malaria Fact Sheet N. 94, March 2014, www.who.int/mediacentre/factsheets/fs094/en/.

6 Claudio Durán, Chile

The opening epigraph can be found in Claudio Durán, *Childhood and Exile*, trans. Francisca Durán (Ottawa: Split Quotation, 2008), 3.

1 A common joke among left-wingers held that any Chilean caught with art literature, specifically books on cubism, would be arrested because thick-headed police thought their contents were about the revolutionary country Cuba, and not the movement of Pablo Picasso.

2 Katherine Hite, "Chile's National Stadium: As Monument, As Memorial," *ReVista Harvard Review of Latin America* (Spring 2004), www.revista.drclas.harvard.edu/book/chiles-national-stadium.

3 Christopher Hitchens, *The Trial of Henry Kissinger* (Toronto: McClelland and Stewart, 2012), 85–96.

4 Valerie Knowles, *Forging Our Legacy: Canadian Citizenship and Immigration 1900–1977* (Ottawa: Public Works and Government Services Canada, 2000), www.cic.gc.ca/English/resources/publications/legacy/chap-6a.asp#chap6-15.

5 Quoted in, Ninette Kelley and Michael Trebilcock, *The Making of the Mosaic: A History of Canadian Immigration Policy*, 2nd ed. (Toronto: University of Toronto Press, 2000), 368.

6 Citizenship and Immigration Canada, "Canada: A History of Refuge," last modified October 10, 2012, www.cic.gc.ca/english/games/teachers-corner/refugee/refuge.asp.

7 On October 16, 1970, the Cabinet of Prime Minister Pierre Elliott Trudeau requested the Governor General to invoke the *War Measures Act*, granting extraordinary powers to the police. At the same time, Canadian Forces deployed at the request of the Quebec provincial government. These acts occurred following kidnappings by the Front de libération du Québec (FLQ).

8 Durán, *Childhood and Exile*, 69.

9 Ibid., 25.

7 Rabbi Erwin Schild, Germany

1 Stephen Evans, "Kristallnacht 75 Years On: How Strong Is Anti-Semitism in Germany?" BBC, November 7, 2013.

2 Erwin Schild, *The Very Narrow Bridge: Memoir of an Uncertain Passage* (Toronto: Adath Israel Congregation/Malcolm Lester, 2001), 170. Erwin also published his experiences in Erwin Schild, *World through My Window* (Toronto: Adath Israel Congregation, 1992).

3 Erwin Schild, "A Canadian Footnote to the Holocaust," unpublished, 5.

4 For a comprehensive history of this period see, Paula Draper, "The Accidental Immigrants: Canada and the Interned Refugees" (PhD thesis, University of Toronto: 1983).

5   Until 1947 when the *Canadian Citizenship Act* came into effect, Canadians
    were defined as British subjects and were governed by the *British Nationality
    and Status of Aliens Act* of 1914. Under the British law, one of the conditions
    for losing citizenship was to marry a non-British subject.

8 Randy Singh, Guyana

1   In religious texts, Sodom and Gomorrah are ancient cities that were destroyed
    by God. They are invoked as examples of divine punishment for homosexual-
    ity, among other so-called vices.
2   *Criminal Law (Offences) Act*, Guyana. L.R.O. 3/1998, Section 354,
    www.oas.org/juridico/mla/en/guy/en_guy-int-text-cl_act.pdf.
3   As of June 2012. See, Citizenship and Immigration Canada, "Backgrounder—
    Summary of Changes to Canada's Refugee System," www.cic.gc.ca/english/
    department/media/backgrounders/2012/2012-06-29b.asp.
4   For insight on the difficult job of an IRB judge see, Peter Showler, *Refugee
    Sandwich* (McGill-Queen's University Press, 2006).
5   Randy received his study and work permits in April 2014 and began part-time
    work in a restaurant. He was to begin a PSW (personal support worker)
    program at City Adult Learning Centre in September 2014.

9 Marguerite Nyandwi, Burundi

1   Philip Gourevitch, *We Wish to Inform You That Tomorrow We Will be Killed
    With Our Families* (Farrar, Straus and Giroux: New York, 1998), 67.
2   "Burundi profile," BBC, last updated March 22, 2014.
3   Immigration and Refugee Board of Canada, "Burundi: Forced Recruitment of
    Females of Hutu Origin by Hutu Militia Groups," September 25, 2002,
    BDI39963.E, www.refworld.org/docid/3f7d4d581f.html.
4   Elizabeth Campbell, Jeff Crisp, and Esther Kiragu, "Navigating Nairobi: A
    Review of the Implementation of UNHCR's Urban Refugee Policy in Kenya's
    Capital City," UNHCR, January 2011, www.unhcr.org/4d5511209.pdf.

10 Andrew Hidi, Hungary

1   Ben Richardson, "Hungary's 1956 Brain Drain," BBC, October 23, 2006.
2   Victor Sebestyen, "Laying Claim to Hungary's 1956 Revolution," BBC, January
    28, 2006.
3   Citizenship and Immigration Canada, "Canada: A History of Refuge," last
    modified December 10, 2012, www.cic.gc.ca/english/refugees/timeline.asp.

12 Tarun, Sri Lanka

1   Name changed to protect identity.
2   Melinda Henneberger, "Waiting, Waiting and Dreaming of Canada; At a
    Shelter in Buffalo, Hundreds of Asylum Seekers Sit Out Their Appeals," *New
    York Times*, August 2, 1993.

3   Colum Lynch, "U.N.: Sri Lanka's Crushing of Tamil Tigers May Have Killed 40,000 Civilians," *Washington Post*, April 21, 2011.

13 Yodit Negusse, Ethiopia

1   Human Rights Watch, "Ethiopia Reckoning under the Law," December 1994, vol. 6, no. 11, www.hrw.org/reports/pdfs/e/ethiopia/ethiopia94d.pdf, 7.
2   "Africa's Horn of Famine," *Economist*, November 14, 2002.
3   "Remembering Ethiopia's Famine 30 Years On," BBC, October 23, 2014.

14 Chairuth (Chai) Bouphaphanh, Laos

1   John Hart Ely, *War and Responsibility: Constitutional Lessons of Vietnam and Its Aftermath* (New Jersey: Princeton University Press, 1993), 72.
2   Mining Advisory Group, "The UXO Problem in Laos: Statistics," www.maginternational.org/the-problems/the-uxo-problem-in-laos-statistics/#.UtgpkdJDvCk.
3   William M. Leary, "CIA Air Operations in Laos, 1955–1974," April 14, 2007, Center for the Study of Intelligence, Central Intelligence Agency, https://www.cia.gov/library/center-for-the-study-of-intelligence/csi-publications/csi-studies/studies/winter99-00/art7.html.
4   Gladys Terichow, "For Lao Refugee, Passion for Photography Began in Small-Town Saskatchewan," *Canadian Mennonite* 14, no. 12 (June 14, 2010): 8–9, http://legacy.canadianmennonite.org/vol14-2010/14-12/14-12small_588_2010-06-14.pdf.

15 Zafar Iravan, Iran

1   "U.S. Asserts 8 Bahai Leaders Have Been Executed in Iran," *Associated Press*, December 31, 1981.
2   Alan Wain, "Fear for Families in Iran Say Oshawa Baha'is," *Oshawa This Weekend*, May 7, 1983.
3   Geoffrey Cameron, "A Quiet Exodus," *Literary Review of Canada*, (July–August 2013).
4   Ibid.
5   Ibid.

16 Samnang Eam, Cambodia

1   Dan Fletcher, "The Khmer Rouge," *Time*, February 17, 2009.
2   Thailand is not party to the UN Refugee Convention, which forbids the return, or *refoulement*, of refugees. See, UN General Assembly, Convention Relating to the Status of Refugees, July 28, 1951, United Nations, Treaty Series, vol. 189, article 33.

17 Marko, Bosnia and Herzegovina

2   Name changed to protect identity.

2 "Sarajevo 1992–1995: Looking Back after 20 Years," BBC, April 9, 2012.

3 UNHCR, UNHCR *Global Appeal 2013 Update* (Geneva: UNHCR, 2013), 253.

4 UNHCR, *Refugees: After the War Was Over*, vol. 2, no. 140 (Geneva: UNHCR, 2005): 10.

5 Alain Bélanger, ed., *Report on the Demographic Situation in Canada 2003 and 2004* (Ottawa: Statistics Canada, 2006), catalogue no. 91-209-XIE, 103.

18 Iren Hessami Koltermann, Iran

1 "The Baha'i Question: Cultural Cleansing in Iran," Baha'i International Community, September 2008, www.news.bahai.org/documentlibrary/TheBahaiQuestion.pdf.

2 "Preliminary Assessment: The Threat of Genocide to the Baha'is of Iran," The Sentinel Project, May 2009, https://thesentinelproject.org/wp-content/uploads/2010/11/Supplementary-Report-Bahais-of-Iran-2010.pdf, 7.

3 "A Faith Denied: The Persecution of the Baha'is of Iran," Iran Human Rights Documentation Center, December 2006, 19.

19 Anwar Arkani, Myanmar

1 "Unforgiving History," *Economist*, November 1, 2012.

2 Akbar Ahmed, "The Rohingya: Myanmar's Outcasts," *Al Jazeera*, last modified January 30, 2012.

3 George Constantine, "Bangladesh: The Plight of the Rohingya," Pulitzer Center on Crisis Reporting, September 18, 2012; "Why Is There Communal Violence in Myanmar?" BBC, July 3, 2014.

4 "'All You Can Do is Pray': Crimes against Humanity and Ethnic Cleansing of Rohingya Muslims in Burma's Arakan State," Human Rights Watch, 2013, 139.

5 "Chronology for Rohingya (Arakanese) in Burma," Minorities at Risk Project, 2004, www.refworld.org/docid/469f3872c.html.

6 "All You Can Do is Pray," Human Rights Watch, 11.

7 Charlie Campbell, "Burma Accused of 'Ethnic Cleansing' of Rohingya Muslims," *Time*, April 23, 2013.

8 Anthony Kuhn, "In Buddhist-Majority Myanmar, Muslim Minority Gets Pushed to the Margins," *NPR*, May 28, 2014.

20 Elvis, Namibia

1 Last name intentionally withheld.

2 "Where Is it Illegal to Be Gay?" BBC, February 10, 2014.

3 "Namibia Gay Rights Row," BBC, October 2, 2000.

4 "Germany Admits Namibia Genocide," BBC, August 14, 2004.

21 Humaira, Afghanistan

1 Name (and names of children) changed to protect identity.

22 Joseph, Sierra Leone

1   Name changed to protect identity.
2   Human Rights Watch reports at least fifty people were killed by shelling by Nigerian vessels. See, "'We'll Kill You If You Cry': Sexual Violence in the Sierra Leone Conflict," Human Rights Watch, vol. 15, no. 1 (A), January 2003, 7.
3   His Jamaican heritage was from free slaves in that country known as "Maroons." In the late eighteenth century, the British deported some of the Maroons including Joseph's ancestors to Canada, and they next sailed from Nova Scotia to Sierra Leone, then still a young British experiment.

23 Christine, Rwanda

1   Name changed to protect identity.
2   Philip Gourevitch, *We Wish to Inform You That Tomorrow We Will be Killed With Our Families* (Farrar, Straus and Giroux: New York, 1998), 52, 154.
3   Russell Smith, "The Impact of Hate Media in Rwanda," BBC, December 3, 2003.
4   Gourevitch, *We Wish to Inform You*, 161.
5   Genocide Archive Rwanda, Nyamata, www.genocidearchiverwanda.org.rw/index.php?title=Nyamata.

24 Mie Tha Lah, Myanmar

1   Central Intelligence Agency, The World Factbook, https://www.cia.gov/library/publications/the-world-factbook/geos/bm.html; "They Came and Destroyed Our Village Again," Human Rights Watch, June 2005, vol. 17, no. 4(C), 21.
2   "Burmese Border Refugee Sites With Population Figures—December 1998," The Border Consortium, http://www.theborderconsortium.org/media/12233/map-1998-12-dec.pdf.
3   Canada first announced the resettlement of 810 Karen refugees in 2006, and opened an additional 2,000 spots in 2007.

25 Max Farber, Poland

1   There are conflicting records of the date of liquidation of the Sokolow Podlaski ghetto. September 1942 seems to appear dominantly, although October 1942 and October 1943 appear in different sources.
2   Testimony by Franz Stangl, former commandant of Treblinka, in *Belzec, Sobibor, Treblinka: The Operation Reinhard Death Camps*, Yitzhak Arad (Indiana University Press: 1999), 120.
3   The Bielski brothers, Tuvia, Alexander, Asael, and Aron, formed a partisan combat group that engaged in armed operations and provided refuge at their camp in the Naliboki Forest. Their story is fictionalized in the 2008 film *Defiance*.

4   "Sempo" Sugihara was a Japanese diplomat serving in Lithuania during the Second World War who issued transit visas to Japan for thousands of Jewish refugees. Israel has recognized Sugihara with the honorific Righteous Among the Nations.

26 Shabnam, Afghanistan

1   Name (and names of children) changed to protect identity.
2   International Crisis Group, "Women and Conflict in Afghanistan," Asia Report no. 252, October 14, 2013, 22.
3   Bruce Riedel, "Afghanistan: The Taliban Resurgent and NATO," The Brookings Institution, November 28, 2006, accessed April 4, 2014, http://www.brookings.edu/research/opinions/2006/11/ 28globalgovernance-riedel.

27 Robi Botos, Hungary

1   "Holocaust Encyclopedia: Genocide of the European Roma (Gypsies), 1939–1945," US Holocaust Memorial Museum, www.ushmm.org/wlc/en/ article.php?ModuleId=10005219; "Roma Holocaust Victims Speak Out," BBC, last updated January 23, 2009.
2   "Romani Porajmos," Newark College of Arts and Science University College—Newark, www.ncas.rutgers.edu/center-study-genocide-conflict-resolution-and-human-rights/romani-porajmos.
3   János Bársony and Ágnes Daróczi, eds., *Pharrajimos: The Fate of the Roma During the Holocaust* (New York: The International Debate Education Association, 2008), 12.
4   Michael Kimmelman, "Simmering Anti-Semitism Mars a Vibrant Hungary," *New York Times*, May 7, 2008.
5   Quoted in: *Identities: The Documentary Series*, Jazz FM, Toronto, 2013.
6   "How to Get Out of a Vicious Circle," *Economist*, August 10, 2013.
7   Phil Cain, "Hungary Nationalists Whip Up Anti-Roma Feelings," BBC, August 31, 2012.

28 Karim Teja, Uganda

1   Michael Molloy, "Uganda Asian Refugee Movement 1972," lecture presented for the 40th Anniversary Lecture at the Centre for Research on Migration and Ethnic Relations at the University of Western Ontario, London, Ontario, October 18, 2012, www.youtube.com/watch?v=NtQPKNhxymY.
2   Tara Carman, "We Did It the Canadian Way," *Vancouver Sun*, September 28, 2012.
3   National Defence and the Canadian Forces, "Details/Information for Canadian Forces (CF) Operation Uganda 1972," Directorate of History and Heritage, Operations Database, accessed December 26, 2015,

www.cmp-cpm.forces.gc.ca/dhh-dhp/od-bdo/di-ri-eng.asp?
IntlOpId=252&CdnOpId=298.
4   Glen Allen, "Army Readies Longue Pointe for Ugandans," *Montreal Gazette*,
September 23, 1972.

29 Avtar Sandhu, India
1   "Indira Gandhi's Death Remembered," BBC, November 1, 2009.
2   Ninette Kelley and Michael Trebilcock, *The Making of the Mosaic*, 2nd ed
(Toronto: University of Toronto Press, 2010), 406.
3   Patrick Brethour, "Why Canada Chose to Unremember Air India and Disown
Its Victims," *Globe and Mail*, June 25, 2010.
4   John F. Burns, "Canada Seizes Freighter Believed to Have Put 174 Sikhs on
Shore," *New York Times*, July 14, 1987.
5   Associated Press, "Canada Frees Last of 174 Sikh Refugees," *Los Angeles
Times*, August 12, 1987.

30 Sabreen, Israel
1   Name changed to protect identity.
2   "Off the Map," Human Rights Watch, March 31, 2008, www.hrw.org/node/
62284/section/4, 4.
3   Jordi Rudoren, "Israel Shelves Plan to Move Bedouins Amid Outcry," *New
York Times*, December 12, 2013.
4   City removed to protect identity.

Then and Now: Would They Get In Today?
1   UN General Assembly, *Convention Relating to the Status of Refugees*, July
28, 1951, United Nations, Treaty Series, vol. 189, 137, www.refworld.org/
docid/3be01b964.html.

Index

About the Authors

Ratna Omidvar was born in India. She moved to Iran in 1975 to start life there with her Iranian partner. In 1981 she and her family (including an infant daughter) fled Iran and found a new home in Canada. Her own experiences of flight to freedom have been the foundation of her work. She has focused on articulating pathways to inclusion for immigrants and visible minorities in host societies, both in Canada and globally. Ratna is both a Member of the Order of Canada and Order of Ontario.

Dana Wagner is a senior researcher at Ryerson University. She studied journalism at Carleton University and global affairs at the University of Toronto. She has worked in Toronto, Ottawa, Hanoi, and Nairobi.